Thinking Voices

Thinking Voices

The Work of the National Oracy Project

EDITED BY KATE NORMAN

Hodder & Stoughton
LONDON SYDNEY AUCKLAND

Cover photograph by John Walmsley

British Library Cataloguing in Publication Data

Thinking Voices: Work of the National Oracy Project
  I. Norman, Kate
  372.6

ISBN 0–340–57312–0

First published 1992

Disc conversion by Columns Typesetters of Reading
Printed in Great Britain for the educational publishing division of Hodder & Stoughton Ltd., Mill Road, Dunton Green, Sevenoaks, Kent by St Edmundsbury Press, Bury St Edmunds, Suffolk.

CONTENTS

CONTENTS

Section 5 Learning Through Talk – Adults Together

Endpiece

INTRODUCTION

This book is one of four publications arising out of the work of the National Oracy Project during its development phase. The other three publications (INSET packs for primary and secondary schools, and a book and video about storytelling) are mainly practical in intention and format, designed to help teachers develop the use of talk in classrooms and schools. *Thinking Voices* is intended to be complementary. We hope that people who have used the packs will want to read further on certain topics. Likewise we hope that readers of the book will go to the packs for practical advice. The packs also contain video material, and many sequences from the videos illuminate issues raised in this book.

The thinking voices published here include children, teachers, project co-ordinators, project officers, LEA advisers and advisory teachers, academics and researchers. Some have been members of, or closely associated with, the National Oracy Project; others have been invited to contribute because their writings and ideas have influenced the Project's work. Some have written as individuals but several articles are collaborations, and even those where one author is named are products of discussion and debate.

The image of thinking voices works on several levels. The articles are accounts of continuing reflective processes; updates on journeys not yet completed, as some questions get answered and others arise. Articles intentionally represent varying experiences, viewpoints, levels of generality and tones of voice. There are, within the book, some dialogues between different authors. We have tried in this way to reflect the interactive nature of talk – the to-and-fro of ideas between people which is the guiding principle of the book.

The articles also contain as evidence many pieces of transcribed talk, getting as close as possible in written form to the actual voices of children and adults. Often in these extracts they think aloud, clarifying their own ideas, assimilating or challenging the ideas of others. In this way, they not only internalise the meanings that emerge, converting knowledge into understanding – they also internalise the processes of effective thinking. This concept of 'thinking voices' is a central message of the book: that talking together, with adults and with peers, is the most important means by which children learn to think. The practical implication is clear. As James Britton said, writing about Vygotsky, whose ideas have greatly influenced the Project, 'if speech in childhood lays the foundations for a lifetime of thinking, how can we continue to prize a silent classroom?' (*English in Education*, Vol. 21, No. 2, 1987).

Each article can stand alone, and readers can select whatever interests them. But the book is not just a collection of articles about aspects of oracy. It has a definite structure, in which articles are grouped and ordered. Some authors make explicit reference to other articles in the book, picking up points made, reinforcing or questioning what others have said. In other articles some cross-referencing has been done editorially. We hope this will encourage readers to pursue a line of thought from a variety of viewpoints.

Structure

Section 1, 'The Richest Resource', is about children's talk and some of the ways which Project teachers found to describe it. It also provides information and reflections on the current state of knowledge about the development of oral language.

In Section 2, 'The Contexts of Oracy', Douglas Barnes has collected articles which explore the relationship between how we talk and the social and cultural contexts in which the talk takes place. The articles range beyond the classroom to examine how factors over which a teacher has little or no control may influence children's perceptions of talk in school and teachers' attitudes to that talk.

Section 3, 'Learning Through Talk – Children Together', attempts to answer the fundamental question: 'How does talking and listening together in collaborative groups actually help pupils to learn?' This is done by establishing a model of the learning process and the place of talk in it, by exemplifying this in some detail through transcripts, and by raising some important questions about the implications for teachers' planning.

In Section 4, 'Learning Through Talk – Teachers and Children', the question about how talk helps learning is raised again, but with a focus on teacher/child interactions. Articles look at flexible teacher response and raise some challenging issues about teachers' own use of talk.

Section 5, 'Learning Through Talk – Adults Together', looks at the National Oracy Project itself, its origins, ways of working and relationship with the National Curriculum. It shows how the principles which support children's learning through talk apply with equal vigour to adults.

Finally, in an Endpiece, Gordon Wells responds to the whole book as an interested outsider, picking up and developing implicit and explicit themes, giving some new information and raising some more questions.

Acknowledgement

This book itself is the product of thinking voices — its structure the fruit of many hours of exploratory talk interspersed with transformations, presentations and necessary 'off-task' talk. A small editorial group of co-ordinators and project officers, to which we were privileged to co-opt Douglas Barnes, took responsibility for planning, commissioning, responding to, and editing the articles in the different sections, leaving to me only the final polishing and pruning. The members of the group were: Douglas Barnes, Jenny Des-Fountain, Roy Corden, Rebecca Hutton and Lynda Yard, and the book would not exist without them.

I also want to thank the authors who co-operated so willingly in the redrafting process and those who read and responded to the writings of others.

Where an article uses material from a particular school, that school has been acknowledged. But many hundreds of other teachers and schools, and all the National Oracy Project co-ordinators and project officers, have also contributed to the developments and discussions which this book attempts to reflect.

Kate Norman
February 1992

Transcripts

Most transcripts of talk have been laid out as simply as possibly, for ease of reading. In some cases, however, authors felt that features such as long pauses or overlapping speech should be shown to emphasise the point being made. Pupils' names have all been changed and in most cases, again to simplify reading, they have been given appropriate pseudonyms.

THE NATIONAL ORACY PROJECT

The National Oracy Project was established in September 1987 by the School Curriculum Development Committee. In September 1988 it became one of the projects administered by the newly formed National Curriculum Council.

The aims of the Project were:

- to enhance the role of speech in the learning process 5–16 by encouraging active learning;

- to develop the teaching of oral communication skills;

- to develop methods of assessment of and through speech, including assessment for public examinations at 16+;

- to improve pupils' performance across the curriculum;

- to enhance teachers' skills and practice;

- to promote recognition of the value of oral work in schools and increase its use as a means of improving learning.

Development Phase

During the development phase from 1987 to 1991, 35 local education authorities in England and Wales were involved in the Project. Between them they covered a wide geographical and cultural range including urban and rural areas. Within each member LEA, a certain number of schools were selected, and they nominated one or, frequently, two teachers to take a leading role. Across the Project as a whole, every phase of education – nursery, infant, junior, middle, secondary, tertiary and special schools – was represented.

Although the majority of the original teacher members had secondary English or primary language responsibility, there was strong and increasing involvement of teachers from other areas of the curriculum. Teachers were asked to identify an aspect of oracy which interested them and to investigate and develop this within their own classroom. They were also encouraged to involve other colleagues.

Each LEA individually, or as part of a consortium, appointed an advisory teacher to co-ordinate local developments. These co-ordinators supported the classroom-based work of the teachers in whatever way was appropriate – working alongside them, providing resources, organising meetings and publishing accounts of their work.

Teachers met regularly in their local groups to share and reflect on their investigations.

The Project had a small central team who supported local development through the co-ordinators and were also responsible for wider dissemination through publications and national conferences. The National Oracy Project published a journal (*Talk*), newsletters, occasional papers and several booklets. It also collaborated with the Open University and the National Council for Educational Technology on joint publications.

Dissemination Phase

During 1991–93 the work of the Project is being widely disseminated and further developed through links with LEAs not previously involved. This is being co-ordinated by two NCC Professional Officers who are also continuing the schedule of publications.

THE NATIONAL CURRICULUM

Several of the articles make reference to aspects of the National Curriculum for England which has been coming on to the statute books throughout the life of the National Oracy Project. To help any readers unfamiliar with the system and its terminology, the main aspects are outlined below.

- The National Curriculum consists of ten subjects – English, mathematics, science, technology, history, geography, music, art, physical education and (for eleven to sixteen year olds) a modern foreign language.

- For each subject there are objectives, setting out what children should know and be able to do at each stage of their schooling. These objectives are called **attainment targets**.

- For each subject there are also descriptions of what children should experience or be taught to help them achieve the attainment targets. These are called **programmes of study**.

- The years of statutory schooling are now known as Reception, Year 1 (five to six year olds) through to Year 11 (fifteen to sixteen year olds). (To find the approximate age of a pupil add five to the Year number.)

- There are four stages for different age groups known as **Key Stages**: Key Stage 1 from age five to seven, Key Stage 2 from seven to eleven, Key Stage 3 from eleven to fourteen, Key Stage 4 from fourteen to sixteen.

- Children will be assessed at the end of each Key Stage. For most subjects this is against a ten point scale, i.e. the attainment target is divided into ten **levels**, each containing one or more **statements of attainment**. Assessment is done through a combination of teacher assessments and national tests known as **standard assessment tasks**. These results must be communicated to parents. School, but not individual, results will be published.

The Richest Resource

1

Introduction

This section is about the range, variety and development of children's spoken language use. Some articles summarise what is known about oral development at different ages, while others give insights into the ways which those involved with the National Oracy Project have found to describe and analyse talk.

In the first article, 'Capturing Talk', John Johnson, Rebecca Hutton and Lynda Yard consider the rich resource that is revealed by increased attention to children's talk. Using the voices of children, teachers and co-ordinators, they explore the complexities of capturing that resource in ways which both do justice to its richness and support classroom practice – 'teachers in the Project have . . . adopted forms of reflective response which have led them to describe in prose what they think is revealed or demonstrated by pupils in their talk'.

In the next article, Maggie MacLure describes the child's development as a talker from birth to five, showing the crucial role of the adult. 'One of the most important insights from contemporary research has been that language develops in the context of sustained interaction with others.' She ends by describing what a five year old can, and cannot, do with talk.

The emphasis on children of this age reflects a concern within the Project to establish how well children can use spoken language at the start of statutory education. Anne Knight and Lynda Yard each observed and reflected on the 'Day of Talk' of a five year old – in one case, a bilingual child. As Shopna and Lucy take part in the learning and social activities of the classroom, we glimpse their wide repertoire of meanings and ways of expressing them.

Greg Brooks's article continues the story of the 'Development of Talk' from five to eleven. He sums up 'what little is actually known', and suggests 'both some reasons for the dearth of information and some strategies for remedying it'.

'Look How Old This One Is!' is an account of how three Project teachers and their local co-ordinator, in a search for aspects of development, gave a similar historical task to children of differing ages. 'We learned that the contexts we create for children's talk and the task design are crucially important in shaping children's responses.'

John Johnson finishes this section by asking 'Some Unanswered Questions' relating to the development and assessment of talk in the eleven to sixteen age-range. He suggests that, while the work of the APU (Assessment of Performance Unit) has shed valuable light on the ways in which the talk of a fifteen year old is 'better' than that of an eleven year old and GCSE oral assessment 'is one of several giant strides forward taken by the English teaching profession', we still do not have the answer to the question: 'How good is this talk?'

Capturing Talk: Description and Development

JOHN JOHNSON

REBECCA HUTTON

AND

LYNDA YARD

Among recent national curriculum development projects in the English-speaking world, the National Oracy Project stands almost alone in its focus on the talk of children and teachers in all curriculum areas and in all kinds of schools. Teachers joining the Project began to listen with increased attention to their pupils' talk in a wide variety of contexts. They were amazed, delighted and sometimes chastened by what they heard. They discovered the wide range of functions and forms of spoken language in the repertoire of every child. This increased attention to pupils' talk immediately raised questions about how to capture, describe and communicate it.

There were no pre-determined answers. The National Oracy Project was not established to carry out traditional research — there were no standard formats for data-collection, no 'control groups', no statistical analyses. Its principal purpose was to support changes in pedagogical practice which benefited pupils' oral work and learning. Thousands of teachers carried out their own personal and school-based investigations and developments, and met together and with local co-ordinators to reflect on the talk already evident in the classroom and to change their pedagogical practice in the light of their reflections. (For more information on the Project's way of working, see Section 5.)

Evidence was an essential and major ingredient of this reflective process, but its form was dependent on the particular needs, knowledge and interests of the teachers concerned. Teachers in the Project did accumulate an extensive body of data. They gathered 'evidence' of oral language used in the classroom in a host of ways. They made their own observations of children's talk – jottings noted on observation sheets, in journals, on file cards or 'post-it' notes – sometimes recording verbatim small snippets of talk, but more often summarising in their own words the conversations which they had overheard or in which they had participated. Many also used audio or video recorders to get exact and replayable evidence, and these were often transcribed and commented upon. From the outset, they became accustomed to using their own words to describe their observations, and their own interests to determine the nature of the description.

The conversation that follows was recorded in a Reception classroom in Dudley, as two boys drew a picture together on an OHP transparency. The tape, with its accompanying picture, was very influential in the early days of the Project, because it demonstrated so vividly and incontrovertibly the communicative resource brought to school by a pair of typical five year olds. The impact of the actual voices, with the awareness that the conversation took place away from the teacher, raised questions about unrecognised oral language potential in a way that no research paper could have done:

CHRISTOPHER: My daddy's had a crash on the way to work.
WAYNE: How?
CHRISTOPHER: I don't know what he's crashed in – I forgot now.
WAYNE: How did he crash?
CHRISTOPHER: Cos – he cos – he was driving properly but he was heading for something and couldn't turn to wheeling steer because it was too stiff and he crashed into something and good he's not injured because he's not injured and nothing's bleeding on him – good he's not in hospital – has your daddy ever crashed?
WAYNE: Yeah.
CHRISTOPHER: What on?
WAYNE: On on on another car.
CHRISTOPHER: My daddy's crashed on a light car – might be another car.
WAYNE: My car's – my dad's crashed in a house.
CHRISTOPHER: Oh – well you'll be bleeding then – was he?
WAYNE: He wasn't injured.
CHRISTOPHER: Nor was my daddy on the way to work today – when he crashed.
WAYNE: Has he got to walk it now?
CHRISTOPHER: What?

WAYNE: Your dad – has he got to walk it?
CHRISTOPHER: No, he can still drive.
WAYNE: But what about his car?
CHRISTOPHER: No, he can still drive, cos it, nothing's happened to his car except it's crumpled, and it can still drive. But he can still drive, Wayne.
(*Pause*)
WAYNE: I don't know.
CHRISTOPHER: Do you know what colour sky is?
WAYNE: Yeah – blue.
CHRISTOPHER: Well, I done it on night time.
WAYNE: Do some more blue on that side.
CHRISTOPHER: Cos mine's – you're on the nother side of the world, and I'm on this side of the world.
WAYNE: And that's the path.
CHRISTOPHER: So it's night on my world, and it's morning on your world.

It is interesting to reflect on the different aspects of this conversation that can be commented upon, depending on the interests and purposes of readers and listeners.

Communication

Wayne's questions and statements elicit from Christopher a powerful evocation of the incident in which Christopher conveys his understanding of the severity of the car crash, its implications and its consequences. In one part, there is apparent error – '(he) couldn't turn to wheeling steer' but many teachers have suggested that there are two or three interrelated concepts within these words, which might be presented as:

– he couldn't turn the steering wheel;

– he couldn't turn the wheels to steer (the car);

– he couldn't turn to full lock.

There are 'echoes' of adult conversation in their talk, perhaps his mother's account to Christopher of the event, or other overheard conversations: 'had a crash on the way to work'; 'good he's not injured' 'has he got to walk it now?' 'nothing's happened to his car except it's crumpled'. (The notion of 'finding voices' from adult talk is developed in article 3.1.)

Social interaction

Christopher's original statement of the incident appears to inspire Wayne to raise further questions, as if realising that Christopher needs to talk about what has happened. He puts himself alongside Christopher by responding affirmatively to Christopher's question ('has your daddy ever crashed?'), but plays the less dominant part in the overall conversation. The transcript shows to an extent what the taped conversation demonstrates better, that each of the boys responds to, and builds very quickly on, the previous utterance. They are socially uninhibited and genuinely collaborative in the relationship which they have built up during the working conversation.

Cognitive understanding and development

The teacher who originally tape recorded the two boys suggested how much this conversation revealed about their knowledge. They appear to know, and can distinguish between, differing degrees of severity of crash, and what the various implications of crashes are. When they return to their drawing task, we can see how they are grappling with concepts of the world as a sphere, and simultaneous day and night. During the two months which the boys had been in school (they are only just five years old) neither concept had been directly the topic of any conversation with the teacher.

Linguistic behaviour

Many aspects of the language used are worthy of comment and can be helpful in analysing its success as communication. It is, for example, revealing to look at the structure of questions and answers and the use of repetition. Some features of the language use betray the boys' youth, and others seem very mature. Many teachers who heard this recording commented on the breadth of vocabulary and looked for local dialect. The use of 'nor' in Christopher's 'nor was my daddy . . .' often aroused surprise, but a teacher with local knowledge told one group that it was common local usage.

Evidence of achievement within the National Curriculum

The teacher was able to consider the tape-recorded conversation as an example of their work in Speaking and Listening (Attainment Target 1 for English). From the programme of study for Key Stage 1, the following requirements are met:

- working with other children and adults – involving discussion with others; listening to, and giving weight to, the opinions of others; perceiving the relevance of contributions; timing contributions; adjusting and adapting to views expressed.

- development of speaking and listening skills . . . when describing experiences, expressing opinions, articulating personal feelings . . .

- development of pupils' powers of concentration, grasp of turn taking . . .

- talking about experiences in and out of school . . .

- giving and receiving simple explanations, information and instructions; asking and answering questions.

Differentiation

As far as their individual achievements are concerned, of course, there are differences between the two boys. Christopher is forthcoming, leading the conversation forward, providing more information and directing and organising the subject matter. He it is who tries to make explicit sense of the picture they have drawn. Wayne, on the other hand, is more questioning and responsive, not seeking to dictate the agenda but rather to maintain the conversation and to play a supportive role in developing it. He does add information, though, and he does extend the scope of their conversation.

Development and progression

As teachers in the Project continued to investigate and capture talk in the classroom, they inevitably became concerned with issues related to the development of spoken language. A lot is known about the development of speech in the pre-school child (see article 1.2), and teachers working in the Early Years confirmed many of these findings for themselves. But there is much less 'hard' information on school-aged children (see article 1.4), and this meant that many teachers found themselves setting forth into uncharted territory.

Teachers were beginning to collect evidence relating to individual pupils over time, partly as a response to the assessment demands of the National Curriculum, and this was raising questions about what actually constituted progress as a speaker and listener. They were also discussing with colleagues the talk of children of different ages, and this stimulated interest in how similar or different the children's work was.

The following extract depicts vividly a group of co-ordinators grappling with the complex issues which are immediately raised by a search for developmental features in transcripts of talk by children of different ages. It was written by Andy Milton, the Cleveland co-ordinator:

We split into four pairs, as planned, trying to look at three different 'kinds' of talk.

- Reflective

- Argumentative

- Story-telling.

Each pair had difficulty in finding any defined features which varied significantly among children of different age groups. As one of us put it, it is possible to come up with models and to find some evidence to support any one of them but there will always be exceptional examples of children's achievements which conflict with hypotheses about neat categories and regular transitional moves.

That said, for what they're worth, we came up with one or two strands.

In reflective talk (children reviewing their activities), five year olds simply recounted what had happened to them, six to seven year olds were able to offer reasons for choices made in the course of earlier work, while ten year olds were capable of suggesting how they, personally, might have acted differently in the circumstances (or in different circumstances). The example of fourteen year olds' talk showed that they had some ability to conceive of and convey how people other than themselves might have dealt with or responded to the situations they had experienced.

The examples of argumentative or hypothetico-deductive talk presented problems – in the case of a group of primary school children discussing the difference between wizards and magicians, it was hard to see what was distinctive about the contributions of the seven year olds and the ten year olds. In fact, it was a seven year old who was able to crystallize the difference and articulate it: '. . . a magician FOOLS you' (while) '. . . a wizard can actually make magic spells'.

It occurs to me, although I don't recall that it was part of our discussion at the time, that a feature of talk in this transcript was children's ability (or lack of it) 'to maintain a consistent position/view throughout the series of exchanges or to change their view in response to questions, objections and so on'.

Is it possible to separate the form of the utterance (as an example of relatively sophisticated talk) from the conception/perception of a difference between magicians and wizards which is constructed out of the child's memory/imagination/knowledge of what magicians and wizards do?

A similar problem arose from the other example of hypothetico-deductive talk (in which three Year 10 boys were trying to decide – before doing it – where to focus a camera in order to get a sharp image of an object's reflection in a mirror). As one boy, who had grasped the principle involved, struggled to communicate his 'knowledge' to the other two, the form of his utterances was shaped not so much by a need to construct a flawless proposition about what was the case as by a sense that it was necessary to help his partners see things in a new perspective; consequently, the surface features of his talk differ little from theirs, and the commentator (without knowing the right answer to the physics) would be hard put to it to ascribe a higher level of development to this boy's talk than to that of the other two. Having said that, his use first of 'I', then 'you', then 'we', then 'it' seems to mark an ability to use language (in this case talk) as a way of shifting/decentring (a precondition for constructing generalisations and hypotheses?).

Two of us looked at a transcript of children's retellings of a story, together with their intervening discussion. One, offered the successive re-tellings out of sequence, struggled to pick out anything which gave a clue to their true order, anything which might be a mark of development. This apparent 'arbitrariness' led us to feel that changes which the children made for each new telling should be seen not so much as 'improvements', but rather modifications to suit the perceived needs of different audiences. So we returned to the idea that development was/is characterised by alterations in the speaker's sense of what is appropriate for herself, her audience and the context, and that progression is marked as much by what any individual ceases to do, as by what she moves on to.

This account demonstrates many of the difficulties faced by teachers, and indeed academic researchers, when considering spoken language development. There are no clear stages or landmarks indicating a new achievement. A younger child may 'succeed' at a spoken task when an older child 'fails'. The particular circumstances in which a conversation takes place, and especially the perceptions of the participants, heavily influence the use of language itself, so that comparisons between children of different ages must be tentative and, to an extent, based on guesswork. Yet it is clear that the content of children's talk, the range of audience and task which they are able to cope with, and the purposes for which they can use talk, do develop in ways which can be proposed tentatively as areas of growth, even if the precise extent of that growth cannot be measured.

Similar difficulties were encountered by teachers who recorded individual children over a period of time in order to consider how they had progressed. One teacher, Joe Powderley from Surrey, recorded three pupils doing the same task that they had undertaken two years previously, so that teachers during a staff training day on the National Curriculum could consider their development. She transcribed the children's talk, and considered for herself some of the differences. In Year 3, one of the children (James) had said this:

Well, today, we're going to talk about worms. Well we're going to test um these leaves with this measuring thing, pot. And um this measuring. Measuring. They kinda use this big round circle pot that hold them and they see if it's a fair test. And if they go in a straight line like them . . . they're um . . . if they go in the same size . . . they go in the same round?

In Year 5, he talks with the teacher:

JAMES: The worm likes the mud best, because it can crawl around inside the mud and can come back out. When it's inside, it stays round and hangs around. And something. On the wet cloth, it just stayed still.
TEACHER: Did you try it on the wet cloth?
JAMES: Mmh!
TEACHER: And it stayed still?
JAMES: It did a bit. It just moved away like that. Its tail was just moving.
TEACHER: Sorry, James?
JAMES: Its tail was just moving (*pauses*).
TEACHER: Its tail was just moving . . .
JAMES: Because it was going back inside. It was like eating the mud.
TEACHER: It was eating the mud?
JAMES: It was like eating the mud.
TEACHER: It went in where, James . . .?
JAMES: Inside the mud . . . (*pauses*)
TEACHER: Inside the mud . . .
JAMES: Its head got in there, but the tail was still up.
TEACHER: What was it in there for?
JAMES: I don't know.
TEACHER: Any ideas?
JAMES: It's nice and cool.
TEACHER: What do you reckon a worm likes?
JAMES: Cold . . . in the ground. No, it doesn't like the sun. It likes cold places.

The teacher's reflections on these two pieces at first focus on the words used: 'The obvious difference is that there were more words spoken in

Year 5 than in Year 3 . . . (when) I don't believe he understood "test". His use of "they" seemed imprecise . . . He was almost limited to one verb – "go".'

She finds his work in Year 5 better:

In Year 5, James was more guarded, reticent to speak. Therefore, I had to ask him more questions. However, what he did say was making more sense. He made simple statements through observations. 'No, it doesn't like the sun. It likes cold places'. He used 'when' and 'because'. Instead of the verb 'go', he was using 'crawl', 'stay' and 'move'. The use of 'round' was more versatile, 'stays round' and 'hangs round'. However, it was his correction of me, 'It was like eating the mud', that gave me evidence to show that James was beginning to understand and control language.

But as her comparison of the children's oral language continues, she gives voice to a rising concern about the contexts in which the oral work was done:

I gaze at James's transcript – there is a glaring unfairness. Why didn't I ask him any questions in Year 3? As I look at my part, my own utterances on paper and my silences, I feel I have done a disservice to the children, who I taught for a year and know reasonably well. I wish it was the only disservice. As I gaze at the children's parrot sounds of 'fair-test' and 'measuring', I become even more aware of the importance and timing of negotiation between the child's experiences and this formalised language that the child must understand and use.

There is a frank honesty in this teacher's realisation of the difficulties of applying 'scientific' or 'experimental' methodology to her pupils' talk. The children do not respond as automata but as social human beings – and behind their responses to the task lie complex issues of power, of schooling and of communicative processes which strike the teacher as being more important than the original research.

Other Project teachers have expressed similar dissatisfaction with other aspects of research methodology. The most obvious of these are the linguistic forms of analysis which researchers have used to try to chart language development. Teachers have used these and noted distinctions and differences in children's phonology, syntax, lexis, language use and so on; and they have noted the lengths and kinds of children's utterances, and tried to put values on these. But they have not often found these detailed processes helpful in marking noteworthy development, nor in indicating how changes might be made to pedagogical practice.

As a general rule, teachers in the Project have either by choice or neglect come to eschew the forms of analysis often favoured by researchers, and have adopted forms of reflective response which have led them to describe in prose what they think is revealed or demonstrated by pupils in their talk. These prose commentaries – in many varied forms such as running records, observation sheets, journals and talk diaries/logs, file cards, etc. – have shown teachers focusing and concentrating on features of the talk and of children's oral development which they can put to educational use. Below is a summary of these observations:

1 The changes most often commented on by Project teachers have been concerned with the social and communicative confidence and 'skills' of pupils. Among the hundreds of case studies written by Project teachers there are examples of:

- the 'quiet child' who feels suddenly prompted to talk;

- the failing or under-achieving child who develops a new identity or self-image when perceived as successful in oral work;

- improvements in the co-operative strategies and work of children in groups;

- new (or hitherto unrevealed) ability to talk with and to people outside the peer group;

- the adoption of new 'roles' within groups – as mentor/guide/tutor.

2 A second area of development often noted by teachers is in the acquisition of new concepts and the handling of specialist terminology. This has most often occurred when teachers have looked back on work done over a period of time and compared children's talk at various points in their experience of a new topic, or particular terminology. These observations and recordings have indicated to teachers how lengthy and complex a process the handover of such conceptual information and terminology is. The words and ideas have to be used and exemplified by teachers (or by other resources such as TV programmes, audio-cassettes, etc.), and explored and processed by children in their own discussions, before they are used with confidence in teacher-pupil dialogue or in more formal presentations.

3 A third aspect of development is the growth in children's repertoire of strategies and uses for talk. Where the organisation and ethos of the classroom is such that a range of purposes for talk can be explored and tried by pupils, teachers have observed changes in the ways in which children learn. Typically, they move readily to

finding partners to talk to about their work, to using more explicit evaluation and reflection during and after work on particular tasks, and to working by choice in groups in structured and purposeful ways.

4 Other aspects of children's linguistic repertoires also develop, of course. In particular, teachers have commented on the growth in both the language awareness and linguistic competence of bilingual children, whose ability to switch codes requires an increasingly sophisticated command of the languages employed, and of the social and communicative demands of the situation. But 'code-switching' is not just a feature of bilingual children. The command of regional and local dialects, the ability to use two or more accents, the understanding of rapidly-changing peer group vocabulary and linguistic forms, are features of all children's linguistic repertoires which teachers have observed.

5 The last aspect of development on which teachers have commented is perhaps more a summary of the whole than a distinctive element. It is the ability of children to interpret, make and communicate meanings of increasing complexity. In order to demonstrate growth in this area, of course, children must have experienced growth in some or all of the previous four areas.

As evidence accumulated and was shared across and beyond the Project, teachers' own confidence in recording and reflecting on talk grew. They became increasingly skilful in observation and deepened their understanding of the processes involved. At the same time, pupils themselves took on more responsibility for reflecting on their own progress by using, for example, talk journals or personal tapes. This expertise provided a firm foundation for further development. Teachers had the evidence to demonstrate that classroom talk, both their pupils' and their own, hitherto neglected as a focus of attention, was in fact the richest resource which teachers could use in improving the quality of teaching and learning in their classrooms.

Acknowledgements

We would like to thank Mary Picardo and Mount Pleasant Primary School, Dudley; Andy Milton, Cleveland co-ordinator; Joe Powderley of Moor Lane Junior School, Surrey.

The First Five Years: The Development of Talk in the Pre-School Period

MAGGIE MACLURE

As far as spoken language development is concerned, the first five years of children's lives are amazingly productive. Children make it seem so easy, too. Compare their achievements with the faltering progress of adults or teenagers struggling to learn a second language. Indeed, so easy does it seem, it was once thought that there must be a genetic programme that inexorably drove us all along the path of language 'acquisition'. Contemporary views of the process are rather different, as we shall see in this article, which considers the conditions under which pre-school language development takes place, and then goes on to profile the communicative resources that we might expect of five year olds.*

---

*Because this chapter deals with broad trends, it does not address individual variation amongst children. Nor does it pursue issues of gender, class and cultural diversity, though these are undoubtedly important for a fuller understanding of pre-school development. To take one example, children's knowledge of stories will reflect the kinds of narrative that are important in their community.

Conditions for communicating: some key aspects of early language experience

This section outlines some special characteristics of children's pre-school experience which seem to be critical for their spoken language development. While it would be neither possible nor desirable to try to replicate the home environment at school, there are still valuable insights to be gained from pre-school practices.

1. Early language development is interactive

Children do not plough a lonely furrow as they learn to talk. One of the most important insights from contemporary research has been that language develops in the context of sustained interaction with others. Without other people to interpret the world for them, to 'make sense' of their earliest attempts to communicate, children would not learn to talk at all. What other people say and do matters. And if it matters at home, it will surely matter in school.

2. Children are active participants

Children are nevertheless key players in their own game. They often take the initiative in their conversations with parents and others; they have a major say in choosing topics; they quickly learn to 'keep their end up' in the to-and-fro of interaction (Wells, 1981). They are active in an intellectual sense too, in that they are constantly reinterpreting and reanalysing the language system and its relation to the world about them (Nelson, 1985).

3. What do adults do?

Adults' talk can be described in terms of four S's:

Shaping: From birth onwards, adults treat children's behaviour as meaningful and reflect back to them modified versions of their own, less sophisticated utterances. This process begins when mothers involve their babies in 'conversations', by treating their cries, burps, smiles, etc. as meaningful and 'replying' accordingly. This is how children discover what it is possible to mean in their culture.

Sharing: Talk is for sharing experiences, ideas, feelings and perspectives. Through talk, child and adult develop 'intersubjectivity'

– the mutual recognition that you and I interpret the world in common.

Supporting: Adults' talk is finely tuned to children's developmental stage (Wells, 1981). Parents and other carers have an intuitive 'feel' for their children's capacities, and an intimate knowledge of familiar events and adventures. So they are able to give their children just the amount of support needed to sustain communication – without doing all the 'work' for them.

Stretching: Within that overall context of unquestioning support, adults also manage to create the conditions which push the child's communicative ability just that little bit further, without posing unrealistic or inordinate demands. Vygotsky (1978), referred to this, rather portentously, as operating in the 'zone of proximal development'.

Though teachers would not wish to replicate the roles of parents, it seems unquestionable that school-age children will continue to need the 'four S's' of interactional support.

4. The centrality of context

Early talk tends to refer to the immediate context and, especially in the early stages, these contexts are highly repetitive – mealtimes, bathtimes, play, dressing, etc. This helps children figure out the links between what happens and what is said. While children continue (as we all do) to use context as an indispensable resource for understanding what people mean, they get better at decoding the language itself as their semantic system develops.

Context is important in a second sense. Precisely because of that close link between events and utterances, only those closest to a child will fully understand everything that she or he says. All families have their repertoire of idiosyncratic words and phrases. My two year old daughter, Martha, will shake her head sagely and pronounce 'that's for the big children' to indicate things that she knows she is forbidden to consume or touch – wine and razors, for example. Parents are inevitably in a better position than teachers to understand the idiosyncrasies of young children's talk and to press the 'buttons' that will unlock conversation.

5. The pleasure principle

From the start, language is a source of pleasure and play. Children orient to rhythm, rhyme, recurrence and surprise – in songs, adverts, stories, games. They also play with language itself, trying out different sounds, substituting one word for another, etc. Play is a serious game, though: it is about discovering the rules and structures of language by breaking them; about getting a feel for different genres and types of language; about developing a metalanguage – i.e. a way of talking about talk itself. As the next section shows, this playfulness continues well beyond age five.

6. *Becoming a person: identity, culture and belonging*

As they learn to communicate, children are woven into their culture. Through language they learn who they are; how people order and classify the world; what counts as important and what can be disregarded in that world. Language anchors children in a shared social world, while teaching them also (in our culture at least) what it is to be an individual.

7. *Power and control*

Language is also about power and control. It can be used to persuade others to act; but it is also about struggle and pain – about being controlled, denied or ignored. While psychoanalysts have highlighted the traumas of childhood, students of child language have perhaps tended to stress the 'soft', caring, supportive aspects of adults' interactions with children, and to overlook the conflict and struggle inherent in relations between adults and children (see Walkerdine, 1989).

8. *The holistic nature of pre-school talk*

In school, we categorise and discriminate: there's 'chat', and there's (serious) talk for learning. There's science talk, and maths talk and something called 'English'. We may distinguish talk for feeling, playing and thinking. Such distinctions don't apply, of course, at home, where there are no 'subjects', and learning and language are wholly intertwined. This is not to suggest that there are no distinctions to be made in the kinds of talk that take place at home. But we do not find the demarcations that are often made in school between 'sacred' and 'secular' forms – for instance, between 'abstract' and 'concrete' language, or between 'on-task' and 'off-task' talk. Or at least we do not find parents consistently giving priority – as has been the norm in schools – to the 'sacred' over the 'secular'.

So what can five year olds do?

The next section opens with a few examples of such 'secular' talk involving five year olds. It is off the record chat of the sort that often goes unremarked by adults. But, as we shall see, such talk reveals (or perhaps more usually conceals) a considerable amount of communicative expertise. We shall 'unpack' some of that expertise as a route into the question of what five year olds can do with talk.

Jack is drawing green dots all over the page on which he has already drawn a house. Liam has a problem: surely the grass should go at the bottom of the picture?

LIAM: What's that? (*pointing to the green dots*)
JACK: Grass.
(*They look at each other.*)
LIAM: Oh. Well, you gotta do it on the **floor**.
(*He points to the bottom of Jack's page.*)
JACK: I 'aven't, that's all the grass far **away**.
(*He points to the top of his page.*)
LIAM: Oh you mean − the grass got cut off an' it's flown up in the air? Like −
JACK: No! Wait, Liam! There's a big **long** garden, right? an' all the − that's all the grass **far away**.
(*Points to the top of the page.*)
LIAM: Oh, an' that's the **tall** grass?
JACK: **Right!**

This snippet of chat was picked up one day in the Reception class. It is not particularly remarkable, but for that very reason it is a good example of the expertise that underlies even the most mundane of conversations. Let us take a closer look, starting with vocabulary: the boys have certainly got the words they need to communicate (though Liam's use of 'floor' rather than 'ground' is a child-like choice). They have no problem with grammar here either: their utterances are well-formed and quite complex. At the level of the interaction between the two boys, the talk is sophisticated. They 'take turns' smoothly, as they try to repair the misunderstanding. This is quite hard work. Each must a) try to understand what the other is getting at and convey this understanding clearly (for example, 'Oh, you mean . . .'); b) express his own ideas comprehensibly, and c) 'check' that the message is getting across (see how both boys emphasise key words, and Jack's use of 'right'). The children are far from 'egocentric', therefore: each is able to put himself in the other's shoes. All this involves the use of a range of linguistic functions: in this short stretch you will find one or more questions, answers, instructions ('Oh. Well, you gotta do it on the floor.'), agreements, disagreements, statements, explanations and clarifications. The talk is also quite complex at a cognitive level. The boys are talking about rather abstract matters – in adult terms, about perspective and the relationship between what you see and how you represent it in two dimensions. Even an innocuous fragment such as this depends upon a complex array of communicative abilities, therefore. It is also a genuinely co-operative effort: the 'sense' that is finally made of Jack's picture is their shared accomplishment.

Meaning is always, in fact, a shared accomplishment. Sometimes, it seems almost to be spun out of thin air. Neil and Joe are sitting side by side on the sofa in the book corner. The sun beats down on them through the window:

> JOE: Ooh, it is hot isn't it, Neil?
> NEIL: **Yeah**. I'm sweatin'.
> (*Another child interrupts.*)
> NEIL: Joe, we're boilin' – we're boilin'. Like roast on the oven, aren't we?
> JOE: Mmm. We're like roast chicken.
> NEIL: Yeah! (*they giggle*) Like peas and carrots roasted, in the pressure cooker.
> (*A short pause*)
> JOE: We – we're like a waistcoat. Burnt.
> NEIL: Yeah, warm. Oh, my, sweaty.
> (*He laughs, rubbing his face.*)
> JOE: Oh, I'm sweaty. I'm sweatin' to bits.
> (*He rubs his face.*)
> NEIL: Oh, I'm sweatin' hot.

This is the pleasure principle at work. It is 'desultory chat' par excellence – but not without its own remarkable features. Like the preceding example, it is a wholly joint enterprise, and a very open-ended one at that. Without any overt negotiation, Joe and Neil conjure a joke, and elaborate it over several turns. Their word play has poetic as well as playful qualities.

Five year olds will also speak in voices other than their 'own', in imaginative role play. With the transition to school, the role of 'teacher' is rapidly added to a repertoire of impersonations that will probably include mummies and daddies, doctor and patient, and others.

Joan has decided to read a story to her 'class', comprising her two friends, Leonora and Susan:

JOAN: Which book would you like today?
LEONORA: I want **this** one. (*in a loud, 'babyish' voice*)
JOAN: Okay. (*she flicks through the book*) Oh, it's too long I'm afraid. I –
   I think you won't like this one.
   (*pause*)
   Now our first one. 'Lucy's Grandma'. Everyone look at the pictures.
   (*she leans over and taps Susan, holding up the book so that all can see*)
   Lucy's Grandma decided me for – to come to tea at our house.

Joan 'reads' a plausible story, working from the pictures. Simultaneously, she monitors the attention of her 'class':

JOAN: Mother has a – a cupboard full of hats, and she tries them all
   on. **And she tried them all on.** (*loudly, as she leans over to tap
   Leonora, whose attention has wavered*) First she tried the old, old
   blue one. **I** didn't like that one very much. Then she tried on the
   boat one. **We** did like that one very much. (*continues . . .*)

These fragments give only a glimpse of the virtuosity of Joan's performance. But you can see that she already has a good grasp of her teacher's crowd control techniques, and some insight into her teaching strategies. She knows, for instance, what is best for her 'immature' charges ('I think you won't like this one'). As the unabridged version of her story shows, she is also well acquainted with the textual features of (written) stories for young children: her 'made up' story might fool the casual eavesdropper. There is a substantial amount of cultural and textual knowledge in children's role play.

Five year olds are also adept, of course, at talking with adults. With empathetic support, they should be able to take their part in conversations with teachers. Tony has no difficulty in telling his teacher all about the 'mequipment car' that he has made out of plastic bricks:

TEACHER: What sort of equipment does it carry?
TONY: It – it carries doctors' and nurses' mequipment.
TEACHER: Oh, I see.
TONY: It's a bit like a ambulance.
TEACHER: Ah. (*nodding*)
TONY: But it takes **blood**. It's – it's a blood car.
TEACHER: Blood transfusion car?
TONY: Yeah.

Tony's teacher provides interested support, taking her lead from Tony. Since the talk relates to an observable object, there are no misunderstandings. Sometimes, however, difficulties can arise, for instance, when children are talking about things that happened at home, or about more abstract ideas. As we noted above, teachers have less access than parents to the child's experiential world. This may be an advantage in the longer term, prompting children to try to convey their experiences more effectively to others, and to envisage other worlds beyond their own. But in the short term, the failure to understand children's utterances can have serious consequences for their progress at school, as Tizard and Hughes (1984) have argued.

Towards a communicative inventory at age five

The examples given above give some flavour of the five year old's communicative abilities, though this is by no means an exhaustive picture. If we were to summarise by drawing up an inventory it would include the following items.

By the age of five many children will:

- draw on a vocabulary of several thousand words;

- control many of the major grammatical constructions of their language – though some aspects of grammar will not be acquired until later;

- speak with a regular, adult-like pronunciation, adopting the speech patterns of their community;

- talk for a range of purposes – including many 'higher-order' ones such as hypothesising, speculating, predicting;

- use talk to further their own learning;

- express their feelings through talk, and understand the feelings of others;

- disconnect talk from the 'here-and-now' where appropriate;

- assess other people's background knowledge and adjust their own talk in the light of this;

- assume joint responsibility for the meanings that are produced through talk;

- know (or quickly learn) many of the cultural and procedural rules for talking with different kinds of people – peers, parents, teachers, strangers;

- engage in role play, and experiment with different interactional 'identities';

- deploy a range of persuasive and rhetorical tactics for increasing the likelihood of securing their own goals, avoiding blame or trouble, etc.;

- have some metalinguistic knowledge, i.e. be able to reflect on, and talk about, talk itself;

- get pleasure out of playing with, and through, language;

- have a developing sense of genres of talk: e.g. jokes, stories, 'news', etc.

There will be individual variation, of course: different children will have their different strengths, and some will be more advanced overall than others. Nevertheless, it would not be unrealistic to expect many children to display many of these abilities, at some level of competence.

So what *can't* children do by the age of five?

But what about those children who come to school seemingly able to say very little, or indeed nothing at all? Research such as that by Gordon Wells (1981) suggests that very few children are wholly unable to communicate. It is probably safer to assume – as an initial working hypothesis – that there is some other reason for their lack of participation. They may be overwhelmed, fearful, disenchanted or uncertain of what is expected of them. Some children who never talk during the 'official business' of lessons may have quite a lot to say 'off the record' – in the playground, or in the gaps between scheduled activities.

Let us end by contemplating some of the things that children probably *won't* be able to do by the time they start school. As already noted, they won't always be good at assessing the listener's state of knowledge, especially when talking about things that are not immediately visible or known to everyone. They may assume, therefore, that the teacher knows more than he or she actually does. And, reciprocally, teachers are likely to be less skilled than family members at 'decoding' the children's messages.

They may not be used to talking in front of, and waiting their turn, among 30 or so other children – although newcomers to school quickly pick up such 'procedural' understanding (Willes, 1983). They may not be used, either, to answering questions to which the teacher seems to know the answer.

Although used to talking with their friends, they may have to learn how to take part in the collaborative, purposeful talk which is required of peer groups as they work together on externally imposed classroom tasks. Similarly, they will be novices at the kind of 'reasoned' argument and discussion that is especially valued in school.

Because their knowledge of the world is still limited, there are many contexts and purposes with which children will be unfamiliar, so they will know next to nothing about talk which is associated with exclusively adult occupations and preoccupations. This is the reason why they would be at a loss if asked to take part, for example, in a simulation of a public enquiry, to chair a board meeting, or to take part in a mock job interview.

Children's existing abilities will also undergo much refinement in the ensuing years. To take an obvious example, they will get much better at telling jokes and stories, and at controlling those other genres which have begun to emerge. They will become more familiar with talk which depends on abstract concepts and which attempts to be 'objective' or dispassionate. They will add further refinements to their grammatical systems, and at the same time become more subtle and sophisticated in their powers of persuasion and expression. Their ability to use talk for learning will develop further too, as they gain more experience in testing out hunches and hypotheses in collaboration with others, in reflecting upon their actions, and in refining, summarising and clarifying ideas so that they can be conveyed to other people.

In conclusion, even the most simple and desultory communication requires all sorts of abilities — linguistic, intellectual, interpersonal, cultural and emotional. Five year olds still have a long way to go in developing those abilities, but their knowledge and expertise is nevertheless impressive. These are the strong foundations to be built on in the school years.

Acknowledgements

The transcribed extracts are all taken from video recordings made during the project 'Language at Home and at School' directed by Gordon Wells at the University of Bristol between 1977 and 1981 and supported by grants from the Social Science Research Council (SSRC, now the Economic and Social Research Council, ESRC).

References

NELSON, K. (1985) *Making Sense: The Acquisition of Shared Meanings*. London: Academic Press.

TIZARD, B. AND HUGHES, M. (1984) *Children Learning: Talking and Thinking at Home and at School*. London: Fontana.

VYGOTSKY, I. S. (1978) *Mind in Society*. Cambridge, MA: Harvard University Press.

WALKERDINE, V. (1989) *Democracy in the Kitchen*. London: Virago.

WELLS, G. (1981) *Learning through Interaction*. Cambridge: Cambridge University Press.

WILLES, M. (1983) *Children into Pupils*. London: Routledge.

A Day of Talk – Two Case Studies

ANNE KNIGHT AND

LYNDA YARD

Shopna – thinking in two languages

I observed Shopna, a five year old girl in my Reception class, during the course of a whole day, and also made tape recordings of her talk. Shopna is bilingual, with Punjabi as her first language.

The day started with greetings and social chat on the carpet, and with Shopna comforting Amina who had a grazed knee. During assembly, Shopna listened intently, shouted out a response to a question and laughed and joked with friends. Back in the classroom, discussing the day's activities, she used talk to confirm understanding:

TEACHER: There are. . .
CLASS: Petals.
SHOPNA: Petals.

and to develop understanding:

TEACHER: These are long and twisty. They take in water so that the plant can drink and grow. They are called roots.
CLASS: Roots.

SHOPNA: Roots. . . like spaghetti.

She continued to use language to develop understanding linking new and existing knowledge as she studied the daffodil bulb more closely:

. . . it's like. . . er. . . er. . . onion.

She used language to express anxiety:

I can't do that drawing.

and to organise herself and others:

I get the pencils. You, you got a pencil? I get them all.

She talked aloud as she drew her dragon and took on the role of expert when Zareena joined the group and Shopna told her what to do.

I noticed that all her actions were accompanied by a mix of instructional and social talk. Redefining, explaining to others, exploring possible outcomes, confirming with peers and adults. Only manoeuvres demanding a high level of physical skill and co-ordination (the tricky bits) were performed silently.

After play, Shopna reflected on the fun:

When it's playtime we play that game again. Is so good. I like it, it's good to do the bus.

She shared a joke with Amarjit, and threatened a friend:

If you don't, you can't play our bus game.

Shopna finished her drawing task and joined the group making plasticine models of dragons. (Activities for the day were based around the theme of St David's Day.) First she looked at the dragons being made, then thought aloud:

Let me see. I like it, your one, what's that? (wings). . . I'm going to do wings – red I do.

She then negotiated with children in the group for the colours of plasticine she wanted. All through the making process she talked aloud as she redefined her ideas:

It's got one, two, three, four legs . . . and a long, long tail . . . is it too long? Is fall off. I make a little one . . . yes.

At the end of the morning the children joined together to reflect on work done. Shopna was generous in her praise:

Oh lovely flower, little flower. Good, Sabra.

She listened hard, answered questions and instigated fun:

TEACHER: And it comes whooshing out of the dragon's nose. It's very
    dangerous. Who knows what I'm thinking of?
SHOPNA: (*shouting*) Bogies! The bogie came out of the nose, all over.
    Monwara say 'bogie'. He say it too!

Shopna and the class collapsed with laughter. During a morning
steeped in listening and talking, Shopna had listened intently,
supported friends socially, shared jokes, developed understanding,
organised herself and others. All in a second language.

On her return to class after lunch, she first explained to the nurse
that she had something in her eye and then joined in quiet reading
time. She chose a book and told herself the story, then decided she
wanted a favourite book, found out who had it and entered into
whispered negotiations to get it.

The afternoon's activities started for Shopna with a group board
game. As they played, the children gave each other instructions in
English and sorted out problems about the game in Punjabi. In the
home corner, Shopna shared jokes with monolingual pupils in English
and, with Punjabi speakers, using her first language.

At the end of the day, I tried to talk to her about talk at home and
other languages, but this fell a bit flat. Perhaps she doesn't see any
need to talk to me about a language I can't understand when she
seems to be able to switch between two with such skill and
appropriateness . . . conveying meaning seems to be the over-riding
criterion for the language choices she was making.

Anne Knight

Acknowledgement

These observations were made in Newport Infants School, Waltham
Forest.

Lucy – a range of voices

At a National Oracy Project co-ordinators' conference, Janet Maybin
told us about her study of a ten year old girl (Maybin, 1991). I was
particularly intrigued by her comments on how children's talk is
'highly populated with the voices of others'. So I was very pleased to
get the chance to observe a five year old girl, Lucy, in a Reception
class.

I spent the day with Lucy in the classroom and playground,
listening to what she said and to the range of voices she used.

Although she rarely speaks in teacher-led group and class discussions and appears initially to be a quiet pupil, it transpired that during the day Lucy spoke to a variety of people: herself, the nursery nurse, me, the teacher, other children individually, in groups and as a class once, and chiefly to two friends, Jane and Andrew. What were the voices she used to make sense of her day?

Lucy used her internal voice to moan to herself as she collected her journal ('I didn't even do anything on Saturday'), and as she realised she had no clock to help her with her clock book ('I didn't even do a clock'). She also used this voice to help spell words in her journal ('I w ... I went ... to ... some, some, some, some.').

Lucy chatted to the nursery nurse using the voice of an adult, echoing her matter-of-fact tones and initiating conversation:

LUCY: My hair was curly yesterday.
NURSERY NURSE: Did you go to the party?
LUCY: Yes.
NURSERY NURSE: Was it good?
LUCY: Yes, we played musical ...
NURSERY NURSE: What?
LUCY: You dance around, then, when the music stops you sit down.

I was also addressed in a matter-of-fact tone when Lucy turned to me at one point and asked: 'Lynda, what's next?'

Lucy made fleeting contacts with a variety of children during the day. One of the voices used in these contacts was that of teacher/ organiser:

Stop it. (*to a boy being silly*)
Get in line. (*to a group at the end of playtime*)
Move back. (*in the assembly line*)

Another voice used was that of making social contacts:

(*to Paula, sorting out party invitations*)
LUCY: Is it your birthday tomorrow?
PAULA: (*nodded*)
LUCY: Have you got a card for me?
PAULA: (*shook head*)
LUCY: Why?
PAULA: Cos I haven't got enough.

(*to Gillian, while putting the journals away*)
GILLIAN: I went to the Water Palace ... on the elephant.
LUCY: I went to South Norwood.
GILLIAN: I've been on the chute.
LUCY: We couldn't do it at night, could we? (*both laughing*)

In the playground, Lucy screamed with her group of friends as they played chase and occasionally shouted:

1, 2, 3, on your marks, get set go . . .

During the wet lunchtime, she joined a group in the role-play area. She was dressed as a Muslim lady and sat saying little but looking dignified in the 'café'. The café changed to a travel agent's, and Lucy suddenly became an expert:

BRIAN: Where do you want to go for your holiday?
ROBERT: France.
LUCY: I went to France one day, on my holiday. I go to France. I live –
    I stay in a tent. Have you been there?
ROBERT: Yes.
LUCY: Really?

Most of the day's conversation was with Jane, a friend she chose to sit with to make the 'clock books'. As equals, they redefined the task and reassured each other:

JANE: I'm not doing it like that, I'm doing it nice and shiny black . . .
    oh, it's brown.
LUCY: She says you can do it any colour.
JANE: But not red, yellow.
LUCY: Red, yellow, brown or black or green.
JANE: I've done it black, hard black.

While they worked, they chatted about the previous day's party, using voices of Mums or older sisters chatting and reminiscing:

JANE: Do you like me at the party, at Vicki's party?
LUCY: But not (*giggle*) when you're crying.
JANE: I know, but did you like my dress and my shoes?
LUCY: (*nodded*) Do you like me?
JANE: Yeah.
LUCY: With my curly hair? Is my hair still curly?
JANE: It's a little bit curly.
LUCY: It was quite straight yesterday. (*laughs*)
JANE: Yeah. (*laughs*) You know what, I had a bath and my hairwash
    with conditioner.

The book took a long time to make. At one stage Lucy adopted a competitive voice, singing:

LUCY: I'm on the other page . . . der, der, der, der, der . . .
JANE: You didn't colour them in.
LUCY: (*singing*) No, I'm on the other page and so very successful.

The teacher came to look at work in progress:

TEACHER: Which one are you on, Lucy?
LUCY: Half past ten.
TEACHER: What happens then?
LUCY: Playtime.
TEACHER: (to Jane) Can you read it? Playtime at . . .? (no answer) Can you read it? Lucy just said it, didn't she? Tell her again, Lucy.
LUCY: Half past ten.
TEACHER: Half past ten. Can you turn your clock to half past ten first? Well done.

The teacher moved to another part of the room. Lucy mocked and then took on a teacher's voice:

LUCY: I'm clever, it's half past ten, and you didn't know it. Say ten o'clock.
JANE: Ten o' clock.
LUCY: Say ten o' clock.

The tape is indistinct for a few minutes, then the girls can be heard cheering each other up, chanting: 'Playtime is at half-past ten. Playtime is at half-past ten'. And later:

JANE: If we get on we can do something, can't we?
LUCY: We've got the last one.
JANE: Look, see, I've only got one more left then I'm done.

During the afternoon, the teacher invited Lucy to share a book with Andrew, a new boy. It was a book Lucy had made at home about her house. Together they teased, reassured, gossiped each other through the task:

ANDREW: The, that says 'the'.
LUCY: House. My Mum wrote it and I copied it.
ANDREW: But a good book. I call it a house book when I make a house.
LUCY: (giggles) My house. My house has got a . . . It is a . . . The . . . It falls it's the gutter.
ANDREW: Your mum writted **this** one down.
LUCY: No, she didn't.
ANDREW: Why is that 'M' there?
LUCY: That says office. (pointing to the picture)
ANDREW: Have you got an office in the bedroom?
LUCY: Yes, my Dad works in the study.
ANDREW: I've got my office already.
LUCY: Boring. All he does is studying. Nearly the end.
ANDREW: (turning a page) This is my favourite one.
LUCY: Read it then.
ANDREW: I don't know it.

LUCY: Well, how come you said it's the favourite one?
ANDREW AND LUCY: (*together reading*) I like my bedroom. I like my
bed. (*giggling*)

Lucy used different voices to make sense of her day: voices of adults chattering, gossiping, goading, teasing, helping, informing. All these are voices she had heard and chosen to use. As she grows and develops, she will add to her repertoire other voices she hears which seem important to her, voices of scientists, historians, technicians, mathematicians, artists, writers . . . As the range of voices she uses increases, so too will her capacity for understanding and for adding to understanding.

Lynda Yard

Acknowledgement

Thanks to Elizabeth Mazzola of Benson Primary School, Croydon for inviting me to observe in her classroom.

Reference

MAYBIN, J. (1991) 'Children's informal talk and the construction of meaning', *English in Education*, Vol. 25, No. 2, pp. 34–49.

1.4

The Development of Talk
From Five to Eleven

GREG BROOKS

As Maggie MacLure has shown in article 1.2, a vast amount is known about the development of talk in pre-school children. But as soon as we look at older children it becomes obvious that:

> There is very little actually known, either about the structure, content and function of children's oral language, or about how it changes and develops over the school years.
>
> (Maybin, J., 1991 p. 34)

In this article, I shall summarise what little is 'actually known' about the spoken language development of five to eleven year olds and suggest both some reasons for the dearth of information and some strategies for remedying it.

Perhaps one major reason for the shortage of information is this. Until the mid-1960s it seemed to be agreed among linguists that acquisition of the language system was complete by the age of five. This was, after all, one of the main pieces of evidence that Noam Chomsky (1959) used in arguing against empiricist accounts of language acquisition, especially Skinner's (1957), and in favour of the theory that some constraints on the form of human behaviour (Chomsky called these constraints 'language universals') are innate. The first evidence that comprehension of some more complicated structures was still developing in primary-age children was produced by Carol Chomsky (1969).

Another reason for the shortage of research evidence on language development after the age of five is the much greater difficulty of undertaking research with school-age children, compared to pre-school children. Not only is their time more occupied, but negotiation of access is more complicated, costs are higher and funds are more difficult to obtain.

So what, despite these problems, is known? No one could seriously doubt that eleven year olds are much more competent language *users* than five year olds. Eleven year olds: can find their way around the world better; are less likely to be naïvely tactless, and/or are better at concealing their thoughts; no longer need to use overt ('egocentric') speech to accompany virtually all thinking; have a larger vocabulary, and a command of more complicated syntax and of ways of expressing abstract ideas; and have learnt a great deal about politeness, formality, relevance, register, and so on.*

At the beginning of that list I said 'No one could seriously doubt', but, as so often, that phrase is an attempt to conceal the lack of evidence. I have sketched a relatively commonsense view about ways in which primary pupils' language develops: shortly I will show how little of that sketch can be substantiated.

First, though, some detail can be given, not about development during the primary years, but about what the competent eleven year old language user is like: a 'static' picture, if you wish, of the end-point of this stage of learning. The evidence for this description comes from the national surveys of oracy performance of eleven year olds in England, Wales and Northern Ireland carried out by the Assessment of Performance Unit team in the 1980s. In three separate surveys, over 4,000 pupils were tested. Each pupil undertook three tasks from a battery of about eight. The results are summarised in Table 1 (p. 36).

With a few exceptions, the tasks in the three categories seem to fall into levels of difficulty. Most of those in the 'High' (= easiest) group require either relatively straightforward responses to simple listening, or an account of directly relevant personal experience. Most of those in the 'Medium' group require either listening to more complex information, or recasting experience or information in some way. And those in the 'Low' (= most difficult) group are probably unusual in most primary pupils' experience of life or the classroom.

---

*For a partly similar list, see Tough, 1979, pp. 22–23.

Speaking and listening tasks on which high (70%+), medium (50%–70%) or low (<50%) of eleven year olds achieved a score of 4 or better on a 1–7 scale:

HIGH
Following instructions to produce a model
Instructing a friend to play a board game
Instructing another pupil to carry out an experiment
Speculating on the reasons for a finding
Reporting the results of an experiment
Re-telling a story heard on tape
Answering questions on a story or anecdote heard on tape
Narrating a personal anecdote
Describing pictures
Telling a story based on a sequence of pictures
Summarising the plot of a book

MEDIUM
From a spoken description, identifying an object among a set of similar objects
Relaying simple information heard on tape
Describing a job
Arguing to justify a point of view
Describing objects for identification
Summarising written information
Discussing to reach agreement
Describing experimental procedures and observations
Appraising technological gadgets
Reporting conclusions on appraising technological gadgets
Inventing a scenario for an imaginary crime or an unusual pictured scene
Predicting events or the continuation of a plot
Reporting reasons for agreed or disputed conclusions
While listening to a tape, making notes for relaying
Explaining use of technical devices on video

LOW
Discussing a technological problem
Discussing reasons for scientific problems
Presenting a point of view based on written notes
Reaching agreement on sequence of pictures for story

Table 1: The eleven year old language user: findings from APU surveys

Source: Gorman, T. P. et al. (1988, Table 2.5, p. 19), supplemented from Gorman, T. P. et al. (1991, pp. 49–50). Both reports should be consulted for further detail.

While performing the tasks, most pupils were also able to:

- organise what they wanted to say clearly;

- avoid undue hesitation and pausing;

- employ appropriate vocabulary and syntax;

- adopt Standard English usage and a widely intelligible accent (Gorman *et al.*, 1988, p. 19).

Much less detail can be given about how this point is reached. I take it as axiomatic that, in order for us to 'know' that an aspect of spoken language develops, that aspect must have been studied in statistically significant numbers of children of at least two different ages, engaged in comparable activities, with findings expressed not just qualitatively but also quantitatively. Such studies would have to be, by definition, either cross-sectional or (preferably) longitudinal.

By far the largest longitudinal study of language development ever carried out in Britain was the Bristol Study of Language Development, directed by Gordon Wells (1985a, 1985b, 1986) and carried out over a period of about fifteen years at the University of Bristol. This provided important data on children's spoken language development from the age of two to the age of five. Once the children were in school, however, the project's focus shifted to written language, and few further data were collected on speech.

With cross-sectional studies, the sum total of the research literature is contained in one tradition and two books. The tradition is that of investigating vocabulary. Since the 1870s, many linguists have published lists of words, organised either by the frequency of the words themselves or by the age of the people studied. In the latter case, an interest in 'vocabulary size' was often the motive. Unfortunately, most of these studies concern written language, or the spoken English of adults. Of those based on the spoken English of children, both those from the USA (Beier, Starkweather and Miller, 1967; Wepman and Hass, 1969), and those from Britain (Burroughs, 1957; Edwards and Gibbon, 1973) are either very out of date or relatively out of date. Even if they were not, they would tell us only about vocabulary size (and then only within the limitations of the methodology used to collect the information). Further work on the compilations would be needed to detect significant changes within the vocabulary (new semantic fields entering, etc.), and an entirely different approach would be required to determine how the words were used.

Page/Chapter

PHONOLOGY

Some details of phonological production still being learnt in
primary years. — Ch 3

In infant years some phonological distinctions still not fully
mastered in perception. — Ch 3

Some aspects of prosody (e.g. perception of intonation and of
contrastive stress) still being learnt in primary. — Ch 3

Eleven year olds already well able to code-switch in accent. — Ch 3

Appreciation of rhythm and alliteration still tenuous at 8.6. — Ch 3

SYNTAX

Passives of mental verbs (know, remember, etc.) less well
understood in primary years than passives of action verbs. — p. 217

Understanding of modal auxiliaries still developing in primary years. — p. 217

Sentences where noun immediately preceding verb is not
underlying subject difficult for many children up to nine and even eleven. — p. 5

Other areas of complex syntax still developing in primary years. — p. 5

Mastery of number markers (e.g. plurals of nouns, singulars of
verbs) still developing in infant years. — Ch. 2

LEXIS

At five, vocabulary growing at nine words/day. — p. 8

Total vocabulary at least doubles between early primary and
mid-secondary. — p. 8

SEMANTICS

Several areas of semantic knowledge still developing in primary years. — p. 8

DISCOURSE

Middle infants already largely socialised into 'teacher initiation –
(minimal) pupil response – teacher feedback' style of classroom
interaction. — p. 177

Seven year olds better than five year olds at detecting and
querying ambiguity. — Ch. 9

LANGUAGE IN USE

Six to seven year olds compare other people on concrete
characteristics, older children on abstract qualities. — p. 222

Table 2: Research findings on spoken language development between the ages of five and eleven reported in Durkin (1986)

The two books which contain all there is of the tiny amount of relevant empirical data are Durkin (1986) and Neville (1988).

In Table 2 (opposite), I present a list of all the findings reported in Durkin (1986) for which quantitative research evidence is presented or alluded to, organised by areas of language and referenced by page or chapter. It should be said that the list is pretty exiguous and ill-balanced as the distillation of a book with such a sweeping title. The last item in the list probably does not belong in an account of language development at all.

Similarly, in Table 3 (p. 40), I present a list of all the findings on oracy presented in Neville (1988), classified as listening or speaking and referenced by page. Neville's findings (like the APU's) all result from the fairly unusual circumstances of a programme of national monitoring of language performance. But then, many of the results reported in Durkin (1986) were also obtained in test/'laboratory' conditions rather than from the naturalistic data that many might prefer.

One other finding from Neville's survey can be inferred from her report, though she does not state it. She includes many pages of transcription of the pupils' responses. Within them, the amount of recognisable Scots dialect is remarkably small: almost all the sentences would be identical in syntax and vocabulary if spoken anywhere in Britain. Whatever their accents, then, it seems reasonable to infer that by the age of eleven or twelve, and even eight or nine, the vast majority of Scottish children can speak Standard English when they perceive the situation as requiring it. For age eleven (and indeed age fifteen), this finding can be generalised to the rest of the UK from APU evidence (as already implied – but, for more detail, see Brooks, 1990, p. 5).

Even taken together, these two sets of findings only begin to sketch out the ground. They put some detail on the commonsense intuition that considerable development occurs in phonology and syntax between five and eleven. They show that between eight and twelve considerable development occurs in several of the purposes for which speaking and listening can be used (at least in test conditions). But:

- the amount of information on several key areas of language (lexis, semantics, discourse) is pitifully small;

- huge areas of linguistic experience and skill are not even touched, such as humour, deception, and all the indirect uses of language (irony, questions used as commands, etc.)

In a national assessment of performance in English in Scotland in 1984, pupils in Primary 7 (aged eleven/twelve) performed significantly better than those in Primary 4 (aged eight/nine) in the following tasks:

Page

A LISTENING

Free and probed spoken recall of a narrative text.	46–8
Free (but not probed) spoken recall of an informative text.	46–8
Written responses to aural cloze tests on narrative and informative texts.	49–51
On these cloze tests, Primary 7 pupils used more sophisticated vocabulary and handled text structure better.	52
(but on same tests Primary 4 pupils made fewer careless responses than Primary 7 pupils.)	52
Multiple choice identification of word in a sentence or in isolation.	55–6
Following directions, following an explanation, interpreting a description, and distinguishing fact from opinion.	58–60

B SPEAKING

Recounting narrative and informative texts	130–1
Giving spoken directions	145–6
Giving spoken explanations	152–4
Stating and justifying an opinion	160–1

Table 3: Research findings on spoken language development between the ages of eight/nine and eleven/twelve reported in Neville (1988)

- interactive talk, which is massively more frequent in the real world than monologue, seems neglected. All of Neville's findings, and many of those reported by Durkin, concern one-way talk;

- not even a start has been made on answering several vital questions (e.g. Do whole fields of vocabulary open up between five and eleven? Are any purposes for language use, absent at five, added to the repertoire by eleven? Are there significant individual variations in the order, rate and even content of acquisition?).

This is clearly the agenda for a massive research programme. Much can and probably will be done by localised and small-scale effort, by research students and others seized with enthusiasm for particular questions. But the overall ignorance will not be much reduced without some coordination of research, preferably by the sort of National Language Centre recommended by the Bullock Committee (DES, 1975).

While research struggles to catch up with the need for information, teaching and learning, of course, have to go on. The good news is that the library of excellent books on the observation, analysis and teaching/learning of oracy continues to grow, and even, in some cases, to inspire.

References

BEIER, E. G., STARKWEATHER, J. A., and MILLER, D. E. (1967) 'Analysis of word frequencies in spoken language of children', *Language and Speech*, 10, 217–27.

BROOKS, G. (1990) 'Assessing oracy', *TOPIC*, 3, item 2.

BURROUGHS, G. E. R. (1957) *A Study of the Vocabulary of Young Children*. Edinburgh and London: Oliver and Boyd.

CHOMSKY, C. (1969) *The Acquisition of Syntax in Children from 5 to 10*. Cambridge, MA: MIT Press.

CHOMSKY, N. (1959) 'Review of Verbal Behavior by B. F. Skinner', *Language*, 35, 26–58.

DES (1975) *A Language for Life (The Bullock Report)*. London: HMSO.

DURKIN, K. (ed.) (1986) *Language Development in the School Years*. London: Croom Helm.

EDWARDS, R. P. A., and GIBBON, V. (1973) *Words Your Children Use*, 2nd edn. London: Burke.

GORMAN, T. P., WHITE, J., BROOKS, G., MACLURE, M. and KISPAL, A. (1988) *Language Performance in Schools: review of APU Language Monitoring 1979–1983*. London: HMSO.

GORMAN, T. P., WHITE, J., BROOKS, G., and ENGLISH, F. (1991) *Language for Learning: a summary report on the 1988 APU surveys of language performance (Assessment Matters, No. 4)*. London: School Examinations and Assessment Council.

MAYBIN, J. (1991) 'Children's informal talk and the construction of meaning', *English in Education*, 25(2), 34–49.

NEVILLE, M. (1988) *Assessing and Teaching Language: literacy and oracy in schools*. Basingstoke: Macmillan.

SKINNER, B. F. (1957) *Verbal Behavior*. New York: Appleton-Century-Crofts.

TOUGH, J. (1979) *Talk for Teaching and Learning*. London: Ward Lock.

WELLS, G. (1985a) *Language, Learning and Education*. Windsor: NFER-Nelson.

WELLS, G (1985b) *Language Development in the Pre-School Years*. Cambridge: Cambridge University Press.

WELLS, G. (1986) *The Meaning Makers: children learning language and using language to learn.* Sevenoaks: Hodder and Stoughton.

WEPMAN, J. M. AND HASS, W. (1969) *A Spoken Word Count – ages 5, 6 and 7.* Los Angeles, CA: Western Psychological Services.

'Look How Old This One Is!'

JENNY DES-FOUNTAIN

DAVID JACKSON

PAULINE LOADER

AND MARK WILLIAMS

In our third year of involvement in the National Oracy Project, having explored and discussed together many aspects of oracy, both practical and theoretical, we felt ready to look for development and progression in children's talk and learning.

David teaches history in a secondary school, and the first National Curriculum history documents were being discussed in Pauline's and Mark's schools, so we decided to focus on talk and learning in a particular sort of historical investigation. Using artefacts seemed to offer good opportunities for looking at oracy in Pauline's Year 1 class, Mark's Year 4 class and David's Year 7 class. The schools are in the same area, near Southend, and most of the children are monolingual English speakers.

It all seemed pretty simple at first: David organised the loan of a box of Victorian artefacts from the local Museum Service, as this period coincided reasonably well with each teacher's plans for the term. We agreed to ask children to handle and discuss the artefacts in small groups. We would tape record their talk and each teacher would then come to the next meeting ready to talk about:

● how the teacher had introduced the work;

● the children's responses to the task;

- the teacher's role;

- any examples of children 'talking history'.

Of course, it wasn't simple at all. When we met we discovered that each of us had given the task a crucially different context. Pauline's five year olds had worked in small groups, at different times, with an adult leading their discussions; she had many interesting observations about the differences in the five adults' approaches to the task and their choices of role with the children. Mark's eight year olds had been introduced to the artefacts box as a 'mystery suitcase' found on board the imagined ship which was taking the class on a trip round the world and had role-played detectives as they described and labelled the artefacts. Many of David's eleven year olds, in their first term at secondary school, were in the process of being introduced to the subject 'history'. All attempted to answer the three questions he suggested historians might ask about an artefact (What was it? What was it used for? What does it tell us about Victorian people?), but many of them were not accustomed to working with tape recorders, and a degree of unease was evident in their group talk.

The different contexts provided by the teachers and the cues they had given their classes about the task made it difficult to begin to unpick any signs of development and progression in the children's uses of talk. We also realised that we needed to think again about what we meant by 'talking history'. We decided that our next attempt should once again use artefacts, but that this time we would:

- agree a common structure for the work in the three classes;

- aim to be more explicit about the context, introducing the Year 1 and Year 4 children to the idea that they were going to be working as historians;

- tape record only one mixed ability group of four children in each class;

- ensure that all the children had had plenty of opportunities to get used to tape recorders.

Because the quality of speculation and discussion had seemed most interesting when the children were examining objects which were less readily identifiable, we decided to use a box of Roman artefacts for our second attempt. We talked about the difficulties that this would create, as we would be asking all the children to work within the context of 'being a historian' rather than within a topic context; this would be a 'one-off' session and we worried about its limitations. We were beginning to grasp just how problematic it is to find a task that could have a real validity in each teacher's classroom yet could establish some commonality of context in order to allow us to compare the children's talk. Each reduction of variables seemed to lead us closer to uncomfortably artificial conditions for learning.

We planned this sequence of work, drawing on the model of learning in *Small Group Learning in the Classroom* (Reid, Forrestal and Cook, 1991). (Peter Forrestal's article in Section 3 describes the evolution of this model.)

1 The teacher showed the whole class one of the artefacts, referring explicitly to the sorts of questions that historians ask themselves when they use artefacts: What is it? Is it old? What was it used for? What does it tell us about the people? The teacher also made explicit the ways that adult historians draw on previous experiences and can go to secondary sources to further their understandings. Finally, the teacher explained the structure for the rest of the sequence.

2 A pair of children was asked to look at three pairs of objects (Roman and replica coins; two pottery fragments; the neck of a wine jug and a glass spout) and to talk to each other about them, using the historical questions.

3 The children had time to prepare what they would say to their partner pair, who would join them to hear what they thought about the objects.

4 The partner pair had been reminded that they could expect the first pair to try to answer the historical questions, but that they should also ask questions, suggest alternative interpretations and so on. The group of four would aim to arrive at a shared explanation of the artefacts.

5 The group would reflect on their learning in the way that was appropriate in their class. The five year olds discussed the work with their teacher and recorded an entry on their class's tape diary. The eight year olds took their observations back to the whole class sharing session. The eleven year olds wrote guidelines on how to work with artefacts, for next year's Year 7 classes.

Other than keeping a discreet eye on proceedings and sending the partner pair to join the group at the appropriate time, the teachers did not intervene in the children's discussions at stages 2, 3 and 4. The session plan worked fairly well; there was some variation, e.g. the five year olds didn't really use the preparation time, but moved directly into discussion with their partner pair after they had made their initial exploration of the objects, but this time we felt that the tapes gave us examples of talk which were more readily comparable.

There was inevitably some interference caused by the presence of the tape recorders. Ironically, this now had more to do with the children's confidence and degree of ownership. Pauline discovered that her five year olds had decided when they would allow the tape to run and when they would turn it off – but we don't know what inspired their decisions, other than one clear example of control over the tape being used to wrest power from a partner in full conversational flow. The older children were conscious of an audience for their talk beyond the peer pair and four, but sounded relaxed and confident on tape.

When we listened to the taped extracts we were struck by the apparent lack of difference between the sorts of talk and learning strategies used at five and at eleven. In fact, when we transcribed sections of talk from the Year 1 class and asked colleagues to guess the children's age, they all suggested that these were much older children.

One possible reason lies with the task design. They were asked to describe the objects, asking themselves some key historical questions; perhaps we would have learned more if we had asked them to use their observations of the artefacts as part of a more analytical task. Another possibility is that, as we have often found in our Project work, we underestimate how easily and skilfully children are able to work in a wide range of curriculum areas, given helpful teacher modelling and the support of peers.

So what did we notice about the children's talk and learning? Over the two terms there was evidence of an increased understanding of what it is to work as an historian or as an archaeologist and therefore of the sorts of discussions which were appropriate. Daniel, aged six, hypothesises with his partner about the discovery of the coins:

Now guess what? They died holding all these coins, right, on the seaside and then the water came in and flushed another load of sand on top of them. Then people . . . then the tide came in . . . then the tide came in again and washed all the sand away and people found them. They didn't find the people but they found the coins, eh?

One element in children's development and progression could be a growing awareness of what it means to work within a particular set of procedures and expectations, for example as an historian, or a scientist, a writer or a designer. We felt that the teacher had a crucial role to play here, modelling and explaining.

Throughout the age range, children drew on previous experiences and understandings in order to make sense of the artefacts. One five year old was able to describe a Roman:

They, like, had these helmets on, and they had the bit under there, it's gold down here, and it comes round here . . . it's all silver this bit, and they have a tall bit up here with a feather in it . . . I've seen 'em.

And, later, the same child says:

I knew they done that, cos I seen it on tele.

An eleven year old reminds her partner:

Yeah, but don't forget their alphabet was a bit different, wasn't it?

One element of development and progression will come simply from children's increasing breadth of experience of life in and beyond school. Once again, we recognised the teacher's role in the introductory stages, encouraging children to make connections between what they already know and new information, observations and explanations.

Both Year 1 and Year 7 children addressed the historical questions and used them to make sense of the objects. At age six, commenting on the pottery shards: 'See, look, this must have been a bowl. There's the bottom bit and it's cracked.' And at age eleven, on the coins: 'They haven't cut it like we do, you know, all accurate.' They described from close observation, and generalised or referred back to other information.

Across the age range, the pairs were able to both challenge and support each other. At six: 'Hold on. Look, look. It's got a Roman helmet on!' And at eleven: 'No, hang on a sec, see if it's got a date.'

We felt that there might have been some aspects of the talk that showed a growing ability to understand the needs of the speaker or listener. However, we were comparing a pair of girls at eleven with a boy and girl pair at five and six, and it is likely that there are issues of gender and power at work.

The Year 7 girls, friends, were more tentative in their discussions, creating spaces for a different sort of collaboration. Natalie and Lorraine are looking at Roman and replica coins:

NATALIE: (*reading*) Are they old? . . . Well the . . . it looks as if it has been printed on a machine, see?
LORRAINE: Yeah, I suppose it is.
NATALIE: Is it old?
LORRAINE: The gold ones . . .
NATALIE: . . . aren't really that old, are they? I mean . . .
LORRAINE: No, they're not that old.

NATALIE: Well, they could be quite old . . .
LORRAINE: Yeah, they could be real coins, but, I mean . . .
NATALIE: They would have cut them more accurately.
LORRAINE: These two big ones, they must be really old because they're
    much different to our ones nowadays.
NATALIE: Yeah, they're big and, like, raised, isn't it?

They seem to be continuing each other's sentences and thoughts, remaining open to suggestions, allowing each other to compare the two sets of coins and to raise alternative interpretations. There seems to be a greater awareness of the value of exploratory talk, and of the ways they could use it to help along the group's thinking.

These eleven year olds were much more likely to use the language of speculation: 'I wasn't sure about these . . .', 'I thought these might be . . .', 'I mean, look at that, right? So what is it?' They also seemed to be more likely to question each other and to seek resolutions to their disagreements: 'If it was a, like, pot, it wouldn't be all black, would it?' The younger children seemed to use questions to check agreement, to signal turn-taking or to check that partners were listening – often at the end of a turn: '. . . can't you?', '. . . yeah?', '. . . right?' When they asked full questions they tended to accept the answer and use it as a springboard for their own ideas. Six year old Daniel asked Mark about the coins:

DANIEL: How do you think they got buried?
MARK: Men, pirates.
DANIEL: Smugglers. Could have done, could have done.

Daniel's 'could have done' sounds exactly like the responses he would have heard his teacher use. We felt that some features of the children's talk had been learned as part of their school life. For example, there was evidence of growing understanding of what is meant to work collaboratively, and the five year olds were able to recognise and set aside off-task talk: 'We're not talking about PE now.' Something of this shaping by schooling may have contributed to the way that the eleven year olds seemed more likely to make their reasoning explicit:

NATALIE: It could have been like a kind of vase, because that looks
    like it's broken, and it goes like that, cos some vases go like that
    and it sticks out at the side like that.
LORRAINE: It starts flat at the bottom and it goes out and comes in to
    a tight neck. I think that bit there might be the handle.
NATALIE: That's probably right, yeah.

Even though we couldn't claim to have reached any new conclusions about progression and development, we rediscovered and relearned some important principles. We learned that the contexts we create for children's talk and the task design are crucially important in shaping children's responses. Here is Laura, at five, deliberately 'naming', as she was engaged in making sense of Roman glass and pottery spouts: 'I know what this is, yeah, what it was when it was big, yeah, it was something to put flowers in. It was a vase.' We suggest that her choice of words grew powerfully from her understanding of what it is to be an historian – and an expert.

We feel certain that all of us, whatever our age, speak and listen according to our perception of our purpose, our situation and our audience. Perhaps the challenge for teachers aiming to track children's development as speakers and listeners is the need to consider the range of roles they model, the tasks they design, the range of contexts and purposes they provide for children's talk and learning.

Acknowledgements

We would like to thank Glebe Infants School, Rayleigh, Essex and King John School, Benfleet, Essex for permission to use transcribed material.

Reference

REID, J., FORRESTAL, P. AND COOK, J. (1991) *Small Group Learning in the Classroom.* English and Media Centre/NATE.

Some Unanswered Questions About the Development and Assessment of Talk in the Secondary Years

JOHN JOHNSON

I remember Richard Landy, who was co-ordinator of the National Writing Project in Mid-Glamorgan, telling me in the early days of the National Oracy Project that teachers entered such projects with many questions in mind, to which they hoped to find answers. His experience had been that rather than finding answers to these questions, they found out what the **real** questions are.

As far as the development and assessment of young adults' talk is concerned, I can only say that Richard's claim has been proved correct. For all the reasons cited elsewhere in this section, it is not possible to state authoritatively what development takes place between age eleven and sixteen. And it is certainly not possible to do so on the basis of the Project's work in that age range. But the four years which I was lucky enough to devote to developing talking and listening in schools have helped me to sharpen my understanding of what the real questions are. Here I want to ask just two. Does the development of oral language – so vital and varied a part of our individual and collective human identity – defeat all attempts to define and to describe it? And are we sure that we know what good **teenage** talking and listening are, and how to evaluate them?

Development eleven–sixteen: the work of the APU

I believe that there are two major problems in trying to answer such questions as, 'How much better are sixteen year olds than eleven year olds at speaking and listening?' Or even, 'How well do sixteen year olds speak?'

The first is the logistical and practical difficulty of running a soundly-based research project on the topic. The second is the difficulty of defining and describing qualitative terms such as 'good' and 'better' in relation to adolescent talk, when talk itself is so infinitely varied in its nature.

The only evidence which deals successfully in the eleven to sixteen age range with the problem of logistics emerges from the national monitoring exercises sponsored by the government. Most notably, during the 1980s the government's Assessment of Performance Unit (APU) conducted a number of surveys in England and Wales of children's spoken language use on a range of tasks at ages eleven and fifteen. In recent years, the work of the APU has been continued by the Evaluation and Monitoring Unit of the School Examination and Assessment Council (SEAC), which has been responsible for issuing final reports on the monitoring exercises.

The 'oracy' surveys, as they were termed, were based on pupils' oral performance on a number of tasks which they undertook in the presence of researchers. The tasks were designed to elicit pupils' responses in such areas as: describing and specifying; informing/expanding; arguing/persuading; focused questioning; evaluation of evidence/collaborative discussion or problem-solving; speculating/advancing hypotheses. (This is fully explained by Brooks (1987).) Three of the tasks were completed by both eleven and fifteen year olds in the national surveys conducted in 1982-3. This comparative work remains unpublished, but I have seen some details of the comparative data for the different age groups.

The three tasks invited the pupils to employ three functions of talk (describing, informing and arguing) and three functions of listening (identification of details, preparation for relaying information, and taking turns in discussion and preparing to respond).

The paper reveals that 100 tape-recorded examples of each task from each age level were marked by a single panel of teachers. The performances were impression marked on a scale of 1 (Bottom), to 7 (Top). This table shows the results in mean scores by age and task.

	Describing	Informing	Arguing
Age 11	3.1	3.5	3.0
Age 15	3.9	4.7	4.1

The paper also provides summary figures for the mean scores for analytic categories on the three tasks. The analytic marking was carried out on a rising 1-5 scale, and the major analytic categories employed were Distinctive Features or Content, Sequential Structure or Strategies of Argument, Register and Performance Features.

a) DESCRIBING

	Distinctive Features	Sequential Structure	Register	Performance Features
Age eleven	2.6	2.5	2.5	2.7
Age fifteen	3.1	3.0	3.0	3.0

b) INFORMING

	Content	Sequential Structure	Register	Performance Features
Age eleven	2.8	3.4	2.7	2.6
Age fifteen	3.5	3.8	3.0	3.2

c) ARGUING

	Content	Strategies of Argument	Register	Performance Features
Age eleven	2.3	2.2	2.5	2.7
Age fifteen	2.9	3.0	2.9	3.2

The paper then analyses the results on each task, indicating, for example, the major conclusions which can be drawn. Thus on the 'Describing' task, the paper states that 'the superiority of fifteen year olds on Sequential Structure means they were judged to have organised their description of the bridges (the task involved describing bridges of different structure and shape) better: in general, this meant giving a clear opening statement, and then progressing from more general features of the bridges to more detailed ones.'

The APU also ran similar matched eleven year old and fifteen year old assessments in 1988, which are reported by SEAC (1991a).

Within the discussion of these surveys, there is further statistical evidence of different levels of performance. There are also direct comparisons of children's performance at the different ages, which suggest that:

- both age groups were most successful at similar activities – instructing, narrating, arguing and persuading;

- both age groups found similar applications of task to be difficult – explaining, reporting and synthesising;

- older pupils were better able to structure and pace an activity by themselves;

- older pupils took the role of chairing a discussion more frequently and effectively than younger pupils, and made more adequate and accurate summaries in that position;

- younger pupils tended to adopt subjective views and to take control of final decision making when they were chairing discussions;

- on science tasks older pupils were inclined to offer more tentative, speculative explanations than younger pupils.

These conclusions, drawing on the judgements of assessors in ways similar to those used throughout the APU's language monitoring work, are important because they are unique as evidence of the oral language development of teenagers. But it is also important to recognise their limitations: they are based on the judgements of assessors who do not know the pupils (but who know their age). Their judgements are largely impressionistic and are related to scores rather than to specific pass/fail criteria. So we cannot say precisely what it is that makes the fifteen year old's talk better than that of eleven year olds, even though the tables indicate that assessors felt it was better.

Development 11–16: defining standards in 16+ examinations

The APU's work was valuable and significant in demonstrating that assessment of oracy could be conducted in a way which could bear comparison with assessment practices in other areas of language development. Just as the first summary reports of the 1982 Oracy Surveys were being published, the Government was developing the National Criteria for the GCSE, the new single examination that would replace the GCE O level and the CSE. The issue of assessing oral communication, as it came to be called, in English was a particularly controversial topic. Many, particularly representatives of GCE O level examination boards, did not want oral communication to be included in the new English examinations. The APU work was influential both in defining the model of oracy which should be assessed – a communicative, functional model – and in providing research evidence of the reliability and validity of the assessment itself.

In 1985, the matter was resolved by compromise – oral communication would feature in the new syllabuses but would be assessed on a different scale – grades 1 to 5 – from the remainder of the examination system. Grade descriptions for candidates' performance were prepared and published by the examining groups. Here are the grade descriptions for grade 5 and 1 from the 1990 syllabus of the Northern Examining Association:

Grade 5

The candidate can be expected to have demonstrated competence in:
understanding and conveying straightforward information at a simple level;
presenting facts, ideas and opinions with a broad sense of order and structure;
commenting on spoken and written material with some sense of relevance;
describing experience and expressing intelligibly what is felt and what is imagined in simple terms;
demonstrating some awareness of the opinions and attitudes expressed by others;
using some variation in speech style according to situation and audience;
speaking audibly and intelligibly. ·

Grade 1

The candidate can be expected to have demonstrated competence in:
understanding and conveying straightforward and complex information;
ordering and presenting facts, ideas and opinions clearly, accurately and engagingly;
evaluating spoken and written material in order to highlight what is relevant for specific purposes and to help the audience appreciate this in a sensible and sensitive manner;
describing and reflecting upon experience and expressing effectively what is felt and what is imagined;
recognising statements of opinion and attitude and discerning underlying assumptions and points of view to which a considered response is given;

displaying through the presentation of material an empathy towards
their subject and sensitivity towards the ideas of others;
showing sensitivity in deploying a range of speech styles appropriate to
audience and situation and taking responsibility for or contributing
considerably to the maintenance of an appropriate atmosphere to
facilitate effective communication;
demonstrating a maturity of vocabulary and phrasing which is not only
appropriate to the task but which enhanced the presentation;
speaking clearly and coherently with such an appropriate combination
of tone, intonation and pace that a telling impact is achieved.

The full hierarchy of grade descriptions is a fairly complete statement
of the kind of communicative objectives which examining groups
thought it appropriate for pupils and teachers to strive to attain. It is
interesting both for the cumulative process it defines – certain 'skills'
are not expected at grade 5, but are included at higher grades, for
example, evaluation – and for the qualitative distinctions between
grades, which indicate what the examining groups thought made
certain forms of talk 'better' than others.

Although oral communication was considered a highly innovative
and therefore problematic development in GCSE, it has not (so far, at
least!) proved to be a controversial one. This is probably the
consequence of the compromise which left it separately (and
differently) graded within the examining system. It has become such
an accepted – or disregarded – part of GCSE that it is actually very
difficult to find out what standards pupils are achieving nationally.
I needed information about 1990 examination results in GCSE oral
communication for a seminar, but I found that this was not available
from SEAC or the DES. I was forced to contact the relevant subject
officers in each examining group in order to prepare a table which was
subsequently published by SEAC (1991b). A slightly amended version
is given on page 56.

The results reveal a very 'bunched' performance by candidates,
considerably over 60% of whom obtained grades 2 or 3. The NEA
(which had by far the highest entry) had only 13.9% obtaining grade
1, while 32.9% obtained a grade 2 result, and 33.5% a grade 3. The
whole history of examining English suggests that teachers consistently
'bunch' their marking around the mean mark. It may be that teachers'
assessments in oral communication have fallen into this pattern of
neither rewarding all those who deserve the top grade nor applying
the lower/lowest grades with proper rigour. If this is so, it is in my
view partly caused by a widespread uncertainty about what is 'good'
sixteen year old talk.

I have here, necessarily, to make assertions rather than to cite
evidence. I have looked very carefully at the examining groups'

EXAMINING GROUP	GRADES					
	1	2	3	4	5	u
Northern Examining Association	13.9	32.9	33.5	15.5	4.2	0
	(13.9)	(46.8)	(80.3)	(95.8)	(100)	(100)
Welsh Joint Education Committee	16.1	35.2	32.7	13.0	2.4	0.6
	(16.1)	(51.3)	(84)	(97)	(99.4)	(100)
Southern Examining Group	20.8	44.4	26.1	7.4	1.1	0.2
	(20.8)	(65.2)	(91.3)	(98.7)	(99.8)	(100)
Midland Examining Group Syllabus A	16.4	41.9	30.7	9.3	1.6	0.1
	(16.4)	(58.3)	(89.0)	(98.3)	(99.9)	(100)
Midland Examining Group Syllabus B	20.3	43.1	26.9	8.0	1.5	0.2
	(20.3)	(63.4)	(90.3)	(98.3)	(99.8)	(100)
London & East Anglia Group: 50% c/work syllabus	13.8	40.0	32.5	9.3	3.6	0.8
	(13.8)	(53.8)	(86.3)	(95.6)	(99.2)	(100)
100% c/work syllabus	12.4	38.1	30.3	10.6	4.3	1.5
	(12.4)	(50.5)	(83.6)	(94.2)	(98.5)	(100)
Dual certification	12.9	32.9	40.0	4.2	3.4	0.6
	(12.9)	(45.8)	(85.8)	(96.0)	(99.4)	(100)

GCSE Oral Communication in English: 1990
Percentage performances by grade (1 to u), cumulative in brackets

procedures and especially at the video material and the procedures for disseminating the standards of the oral examination which the groups have put into place. I believe that the video material, the examining groups' commentaries, and the procedures for applying standards are based on the false premise that sixteen year olds should talk like adults.

Let me give one small example of this. In a standardising video published by one examining group, four candidates are shown participating in a role play of a court case. They then take part in a discussion of the rights and wrongs of the case.

One of the candidates, it is suggested, merits the award of a grade and level of 2+ (the + indicates that she might be on the borderline of a grade 1). Some of the commentary on her performance in the discussion is very revealing. The commentary is in general very positive: it talks of the candidate's 'speech style, clarity and structure of explanation, ability to highlight relevant issues and to evaluate the arguments she is confronted with', and words such as 'sharper', and 'very effectively' abound. But in two places the commentary strikes a cautious note, first when it says: 'In this situation she is less formal, which in a way is regrettable as the discussion needs to be chaired', and later: 'Her arguments with Lian are perhaps the highlight of a lively discussion which unfortunately suffers from the lack of a chairperson'. Now I know that in adult life many meetings are chaired by particular people. And I know that National Curriculum English has placed the role of chairing group discussions as a high level activity. But there was nothing in this particular task, nor in the hundreds of similar discussions which I have witnessed as a teacher and as a participant in the National Oracy Project, which suggested to these sixteen year olds that one of them needed to chair the discussion. They were simply having an open discussion of an issue, and to penalise them for a criterion which was not made clear in advance, or by the task, is an example of bad assessment practice.

This example is one of many which I have found in the materials issued in the first four years of GCSE English. I have come across young people being criticised for: using anecdote to back up argument (a strong feature of adolescent but also much adult talk); for not being clear in their statements (and yet deliberate ambiguity as a device to create tentative rather than firm 'positions' seems to be another feature of adolescent talk); and using peer group language (when they are talking to their peers in an informal way!).

I do not mean to be over-critical of the examining groups, however, and especially not of teachers. Putting the oral communication element of GCSE into place so comparatively successfully and professionally is in my view one of several giant strides forward taken by the English teaching profession in recent years. It is an achievement much admired by visiting educationalists from the English-speaking world and from Europe. I only want to argue that we must not be complacent about it, but be critical of the model of talk which underpins the examining process and focus more on how sixteen year olds do communicate successfully rather than on how we as adults (often far removed from them in age, interest and experience) believe that they should.

Development eleven to sixteen: future work

I believe that the combination of all the work mentioned in this section – especially the work of the APU and the general findings of the National Oracy Project – has in effect cleared the ground of the débris and rubble of prejudice and misunderstanding which surrounds the development of talk in the secondary years. It is now much clearer that teachers do not want, and cannot use, information about the precise growth of syntactical forms, vocabulary, use of abstractions or whatever else might be narrowly compiled through statistical analysis of young people's discourse. Rather, it seems to me, they want information about the kinds of experiences and choices which young people should have and be able to make in talk, about the general development of young people as social learners, and about how to evaluate and assess these developments within the educational framework of the classroom and of the National Curriculum. Other sections of this book describe both the Project's findings and other academics' views on these matters in some depth. At the heart of it all is the wish that pupils and teachers should take part in the classroom in what Gordon Wells (in a presentation at UEA in 1991) termed 'institutional conversations'. In such conversations the framing and development of the task itself, the roles and relationships of participants, and the shared process of making meaning (in which the previous knowledge and experience, and linguistic resources, of participants are put to work) are all relevant. How we as teachers determine some of these highly variable factors will in part be based on our view of the pupils' development. For example, the choice of speech activity is highly complex. Douglas Barnes provided the 'map' on the page opposite of the choices made by teachers and pupils determining the nature of speech activities.

At each stage of such a process, and hence of planning or negotiating the activity, we as teachers will be matching the choice made to what we know of the linguistic abilities, previous knowledge and experience of the pupils, while also trying to support their entry into new areas of experience and understanding. And each choice made may, we know, help or hinder this development.

Last of all, what of assessment? Here I want only to recommend two pieces of further reading. The work of secondary school teachers in the

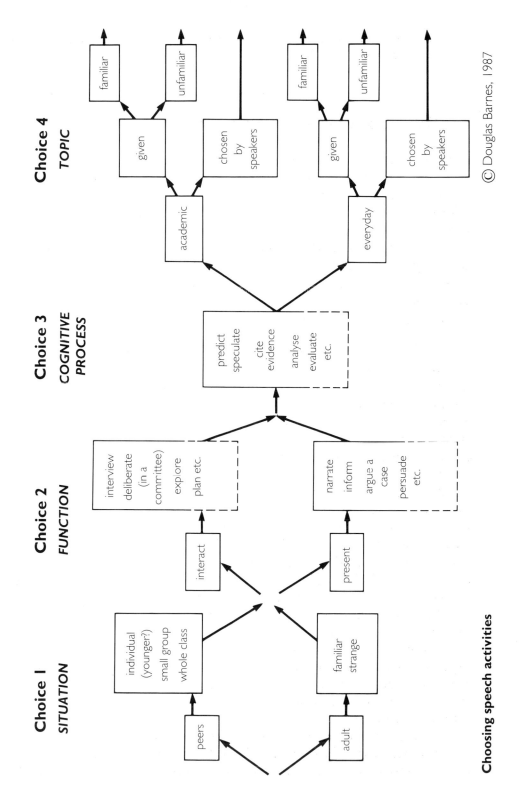

Choice 1
SITUATION

Choice 2
FUNCTION

Choice 3
COGNITIVE PROCESS

Choice 4
TOPIC

peers

individual
(younger?)
small group
whole class

adult

familiar
strange

interact

interview
deliberate
(in a committee)
explore
plan etc.

present

narrate
inform
argue a
case
persuade
etc.

predict
speculate
cite
evidence
analyse
evaluate
etc.

academic

given

familiar

unfamiliar

chosen
by
speakers

everyday

given

familiar

unfamiliar

chosen
by
speakers

© Douglas Barnes, 1987

Choosing speech activities

59

National Oracy Project in assessing talk is summarised in a co-publication of this book – an INSET pack called *Learning Together Through Talk; Key Stages 3 and 4* (in press). A general process is defined and explained in that pack (and in other National Oracy Project publications) of basing final evaluations on the considered but selective sampling of valid evidence. And a model for 'assessing oracy' is contained in an article by the late Andrew Wilkinson and Deborah Berrill – 'Truth to Tell: criteria for judgement' (1990). This model looks closely at three aspects of any talk: Ideational (what is said); Interpersonal (how it is said); and Textual (the form chosen). In this model, the two writers came as close as anyone has done to summarising in one place all the issues which should be considered when trying to answer the question, 'How good is this talk?' It is a good testimony to the quality of thought and insight which Andrew Wilkinson brought to this field – a field which he himself marked out a quarter of a century ago. It certainly provides the starting point for an attempt to answer some of those unanswered questions.

Acknowledgement

Thanks to Douglas Barnes for permission to use the diagram 'Choosing speech activities'.

References

BROOKS, G. (1986) *Primary/Secondary Oracy Comparisons* (unpublished).

BROOKS, G. (1987) *Speaking and Listening. Assessment at Age 15.* Windsor: NFER – Nelson.

NCC (in press) *Learning Together Through Talk; Key Stages 3 and 4.* Sevenoaks: Hodder and Stoughton.

SEAC (1991) *Assessment Matters: No. 4, Language for Learning.* London: SEAC.

SEAC (1991) *GCSE English Chief Examiners' Conference Report 1990.* London: SEAC.

WILKINSON, A. AND BERRILL, D. (1990) 'Truth to Tell: criteria for judgement' in Wilkinson, A. , Davies, A. and Berrill, D. *Spoken English Illuminated.* Milton Keynes: Open University Press.

The Contexts of Oracy

2

An Introduction to Section 2

DOUGLAS BARNES

This section explores some of the relationships between how we talk and the social and cultural contexts in which the talk takes place. It is important for teachers to be aware how pupils' interpretations of what is going on in a lesson will affect what they say and how they say it, since this will help them to understand better some of the more puzzling aspects of classroom talk and to plan for effective participation in lessons by all pupils. It is equally important to understand how language affects people's lives in the community outside school, for pupils bring to school attitudes and expectations which may affect their success as students.

How we talk is greatly influenced by the immediate context in which we find ourselves. In this sense, 'context' is not a matter of the physical situation but rather of how we perceive the identity and purposes of the other persons present, how we interpret whatever activities are currently being carried out, and our own place in them. For example, if we are expecting our speech to be judged, this will have an effect not only on what we say but on how we say it. Two of the articles in this section point out that young children may be silenced by uncertainty about what is expected of them in the classroom; this is probably the source of the myth of the child who 'comes to school without language'. Contributors to the section discuss some of the unspoken expectations that may face children not only when they first come to school but later as they meet the specialist language forms in which certain curricular subjects are commonly discussed.

Talk is closely related to context in a wider sense, for 'context' here includes not only the immediate situation but the practices, assumptions and beliefs that make up a way of life. What we say communicates more than the overt message: every time we speak we also transmit messages about who we are, and where we belong. Different languages, and even different accents and dialects, become linked to groups of people of different standing in the community. Tony Edwards, in his article, points out that language differences may provide 'a basis for judgements not only about the cultural origins of speakers but also about their capabilities and prospects'. Since some of these latter judgements are likely to be inaccurate and harmful this is a matter of considerable importance in schools, especially for those children whose home language is not English and for those others whose accent or dialect is associated with low status in some people's minds.

It is important not to think of children's talk on a particular occasion as an unambiguous indication of their language abilities. How children talk in school depends both on their experiences outside school – the different roles and purposes for which they have used language – and on how they interpret the requirements of the classroom situation. Teachers need to understand that their behaviour as listeners and respondents sends tacit messages to children about the role they are expected to perform as learners. How pupils talk in a lesson depends not only on the context and purpose set up in that lesson but on their previous experiences of taking part in classroom talk. It is thus useful for teachers to discuss explicitly with their pupils the reasons for asking them to engage in different kinds of talk and why it is important.

'Learning to talk is part of learning to be a member of a particular culture' (Wells, 1989). That is, learning to talk is not just a matter of learning how to construct sentences but of learning how to engage with other people, to respond to what they say, to influence what they think and do – in Halliday's phrase, 'to make meanings'. Because talk is part of social action it is essentially purposive: if we ask children to talk for purposes that they have not themselves accepted they are unlikely to excel. Our ability to talk well is not independent of our understanding of what we are talking about and our commitment to it: good talk 'about nothing' is inconceivable. Nor is the ability to talk independent of sensitivity to the perspective of the persons we are talking with. This suggests that attempts to 'teach talk' out of context are likely to meet with limited success.

The National Oracy Project has on principle favoured the development of pupils' spoken language through activities that are worthwhile in their own right, including talk as part of the learning activities throughout the curriculum. Young people are most likely to 'stretch' their oral competences when they are struggling to say something that matters to them to someone who wants to hear. Janet Maybin cites several pieces of research that demonstrate the truth of this for younger children: it is equally true for adolescents and adults.

An important pointer for the classroom is provided by Tony Edwards' reminder that 'communicative competence includes being able to draw upon a repertoire of ways of speaking'. Since effectiveness in talk is so closely related to the expectations and purposes of those to whom we talk, it is essential that young people become sufficiently aware of what is expected in different situations to be able to switch appropriately, for example, into a spoken version of Standard English or to a less formal style, whenever each of these is appropriate. (Such awareness would also allow them to choose to speak 'inappropriately', if on some occasion they thought it essential.) Flexibility, sensitivity to context, and the ability to reflect on the implications of other people's responses are important aspects of oral competence.

The phrase 'language practices' which occurs frequently in these articles indicates that attention is focused more on the purposes for which language is used than on the forms – the vocabulary and grammatical structures. However, the forms cannot be ignored. Tony Edwards's article, 'Language, Power and Cultural Identity', sets the scene for the whole section by discussing some of the ways in which the forms of language people use identify the groups to which they belong. Such stereotyping is a matter of considerable importance in education for, as he writes, 'People can be disadvantaged by sounding disadvantaged – by speaking haltingly, or declining to use, whatever language is associated with "getting on" in the world'. Thus, speech is involved in the processes by which status, power and wealth are allocated. Half aware of this, some older pupils may deliberately stress their home accents as a way of demonstrating their separation from the goals and values of school.

One kind of stereotyping that can be observed in classroom talk is that which differentiates girls from boys. Hilary Kemeny discusses gender and oracy in her article, 'As Near to Life as Possible?' She points out not only the well substantiated differences between boys' and girls' oral participation in lessons, but also shows how 'the hidden curriculum of gender roles' may be unintentionally reinforced during lessons. Her examples show how, even when equal participation in discussion has been achieved, some boys may marginalise and even ignore girls' contributions, sometimes devaluing them in their own eyes. But, as Gemma Moss also argues in a response to this article, this evidence does not mean that teachers should encourage girls to behave more like boys. Rather, they should, with their pupils, look more closely at the different conversational strategies used. 'If girls and boys are using different ground rules, who gets to decide which set of rules is most appropriate?'

Tony Edwards also refers to the power that resides in a teacher's hands by virtue of his or her right to determine the nature and content of the talk that constitutes so large a part of lessons. This function of talk is analysed further by several authors in Section 4.

Richard Bain, in 'Striking Attitudes', discusses some of the ways in which teachers' and pupils' attitudes to spoken language may impede learning. No one doubts that there are linguistic differences between the language spoken in many homes and the various language practices expected in school, but it is no longer believed that some language styles carry an inherent intellectual disadvantage. There are two processes that may nevertheless create disadvantages. We have already pointed out that certain language styles are perceived to be linked to a lower status and a more restricted education. Such perceptions can themselves carry educational disadvantages, particularly if the children themselves believe their spoken language to be inferior. Moreover, some uses of language are implicitly linked with particular ways of understanding the world. Children whose homes have not given them ready access to those ways of talking and thinking that are expected in school may be disadvantaged because it takes them longer to tune in to what is going on in a lesson.

Janet Maybin develops this line of thought in her article, 'Children's Language Practices at Home and School'. What children learn at home is not just the forms of a language but also social roles and behaviours. These may carry with them a higher valuation of certain ways of thinking and knowing. When they go to school, all children face a greater or lesser disjunction between their home expectations and those of the classroom. For almost all children, talk at home is embedded in a rich web of shared purposes and experiences, stretching from the past and reaching out towards the future. The meanings celebrated in lessons are necessarily more isolated, less embedded in experience shared by teacher and children, however hard the teacher tries. She goes on to suggest that one result of the gulf between language practices at school and home is that much of children's language resources may be untapped during their hours at school.

Mary Morrison and Perminder Sandhu, in 'Towards a Multilingual Pedagogy', stress the links between a child's mother tongue and his or her basic strategies for thinking and learning. They illustrate how a classroom that is designed to encourage and support bilingual children's use of their mother tongue alongside English enhances their ability to engage in complex thought. They go on to discuss sympathetically the anxieties faced by monolingual teachers in making this possible. Bilingualism, far from being a disadvantage, can be advantageous. Janet Maybin too shows that, though the cultural gap between home and school may seem to be a particular problem for bilingual children, their knowledge of more than one language may become an advantage for some, as it heightens their awareness of the necessary adjustments to school talk, which other children may not even perceive.

Yanina Sheeran and I deal with the spoken language requirements of particular school subjects and with the vexed question of whether there are linguistic genres which are so important to school success that they should be taught. At the centre of the debate is whether thinking in science, history or mathematics is indissolubly wedded to the special terminology and stylistic characteristics that can be found in the writings of specialists in those subjects. Can the concepts that underlie school subjects be learned without adopting specialist language? Another consideration is that our style of speaking often has considerable influence on our standing in other people's eyes: if we do not talk about science as scientists do, many of our hearers will think we do not know what we are talking about. We discuss the functions that specialist language plays both in and out of schools, and go on to discuss what might be done in lessons to help children be more aware of the kinds of talk expected of them.

Reference

WELLS, G. (1989) 'Language in the classroom: literacy and collaborative talk', *Language and Education*, 3:4, 1989.

Language, Power and Cultural Identity

TONY EDWARDS

'Standard English' was discussed by the Working Group for National Curriculum English as a dialect 'of a special kind', not to be confused with 'good' English, because its speakers 'can use English just as "badly" as anyone else'. But all children should have opportunities to 'learn to use it competently' because, unlike regional dialects, it is 'conventionally used for a wide range of public purposes', (DES, 1989, Chapter 4, § 9–12).

That view of Standard English as a social dialect with particular uses and particular advantages bitterly disappointed those who had hoped for a reassertion of respect for the inherent superiority of 'correct' English 'properly' spoken. The accompanying insistence that non-standard forms are governed by different rules rather than being haphazard departures from correctness, and that they can be a 'social irritant' without being structurally defective, was intended to mark out a sensibly moderate position in what has been a long, heated debate frequently distorted by a tendency to treat departures from linguistic 'correctness' as evidence of cultural and even moral decline (Graddol and Swann, 1988: Milroy and Milroy, 1985: Stubbs, 1989). Much of the heat has come from confusing different kinds of superiority. For languages, and varieties of 'a' language, may be 'equal but different' from a linguistic perspective, yet very unequal in the social worlds to which they give ready access.

This is most obvious in multilingual societies where language is a heavy weapon in a continuing contest for spheres of influence. Whose language is normally expected on public occasions, and is expected to be heard from those in authority? Which language has normally to be spoken with some fluency to be taken notice of by those in positions of power and influence, or to allow speakers of that language to be taken seriously as contenders for such positions? If one of the competing languages is socially and politically privileged, then its use or non-use is likely to be a basis for judgments not only about the cultural origins of speakers but about their capabilities and prospects. The danger of stereotyping is therefore high. People can be disadvantaged by sounding disadvantaged – by speaking haltingly, or declining to use, whatever language is associated with 'getting on' in the world. Similarly, their failure to 'get on' in the world may be conveniently explained away by treating their speech as evidence of poor ability or low ambition.

Differences within the same language convey similar social information, with similar dangers. Dialects have become less distinctive in vocabulary and certainly in grammar under the standardising influences of mass education and the mass media. But regional accents persist, as do many local words and phrases. Where the social networks within which children grow up are populated largely by local people, then that fact will be pervasively evident in their own adult speech unless they make conscious efforts later to conceal their origins. Even then, particular features of pronunciation are likely to persist and 'betray' them. Where families are themselves mobile, or live in areas of diverse and shifting population, then the variety of linguistic influences is likely to produce speech patterns which are less consistently distinctive and so much harder to place. Regional accents are strongest among those in manual occupations and in traditionally stable working-class communities. In contrast, what is called Received Pronunciation (or RP) is that version of 'top people's' English which is regionless (though emphatically not classless), and which used to be associated with the BBC until regional accents came to be accepted, and even encouraged. It should not be confused with Standard English. RP speakers have always been a very small minority, however conspicuous in various branches of the 'establishment', and are far outnumbered by speakers of regionally-accented Standard English. Even they seem hard to find in London classrooms among the 60 or more varieties of English and the substantial minority – as high as one third in districts like Haringey – who speak at least one other 'named world language' (Linguistic Minorities Project, 1985).

London schools represent, in heightened form, a common reality in urban areas. What is accepted or tolerated as an appropriate way of speaking in the classroom, for at least some educational purposes, is therefore a critically important matter. The existence of first languages other than the 'authorised' language of schooling may present problems of mutual comprehension which are too obvious not to be tackled directly, but can also be a valuable resource in extending pupils' linguistic and cultural understanding (Miller, 1983; National Curriculum Council, 1991). Non-standard varieties of the same language are unlikely to be used in that positive way. Less obviously a 'problem', they may present barriers to learning which are all the greater for being insidious. For example, their association with low-status occupations may be treated as a causal relationship, linguistic differences being used to 'explain' high rates of educational and occupational failure among some social groups on the grounds that their language is deficient, limiting, or at best inappropriate for 'public purposes'. Such judgments then create their own reality, shaping the expectations of teachers and pupils alike. The fervour with which non-standard varieties of English have been defended as being linguistically different, but not cognitively deficient, reflects concern at the denial of educational opportunity which linguistic intolerance can produce. This is well expressed in a statement on the issue which has been much quoted: 'what is at stake is not logic, rationality, reasoning power, but what we think of each other and of ourselves' (Hymes, 1972, p. xxxi).

For many pupils, the language of the home is not very different from the language thought appropriate to the classroom. They face no great test of linguistic adaptability, or of cultural affiliation, as they move between those social worlds. But where success seems to depend on learning a new language, or a more prestigious variety of the same language, then its adoption is not only a linguistic challenge. It may mark a considerable and growing cultural distance from the home, being taken as evidence of assimilation into another culture or sub-culture, and suspected or resented by those 'left behind'. Where its acquisition brings prized occupations within reach, it may be welcomed for that reason by parents, who at the same time regret the uprooting it threatens. Their children's awareness of that regret may lead them, when at home, to depress their otherwise skilled performance in the second 'language' and display a deliberately cultivated incompetence as a reassuring sign of loyalty to their culture (Miller, 1983).

That phenomenon is a necessary reminder that communicative competence includes being able to draw on a repertoire of ways of speaking. For those fluent in several languages or dialects, the repertoire is linguistically wide and the code-switching will be obvious. Even apparently monolingual speakers can choose – whether consistently or on certain occasions and for particular purposes – to highlight or suppress items of speech so as to display or emphasise a particular identity, cultural loyalty or social aspiration. What socio-linguists call 'hyper-correction', for example, is the tendency among the socially ambitious or socially insecure to overdo the 'correctness' ('between you and I' being a familiar example) or exaggerate prestige forms of pronunciation.

It would be quite wrong, however, to suggest that social movement and social aspiration are always 'onwards and upwards'. Loyalty to cultural origins may be strong, and linguistic differences can be a powerful expression of resistance to assimilation or subordination. Thus Black English Vernacular in the United States became a powerful political instrument: it was a means of marking a sense of cohesion within black communities and their sense of distance from the white 'mainstream'. 'Monitoring black' was used to describe this deliberate highlighting of linguistic differences. London-Jamaican and other regional vernaculars serve the same function, as, of course, do the languages preserved and fostered within ethnic minorities. Whether they are linguistically large or slight, speech differences represent an infinite resource for expressing a sense of similarity or otherness and so for maintaining, reducing or extending social distance. Thus, non-standard forms may be deliberately accentuated, in classrooms as in other social situations, so as to make the statement: 'I am unlike you, my world is different, this education has little or nothing in it for me.' Or they may be modified, in the classroom but not in the playground or street, so as to indicate a willingness to meet the school's expectations, if only for practical purposes.

This dynamic view of speech differences emphasises that talk does not simply take place 'in' particular contexts. It often serves to define the situation – for example, to mark it as formal or informal, as an occasion for official business or personal exchanges. Choice of language or social dialect can have that effect. Forms of address (Sir, Miss Smith, headmaster, Jane, Smith) and, in many languages, the choice between formal or intimate forms of 'you' display the speaker's sense of hierarchy or equality – of whether respect is called for or can be claimed, or whether there is a proper social distance to be maintained. That perception may then be confirmed or challenged by the other speaker's choice of words.

Such analysis can be extended beyond the formal characteristics of speech to questions about who can appropriately do what with the words that are being exchanged. A general contrast can be drawn between ordinary conversation, broadly defined as 'talk between equals', and talk in which the age, gender, social status or role of one or more participants normally carries certain communicative privileges and responsibilities. In the former, talk is organised by the participants as it goes along, because none of them has any special right or obligation to ensure its smooth running. In the latter, someone is 'entitled', for example: to speak first, most often and last; to decide who else shall speak, when, for how long and about what; or even to interrupt the turns of others without risking complaint or retaliation. The constraints on who can 'properly' do what may arise from particular roles in a particular situation, as with the special rights enjoyed temporarily by those asked to chair meetings. Constraints may also be pervasively attached to social identities. Those being introduced to the Queen are expected to answer questions, but not to ask them. Females commonly claim, or are 'allowed', less than their 'share' of talking time even in mixed groups of supposed equals; they take or are allowed to take fewer initiatives; and they are more vulnerable to interruption. Young children often have to work hard to attract and keep the attention of an adult conversational partner, who may end the conversation ('I'm busy/tired') much more abruptly and unilaterally than would normally be permissible with another adult. Classrooms have traditionally been marked by highly asymmetrical relationships, the transmission of knowledge creating very unequal communicative rights. This is evident, for example, in the amount of talking which teachers do, the frequency of their questions and the frequency with which they approve, amend or discard the answers.

Knowing how to manage unequal relationships, to choose the 'right' forms and do the 'right' things, is an important part of being communicatively competent. More generally, 'the process of learning how to negotiate communicatively is the very process by which one enters the culture' (Bruner, 1984, p. 1). It is largely through talk that children develop their sense of identity as members of various social worlds. As they listen and talk, they learn what it is appropriate to know, do and say in that particular relationship or setting. In complex, multicultural societies, however, it is very unlikely that this will be 'common' (in the sense of 'shared') knowledge. This powerful notion of talking one's way into forms of social relationship raises questions about how closely what is learned in the 'home world' corresponds to the communicative demands of critical contexts in the wider society. Since school represents the first and most important move out of the home world, those children who experience a great deal of continuity between how language is used in their classrooms and in their homes stand a much better chance of being identified and sponsored as successful pupils. Ignorance of, or resistance to, those communicative demands – whether the demands are for 'appropriately' standard or formal speech, or for particular ways of taking turns or answering questions – may be interpreted as indicating a general unfitness for learning. As one black mother complained about the language difficulties attributed to her son at school: 'My kid, he too scared to talk, cause nobody play by the rules he know. At home, I can't shut him up' (Heath, 1983, p. 107). Predominantly monocultural classrooms in a multicultural society are a powerful and pervasive source of educational disadvantage.

References

BRUNER, J. (1984) 'Interaction, communication and self', *Journal of the American Academy of Child Psychiatry*, 23 (1), pp. 1–7.

DES (1989) *English for Ages 5–16*. London: HMSO.

GRADDOL, D. AND SWANN, J. (1988) 'Trapping linguists: an analysis of linguists' response to John Honey's pamphlet, "The Language Trap"', *Language and Education*, 2 (2), pp. 95–112.

HEATH, S. (1983) *Ways with Words: Language; Life and Work in Communities and Classrooms*. Cambridge: Cambridge University Press.

HYMES, D. (1972) 'Introduction', Caszden, C., John, V., and Hymes, D. (eds.), *The Functions of Language in the Classroom*. New York: Teachers College Press, ILEA.

LINGUISTIC MINORITIES PROJECT (1985) *The Other Languages of England*. London: Routledge and Kegan Paul.

MILLER, J. (1983) *Many Voices: Bilingualism, Culture and Education*. London: Routledge and Kegan Paul.

MILROY, J. AND MILROY, L. (1985) *Authority in Language: Investigating Linguistic Prescription and Standardization*. London: Routledge and Kegan Paul.

NATIONAL CURRICULUM COUNCIL (1991). *Linguistic Diversity and the National Curriculum (Circular No. 11)*. York: NCC.

STUBBS, M. (1989) 'The state of English in the English state: reflections on the Cox Report', *Language and Education*, 3(4), pp. 235–50.

Children's Language Practices at Home and School

JANET MAYBIN

Introduction

When children first enter the classroom, they have to learn particular ways of using language which are closely tied up with the socialising and educative function of schools. These ways with language have deep roots which extend beyond institutional purposes to underlying cultural beliefs about the nature and purpose of different kinds of knowledge, the ways people's relations with each other should be structured, and the relationship between language and learning. Children are not just learning, for instance, that the teacher will ask them questions to which he or she knows the answer, or that responding to a story involves having a particular kind of conversation about it. They are also learning which kinds of knowledge are marked as important, and what it means to be a reader and to be a pupil in a particular culture.

Most research into the differences between children's language practices at home and school has been interested in identifying the reasons for particular children's 'problems' in coping with school uses of language, or with identifying those home practices which seem most closely associated with school success. This research suggests that certain ways of using language in relation to literacy, and for analytical reasoning and reflection, are significant for educational achievement. Some of the research also indicates home uses of language which are not tapped by the school, and which have considerable potential for enriching the classroom environment and individual children's learning experiences.

How should the teacher respond when faced with children whose home language practices are different from, and even at odds with, those of the classroom? I want to start with two examples of American research which highlight the cultural complexities involved in this question, before moving closer to home.

The children of Warm Springs

About twenty years ago, an anthropologist, Susan Phillips, made a study of Native American children's talk in the classroom, in the Warm Springs Reservation school in Central Oregon. Many teachers had been complaining that Native American children wouldn't talk in class, and that the problem seemed to get worse rather than better as they got older. But when Phillips started observing the talk more closely, she found that there were times in the classroom when the children were willing and, indeed, eager to talk. She related the children's extreme reluctance to participate in certain kinds of classroom talk – and their preference for others – to their experience of talk and learning outside the school. Because the community placed importance on learning through silent watching and listening, and on privately practising skills before demonstrating them in front of others, children felt acutely uncomfortable when teachers asked them questions in class, since this meant making mistakes and demonstrating their ignorance publicly. In the community, social activities were not organised by particular individuals and did not involve a distinction between audience and performers; the drumming, dancing or singing could be initiated by anyone, with others joining in as they wished. Similarly, anyone who wanted to speak at a political meeting could do so; people were accorded respect in relation to particular abilities and knowledge rather than because of some position they held. So in the classroom children responded negatively to the teacher's control of their contributions and talk, and to situations where they were being asked to 'perform' in front of others. But when they were asked to work on a project co-operatively in small groups, then they collaborated very effectively, and talked together with great concentration in the course of their work.

This study raises interesting questions about the meaning of different language practices for children. For the Warm Springs children, it was not just a case of having to learn new vocabulary, or particular kinds of question and answer routines, but rather of being faced with ways of using language which seemed to go directly against fundamental community beliefs about how people should relate to each other, the constitution of authority and the nature of learning. The ways they had learned to use language at home were closely tied up with particular cultural beliefs and social practices, which were different from those which underpinned the language practices in the classroom.

How did the Warm Springs teachers, who were not Native American, respond to the children's behaviour? Phillips found that they had moved towards using small group project work for most of the time, avoided whole class discussion and had abandoned activities, such as 'show and tell', which involved children speaking out to the whole class. This resulted in an easier and happier working atmosphere in the reservation school classroom. Phillips points out, however, that it did not seem to help the children when they moved on to the larger, racially mixed school in the town; here, the problem of non-participation became more pronounced and was exacerbated by racial tension. This leads Phillips to ask if reducing the kinds of talk contexts is also reducing children's opportunities for particular kinds of learning. In other words, although the Warm Springs children may have more opportunities for learning from each other, they may have fewer opportunities for being 'scaffolded' by their teacher. (Article 4.2 explores the concept of 'scaffolding' in depth.)

The children of Trackton

More recently, Heath (1983) studied the language experience of pre-school children in three local communities in the American Piedmont Carolinas. She wanted to show that children in modern America could come to school not only with different experiences of books and reading, but also with different ideas about the relationship between spoken and written language. She found that children from black and white urban middle-class families came to school expecting to make connections between their own experience and the books they read, and to use the ideas and structures from books for their own imaginative explorations and fantasies. Children from a nearby working-class white community, where religious practices included an emphasis on written scriptures, came with experience of number and alphabet books, Bible stories and real life stories about children like themselves, but saw texts as inflexible records of 'the truth' which shouldn't be played about with. But it was children from the third community, Trackton, who seemed to have most difficulty in adjusting to school language practices. These black working-class children were unfamiliar with story books, but were skilled in oral story telling, and in performing and interacting with an audience. Their experience of written texts was of adults reading and discussing together the meaning of newspaper articles, letters from school, advertising brochures and church-related materials. In school, these children were faced with unfamiliar kinds of questions, asking them to identify and label individual features such as colour, shape and size, in relation to pictures and written texts which were strange to them. These children were not used to responding to utterances which sounded like questions, but were really directives (for example, 'Why don't you use that one on the shelf?'), or to questions which required a direct feeding back of information already known to the teacher, or to questions which asked for a display of specific skills and content information acquired primarily from books and ways of talking about books. For instance, Heath (1982) quotes the following dialogue, which occurs just after the teacher has read a story to her class of seven year olds:

TEACHER: What is the story about?
CHILDREN: (*silence*)
TEACHER: Uh . . . let's see . . . who is it the story talks about?
CHILDREN: (*silence*)
TEACHER: Who is the main character? Um . . . what kind of story is it?
CHILD: Ain't nobody can talk about things being about theirselves.

Heath explains that this child was reacting to the fact that teachers' questions so often asked for labels, attributes and discrete features of objects and events in isolation from the context. In the child's community, people asked questions about whole events or objects and their uses, causes and effects; answers usually involved telling a story, describing a situation or making comparisons with other events and objects known to the audience. But this ability to link two situations metaphorically and recreate scenes was not tapped in school – in fact, it could often be a nuisance to the teacher. By the time these children reached the stage in their school career when reasons, explanations and effective statements called for the creative comparison of two or more situations, it was too late for many of them; they had not picked up the particular kinds of composition and comprehension skills needed to translate their analogical skills into an acceptable channel. What is more, the rejection by the school of these young children's ways of using language often resulted in the child losing confidence, and eventually switching off school altogether.

How does Heath suggest their teachers should respond to the children of Trackton? She makes two suggestions. First, that teachers should find out about the home language practices of their pupils and, secondly, that they should try to discover ways of organising their classrooms and teaching, in order to bridge the gap more effectively between children's home experience and the 'mainstream' language practices they will need to acquire in order to cope with school. Interestingly, she doesn't seriously address the question of changing school language practices to the extent where the Trackton children's skill in using language metaphorically and analogically might contribute directly to their early learning in school.

British research

The two best known British studies of children's language use at home and school have both focused on monolingual children. Wells (1985) was interested in how children's pre-school language experience contributed to their learning and to their later school achievement, and Tizard and Hughes (1984) contrasted young girls' language at home with their mothers with their language experience at nursery. Both looked particularly at adult-child dialogue, and found that whereas children at home had extensive conversations with adults, in which they built up shared meanings and tested out ideas, similar conversations seldom occurred at school or nursery. This was partly because there wasn't the time and partly because the teacher and child didn't have the initial shared experience and understanding that make such conversations possible. Both studies concluded that in order for children to learn through conversations with adults, such shared understanding and experience are vital.

Wells identified certain pre-school experiences of literacy as being closely related to children's later achievement, especially the experience of listening to stories. He suggests that learning the structure of stories helps children to be literate and to use language for intellectual exploration. For this reason, he argues that story and narrative should play a much larger part in classroom language practices.

What about the experience of bilingual children in Britain? How does their pre-school language experience prepare them for classroom uses of talk? It would appear that these children are even less likely to find the all-important basis of shared experience and understanding with their teachers, or to receive positive affirmation of their own competence in language use. As Miller (1983, p. 5) points out, 'a child with two or three non-European languages, in some of which he may be literate, could be regarded as quite literally languageless when he arrives in an English school, where "not a word of English" can often imply "not a word"'. However, research (e.g. Saunders, 1983) suggests that bilingual children have greater and earlier awareness of language as a symbolic system (for example, that objects and ideas can be represented by different words and in different ways, depending on which language is being used) and that they also have greater sensitivity to the relationship between language and context. This should put bilingual children at an advantage in recognising and coping with the specialised uses of language in the classroom. The following example illustrates the kind of awareness of, and sensitivity to, language use which Saunders is talking about.

Fifteen year old Rahilla is introducing her four year old sister Asiya to an English picture book one afternoon at home. She is also introducing her to a kind of language practice which she knows Asiya will soon encounter in school and to some important metalinguistic knowledge. Rahilla and Asiya usually talk to each other in Urdu at home but here, where Rahilla is drawing her sister into a type of school reading activity, most of the interaction is in English. Rahilla taped and transcribed the talk while researching her own language development, and her current language use in different contexts, for a GCSE English assignment:

RAHILLA: What colour is the flower?
ASIYA: White and green.
RAHILLA: White and green. OK. What's beside the . . . erm . . . girl?
   What's beside her?
ASIYA: The thing.
RAHILLA: The red thing. What's that?
ASIYA: Ladybird!
RAHILLA: What colour's the ladybird?
ASIYA: Red and black.
RAHILLA: Oh, look, there's a feather there!
ASIYA: Yai! . . . white!
RAHILLA: What's on the page? What's this?
ASIYA: Boy teacher.
RAHILLA: A boy teacher. What has he got in his hand?

ASIYA: (*pause*) . . . a . . . a sohti.
RAHILLA: A sohti.
ASIYA: Yai!
RAHILLA: That's a stick. (. . .) Oh look, here's a teacher. What's he doing on the board?

The way in which Rahilla talks to Asiya about the pictures in the book teaches her to focus on particular features (for example, the name and colour of items) in exactly the same way that Heath observed teachers operating in her study. Asiya starts to internalise and anticipate particular types of questions: for example, she spontaneously gives the colour of the feather without being asked. Rahilla is also preparing her for the school practice of responding to stories through conversations about them. And Asiya is learning that language is a symbolic system, where words can represent pictures and can be translated from one language into another: for example, a 'sohti' is a stick.

In her GCSE assignment, Rahilla describes how, as a young child, she first became fluent in Punjabi but was also picking up words in Urdu and English from people, books, newspapers, videos and television. Rahilla now slips easily in and out of her three languages, depending on where she is and to whom she is talking. And, of course, there are different styles and registers within these languages, which are closely tied up with different cultural and social practices. It may, in fact, be difficult to think about language use in isolation from these practices. As Rahilla puts it, 'When we were younger we were not told how to speak to someone, we were only told how to behave. I was recognising that there were some situations where I had to completely change the way I spoke.'

Conclusion

From these studies in Britain and America, we can draw some general points about the differences between children's language experience at home and school.

1 All children bring considerable language resources with them to school. Certain children, however, are not familiar with some of the ways in which language is used in the classroom to construct shared meanings. In particular, they may not be used to the kind of labelling activities which are a central part of teaching early literacy and numeracy, and they may not be used to talking about 'things being about themselves' – what has been termed a 'disembedded' or

'decontextualised' use of language. They may also be unfamiliar with the rather specialised ways in which the teacher uses language to organise and control the class.

2 Children learn best where they are treated as equal conversational partners and are encouraged to explore their own concerns and interests in extended conversations. This needs to be done in a context where there is shared experience and understanding, and where the child is respected and encouraged as a speaker.

3 A large part of some children's oral language resources for learning is not being tapped in the classroom.

We need, however, to remind ourselves continually of the questions raised by the studies described here, as we respond to the language practices which children bring with them to school and attempt to introduce children to the different ways with words which seem to be important for their educational success. If we believe it is important to give all children access to mainstream language practices, how can we do that in a way which recognises that this is not a simple case of skills training, but an activity which impinges upon important underlying cultural assumptions about knowledge, authority and learning? And, if we believe that children's own communicative practices (for example, the Warm Springs children's co-operative talk or the Trackton children's metaphorical and analogical storytelling) should be encouraged to flourish and enrich the classroom language environment, how can we do that without, on the one hand, draining these communicative practices of their meaning through transposing them into the school context or, on the other, calling into question those structures of power and authority on which our educational system rests?

These are difficult questions, but I believe that we must address them. If not, then our dialogues with children in school will remain all too often a ritual of 'going through the motions' rather than a joint exploration for meaning and knowledge.

Acknowledgement

With thanks to Rahilla Faruk for allowing me to draw on her GCSE coursework.

References

EDWARDS, V. (1986) *Language in a Black Community*. Clevedon (Avon): Multilingual Matters.

HEATH, S. B. (1982) 'Questioning at home and at school: a comparative study' in Spindler, G. (ed), *Doing the Ethnography of Schooling: educational anthropology in action*. New York: Holt, Rinehart and Winston.

HEATH, S. B. (1983) *Ways with words*. Cambridge: Cambridge University Press.

MILLER, J. (1983) *Many Voices*. London: Routledge and Kegan Paul.

PHILLIPS, S. (1972) 'Participant structures and communicative competence' in Cazden, C. B., Hymes, D. H. and John, V. D. (eds.) *Functions of Language in the Classroom*. New York: Teachers College Press.

SAUNDERS, G. (1983) *Bilingual Children: guidance for the family*. Clevedon (Avon): Multilingual Matters.

TIZARD, B. AND HUGHES, M. (1984) *Young Children Learning*. London: Fontana.

VYGOTSKY, L. (ed. Cole, M. et al.) (1978) *Mind in Society: the development of higher psychological processes*. Cambridge, MA: Harvard University Press.

WELLS, G. (1985) *Language at home and at School*. Cambridge: Cambridge University Press.

WELLS, G. (1987) *The Meaning Makers*. Sevenoaks: Hodder and Stoughton.

2.4

Striking Attitudes

RICHARD BAIN

In my work as co-ordinator for the LINC (Language in the National Curriculum) Project in the North East of England, I have become acutely aware of the impact of society's attitudes to spoken language on children's speech and on children's attitudes to the speech of others. As a literate society we put very great emphasis on what is written. Our examination system has only just begun to acknowledge that children can display their understanding through speech as well as writing. Within this context, the success of oracy teaching will depend on helping pupils to develop positive attitudes to their own speech and to the speech of others. If pupils regard themselves as poor speakers, if they feel that discussion activities are not 'real work', or if they fail to see the value of listening to their peers, they are unlikely to use oracy effectively as a tool for learning.

In working to develop positive attitudes to speech, teachers may be working at variance with attitudes to speech expressed by society, the children's families, the peer group, and even the school itself. Teachers need to be aware of this disjunction between educational values and dominant social attitudes if they are to be able to support pupils in the difficult task of countering and challenging such attitudes.

Attitudes to spoken language within our society

Many people feel very strongly about language issues, and especially about what they see as a decline in 'standards'. Their views are often found in the letters pages of newspapers, and in newspaper editorials. People frequently complain about the use of clichés and jargon, about accents and pronunciation, about Americanisms and about words misused. The novelist P. D. James, speaking about Standard English in the House of Lords recently, argued that we would never achieve equality of opportunity in this country when 'so many people proclaim their disadvantage every time they open their mouths.' The implication of her comment is that we could achieve equality of opportunity if all people were taught to 'open their mouths' in the same (advantaged) way, rather than by learning to value and respect people's differences.

Not all our attitudes are as openly expressed. Underlying attitudes to language can often be seen in what is accepted as being 'ordinary' or 'normal'. Standard English, for example, is seen by some as being 'normal' English, and all other forms as deviations from that norm. Twelve year old pupils in a classroom in Wallsend described the speech of their teachers as 'normal' in contrast to their own speech, despite the fact that they, their parents, and almost everyone else they knew, spoke in Tyneside dialect. The mirror image of this is that speakers of Received Pronunciation will often claim to have a 'neutral' accent, or even no accent at all.

Attitudes to spoken language in the home

Many parents' attitudes to education are based on a 'common sense' validation of their own experiences as pupils. 'Common sense' tells them that it is difficult to concentrate in a noisy environment. This 'common sense' perception validates their own experience as passive learners in silent classrooms. 'Common sense' tells them that writing is valued more than speech in our society, and this validates their schooltime experience as writers of prodigious quantities of notes to be memorised for written examinations. 'Common sense' tells them that teachers know more than pupils, and this validates their experience of a system in which teachers spoke and pupils listened. 'Common sense' tells them that Standard English has power and prestige in our society, and this validates their experience of classrooms where forms of local dialect were 'corrected' and suppressed.

Some nine year old pupils in a classroom in Hebburn, in a discussion about their dialect, were quite clear about the use of Geordie at home – although their parents used it, its use was frowned on:

> It's not pleasant; me mam says that accent's not very good.
> They're worried you might get into the habit and forget posh words.
> They think they'll be shown up if we speak Geordie.

They identified a clear difference between their mothers and their fathers. One little girl said that her mother tried to stop her father from speaking Geordie, but her father said, 'If you pack smoking in, I'll stop speaking Geordie.' The girl's sympathies clearly lay with her father on this issue.

The consequence of such attitudes to dialect is that children are likely to follow the model of their parents and their peers: to use the local dialect, but to feel guilty about its use and to feel that their own speech is somehow 'second rate'. This runs directly counter to the aim of our schools to foster a pride in local speech and a self-confidence in children's own abilities as speakers.

Attitudes to spoken language in the peer group

At one level, the peer group may have a very lively and positive attitude to language diversity. Children delight in jokes, slang, wordplay and in the process of changing and challenging accepted language conventions. Peer group attitudes to dialect are mixed. In cases where pupils feel that their language and culture are discouraged and rejected by the school, this can lead to the development of a counter-culture, where broad forms of dialect are deliberately cultivated in defiance of the school's desires and expectations.

Children can also be extremely intolerant. Newcomers from another part of the country are often teased and ridiculed because of their accent. Where the new accent is familiar – perhaps from television programmes like *Eastenders* or *Brookside* – it may be more acceptable. Often, however, children with different accents are simply identified as being 'posh', and they may have to work very hard to live down such stereotyping. Bilingual children face even more severe intolerance. Monolingual pupils may feel threatened and excluded when bilingual pupils use their mother tongues; rather than recognising their remarkable skill and understanding across two or more languages, they may assume that bilingual pupils have deficient English. Such attitudes often arise from ignorance: fifteen year olds in South Shields referred to other pupils who 'speak Muslim'.

Attitudes to spoken language within school

Attitudes to speech within schools have changed tremendously over the past ten years or so. Though there are still schools where pupil talk is viewed with suspicion and where silence is seen as essential for learning, the requirements for talk within the National Curriculum and at GCSE make such attitudes hard to maintain. Speaking and listening constitute a third of National Curriculum English, and the National Curriculum requirements for the other core and foundation subjects presuppose opportunities for small-group discussion, problem-solving, and the assessment of learning through talk.

But attitudes to speech within schools are by no means as consistent as they might be. English teachers and primary language co-ordinators will often turn in frustration and say that it's all very well for *them* to encourage children to take a pride in their local dialect and to value their speech, but what happens when another teacher 'corrects' (or indeed punishes) dialect uses, or when the headteacher objects to the noise of discussion? English teachers themselves may lack the courage of their convictions, for example by insisting on a written outcome to the work of small groups.

Attitudes to language may be expressed in any of the activities and interactions that make up the life of a school. Assemblies, for example, may in some schools appear to suggest that it is the children's role to sit in silence, passively listening. Conversations between teachers and pupils in corridors, on the games field, or during a visit, show how pupils' talk is, or is not, valued.

The style of teaching in lessons also gives many implicit messages about speech. The traditional 'didactic' lesson where the teacher has all the answers, and the children only speak in order for the teacher to check their understanding, implies that pupils' speech is of little worth: their role is to listen and respond. Even in classrooms which have been reorganised to encourage more interaction between pupils, the teacher's style of questioning can easily inhibit and devalue pupils' speech. In a recent lively and interesting lesson about the history of the language I heard a child plead 'Give us a clue, Miss!' as the teacher tried desperately to elicit the 'right' answer. Pupils may have the opportunity to explore, think and learn in small groups but, if the classroom has a strong competitive ethos, this may simply take the form of pupils competing to demonstrate their own abilities at the expense of others.

Correcting children's speech

The correction of children's speech is an important feature of a school's attitudes. Children's speech is closely associated with their sense of identity and self-worth. 'Correcting' children's speech is a risky and ineffective way of developing their spoken competence, but a very powerful way of imposing school discipline. Some schools require the use of formal Standard English in the same way that they require the wearing of a formal school uniform, and it is quite common for children's speech to be 'corrected' when they are being admonished for some other misdemeanour: 'Don't speak to me like that.' What is being required has little to do with clarity or meaning, it is an assertion of power, imposing a language of subservience in place of a language of independence. Children speak feelingly about the humiliation of having their speech corrected, and of how they will retreat into silence rather than expose themselves.

The English Working Group Report argued that:

> There is little point in correcting the spoken language of pupils in any general way and as part of their routine language use, because it is unlikely to have a beneficial effect: against the pressures of home and the peer group, teachers can have little hope of changing how pupils speak. Moreover, criticism of pupils' spoken language will be interpreted as criticism of their family and friends.
>
> (DES, 1989)

Such an approach has certainly not been accepted by all schools, but it does form part of the background of opinion against which schools have to justify their policies. In preparation for this article I asked a number of teachers about their current practice. Most said that they *do* correct children's speech, but that they correct grammar and vocabulary rather than accent. Correction would usually take the form of 'remodelling', i.e. contriving to use the expression that the child has used wrongly in a sentence of his or her own, so that the child can hear the correct form without the flow of conversation being interrupted, and without the child being criticised. Many were at pains to emphasise the need to 'correct' in a positive way, to raise awareness and understanding, rather than negatively. They said that they would *not* correct children in circumstances where a correction would interrupt the flow of discussion or debate, or where a correction might undermine a child's confidence or expose the pupil in front of his or her peers.

Though the teachers I spoke to all agreed that they would not attempt to 'correct' regional accents, many of them objected to 'sloppy' pronunciation, as, for example with 'nah' for 'no', 'cos' for 'because', 'could of' for 'could have', 'wa'er' for 'water'. They argued that 'sloppy' pronunciation leads to problems with spelling: pupils pronounce the words 'there', 'their' and 'they're' as 'they', and they write them all as 'they' as well. The 'careless' pronunciation of ' 'ouse' for 'house' leads pupils to write it without the 'h'. But they didn't complain that the 'careless' pronunciation of 'our' for 'hour' leads pupils to spell that without the 'h'! The problem is that English spelling and English pronunciation are notoriously dissonant in all dialects of English, but that the particular difficulties vary from dialect to dialect. It does not help to compound a child's spelling problem by attacking his or her pronunciation as well. In its introduction, *The Oxford English Dictionary* states:

> The pronunciation is the actual living form of a word, that is, the word itself, of which the current spelling is only a symbolisation.

Received Pronunciation, which is often appealed to as a guide for pupils' pronunciation, is as distant from spelling as any regional accent, and no clearer or easier to understand.

Teachers who choose not to correct children's speech are by no means abdicating the responsibility for developing their pupils' spoken competence. Correction is reassuring for the teacher, but may not be very effective for the pupil. Much more effective is the provision of opportunities for children to use spoken language in a wide variety of contexts and to reflect on their use. I have never come across a child who, when asked to take the role of a monarch, or 'to read the news' on class radio, cannot produce a very acceptable version of RP.

Striking new attitudes

There is little that schools can do in the short term to change the attitudes of society as a whole, since teachers are unlikely to influence views on such matters as dialect and Standard English. However, they can inform parents about the place of talk in the curriculum and encourage them to recognise and value their children's achievements as speakers.

Developing a consistent policy towards speech within a school is a worthwhile task. Many teachers' views on correction, on regional dialects, and on talk for learning may coincide with the views and prejudices of society as a whole. Schools can aim to influence the attitudes of staff in several ways. Teachers can be helped to be more conscious of the models they themselves offer for speech, both during lessons and in other school activities. Staff can discuss together the purposes and likely effects of 'correcting' speech. They may need more information about dialects and other languages within the school, and about the value of bilingual skills. Attention to the ways in which oracy can improve learning in all subjects can also help teachers to review their attitudes to pupils' speech.

Schools can foster awareness of the importance of language and excitement at its diversity. This includes greater knowledge about English and other languages, other dialects, and the variety of forms and purposes for speech in our society. The National Curriculum makes this task explicit. Pupils are required to talk about 'variations in vocabulary between different regional or social groups', and about 'grammatical differences between spoken Standard English and a non-standard variety'. One of the most exciting features of the National Curriculum is the requirement that children should understand 'some of the factors that influence people's attitudes to the way other people speak.' This is one way to extend understanding of and sympathetic insight into other people's uses of speech. Teachers can encourage pupils to stand back from the prejudices of their elders and to strike new attitudes of their own. When Alan, a twelve year old pupil from Wallsend, was asked if there were any accents he disliked, he looked back in incomprehension. 'How can you dislike an accent?' he asked. 'That's just petty.'

References

DES (1989) *The English Working Group Report: English for Ages 5–16*. London: HMSO.
(1933) *The Oxford English Dictionary*. Oxford: Oxford University Press.

Oracy and Genre: Speech Styles in the Classroom

DOUGLAS BARNES

AND

YANINA SHEERAN

Both teachers and pupils sometimes delight in the power which their knowledge of a particular academic 'argot' brings. Fluent in the tongue of their chosen subject, be it physics, geography or sociology, they baffle the outsider with their casual use of technical jargon. Such use of a specialist language signals membership of a particular group within the academic world and is a source of status and identity. People who do not command certain genres are likely to be excluded from taking part in certain activities because they sound as if they do not fit in. If you sound like an outsider you will be treated as an outsider. Specialist language, therefore, performs an important socio-cultural function for those who use it. However, many people consider that specialist language is also necessary for the development of 'disciplined' thinking. In this article, we attempt to explore and clarify some of the central issues in this debate, through a consideration of two main questions: are the language and thought patterns of specialist subjects somehow inextricably interwoven? And should we, as teachers, initiate children into the mysteries of technical jargon, or should our efforts be mainly directed towards the demystification and demotion of language so remote from everyday living?

Underlying the first of these questions is, of course, our conception of a subject discipline. One influential view is that disciplines should be seen as different 'language-games'. The concept of a language-game was applied to the study of school knowledge and the curriculum by Hirst and Peters (1970). They argued that there are seven fundamental realms of knowledge. Either singly or in some combination, they form the basis of any curriculum subject. To understand each discipline, a person must master the appropriate language-game, which consists of characteristic logical structures, particular concepts and distinctive kinds of test for the truth of propositions.

More recent writers are less convinced that the fundamental forms of knowledge can be so discretely categorised. However, there is increasing agreement that successful learning in school involves intellectual shifts in perception which can be likened to learning new rules and playing new games with language and thought. Mercer and Edwards (1981) argue that in school there are conventions of language and thinking (which they call 'educational ground rules') governing cognitive processes. Successful learning in specialist subjects is partly a matter of gaining access to distinctive clusters of educational ground rules (Sheeran and Barnes, 1991). Children must learn to play intellectual games whose ground rules may be very different from those to which they are accustomed. Most disconcertingly for them, they often have to abandon 'taken-for granted', 'everyday' or 'common-sense' interpretations and explanations, and learn to 'see things differently'. For example, in science, one rule of the game is that giving a scientific explanation hinges on the exposition of basic principles, rather than considering the practicalities of the activity in an everyday context. Some children tend to confine their thinking to real life contexts only. One pupil, who was asked what elements were essential in photography, challenged the teacher's reply that it was light plus chemical change. He insisted that his camera needed a battery too. The Children's Learning in Science Project (CLIS) at Leeds University (Brook and Driver, 1986) has shown how children often cling to such 'common-sense' ways of thinking when given scientific problems.

If what distinguishes a subject is its distinctive conventions of thought and particular conceptions of phenomena, the task for teachers is to communicate those conventions and conceptions as useful, albeit provisional, ways of understanding the world. This means that teachers need to allow time and opportunity for the process of constructing and transforming meaning. They frequently set up discussions in which they encourage their pupils to express their ideas 'in their own words'. In the following transcription, four thirteen year olds have been given a topic to discuss in the course of a physics lesson concerned with 'work' and 'energy'. They have been told that 'work' (in the technical sense) is a measure of how much energy changes from one form to another. In this extract, the four pupils (two boys and two girls) are considering a question set by the teacher: 'Is work always done when energy changes form?' They have also been told to consider several situations, such as 'the conversion of food to movement on a bicycle':

PUPIL 1: Is work always done when energy changes form?

PUPIL 2: No, not always. It depends to what you'd classify as work.

PUPIL 3: Well, I don't really understand this.

PUPIL 4: (*at the same time*) I think work is done when a force moves.

PUPIL 2: Food to movement on a bicycle. Well, work is done when you're eating the food and when you're driving the bicycle.

PUPIL 4: Work is done all the time. You're always doing work. When you're sleeping you're breathing, aren't you?

PUPIL 2: Well, you're not using much energy.

PUPIL 4: Not much, but you're using a bit.

PUPIL 1: (*at the same time*) Well, you just, you just think of everything really. Energy needs to keep . . . go on moving. It can't just go, then stop, can it? Like when you eat food, you can't just stop for a week and just get started, can you? You'd be dead already.

(Barnes, D. and Todd, F., 1976)

It has been a fundamental tenet of much oracy work that children will learn effectively through such experiences. Teachers who advocate this approach believe that it is important for all pupils to be given opportunities to use their everyday language resources to solve problems, conduct investigations and reach understanding. But the appropriateness of this has been challenged. Recently, a group of Australian linguists has been arguing forcefully that such a child-centred approach, with its emphasis on everyday language, denies pupils access to important discourse modes or 'genres', language forms which are essential for carrying the meanings of specialist subjects:

Schools are . . . responsible for teaching ways of meaning, ways of knowing, ways of working and ways of enquiring . . . Those pupils who fail in schools are those who fail to master the genres of schooling: the ways of structuring and dealing with experience that schools value . . . Children who fail in schools are those who operate with ways of meaning different from those of schooling.

(Christie, 1985, pp. 22 & 24)

People who collaborate in work or play develop shared ways of going about things, and ways of talking about them. This applies as much to garage mechanics and fishing enthusiasts as to researchers in atomic physics. It applies to small groups such as families, and to much larger groups such as the teaching profession, whose staffroom talk must appear mysterious to outsiders who are not familiar with teachers' jargon and even less with the ideas lying behind it. What all such groups come to share is a way of understanding the world and acting upon it. If we call this a 'discourse mode' or 'genre', we are referring not only to the language used, but equally to the meanings the members share, and to their ways of doing things and relating to one another. At the centre of a genre or discourse mode is a shared way of living and the common understandings that go with it.

The presence of genres, of standard ways of going about tasks and of talking about them, is, Frances Christie says, of crucial importance in schools, since all pupils need to cope appropriately with such expectations in order to succeed. If a child fails to fit in with a teacher's expectations, he or she is likely to seem either stupid or unco-operative, and this is true at all phases of schooling. Christie (1985, pp. 27–9) gives a persuasive example from an infant classroom of a 'news telling' session, in which some children are noticeably more capable than others of dealing with the tacit expectations built into the activity.

Certain people have the power to act as language definers, and they become the carriers of the 'public' or dominant meaning of language in each setting. In school, teachers are the powerful 'language definers', and the process of successful learning in specialist subjects is seen by many as one of taking on the teachers' definitions. (Neil Mercer develops this idea in his article, 'Talk for Teaching-and-Learning' in a later section.) When children and teachers talk together in the classroom, the contrast between the 'public' meaning and children's pre-existing or 'alternative' meanings often lies at the root of misunderstandings. The school may be 'foreign territory'. The cultural norms, the language and experiences of the teacher may be different enough from children's life at home, on the street or in the playground, to cause significant problems and involve the participants in 'repair' work in order to create shared understanding. Some children seem unable, or even unwilling, to take on the dominant 'public' meaning of the subject. Instead, they continue to use meanings shared within one of their other cultural groups. Others may well understand, for example, the principles of scientific discourse, but lack the habit of moving into a scientific way of seeing the world when required. This is why some teachers fear that, if children 'use their own words', instead of employing the genre of a specialist subject, this will lock them into everyday ways of thinking and thus bar them from the special kinds of thinking represented by many school subjects.

There is an ambiguity in the idea of genres or discourse modes. Are they structures of words or structures of meaning? The answer must be that they are both. However, it has tended to be linguists who have drawn our attention to them, and this has emphasised that from one point of view they are made up of identifiable language, both vocabulary and grammatical forms. Janet White, for example, when discussing transcripts of children talking about a scientific topic, writes not just of vocabulary ('lexical density'), but of grammatical patterns, such as 'impersonal constructions', 'options in the mood system', and so on (White, 1988, p. 11). Her contention is that the use of these linguistic forms directed certain pupils to differing ways of thinking about the topic. Switching into the science genre implies (in her opinion) switching into scientific ways of understanding the world.

Genre is partly a matter of specialist vocabulary. It is clear that, in order to join in talking with a group of specialists, perhaps in history, it might be important to understand and use terms such as 'socio-economic change' or 'conspiracy theory': such terms are economical because they encapsulate (for those who can use them) complex sets of ideas and evaluations. The crux comes when we ask whether such language is *necessary*; can one think about history and discuss historical issues without them? Clearly one can: circumlocutions are always possible. However, not being able to use such language might exclude one from collaborating with other historians, and it is true that the inability to adopt appropriate speech styles prevents some people from having full access to life in our society.

But genre is also crucially about ways of meaning. When we talk, we are driven by intentions which arise from the situation we are in, the persons we are talking to, and those of our own concerns that are relevant. Our sense of the needs and interests of the persons we are talking with is important, too. It is on the basis of these intentions that we select from our repertoire of language forms. Christie (1988, p. 27) writes that a scientific genre 'builds its meanings through a series of linguistic choices'. But both 'select' and 'linguistic choices' are potentially misleading terms, since what we are aware of as we talk are our purposes and not the language forms we are using to embody them. That is, our speech is not directed by deliberate choice from the repertoire of linguistic means at our disposal but by the meanings that we and others are working towards as we talk.

Is it helpful to teach the genres that pupils need in school? It has already been suggested that there is a danger that genres are seen as composed of words and grammatical structures rather than of meanings, priorities and ways of understanding. Christie writes of 'uncovering schematic structures' in speech – a very proper activity for a linguist, but what about schoolchildren? She recommends that:

> the generic structures to be used in language (should) ... become much more overtly an aspect of the educational agenda, negotiated between teacher and students, and forming an essential element in the teaching/learning process.
>
> (Christie, 1985, p. 32)

Although we commend the insistence on negotiation, this emphasis on linguistic forms carries with it the possibility that some teachers may be so ill-advised as to try to teach a particular genre as a set of forms rather than as a way of thinking, even though Christie herself may not intend this. For example, to teach children of any age the language forms used by literary critics is not going to help them to read a novel as a skilled adult does. It is all too likely that any changes that result from such teaching would 'lie on the rhetorical surface', as Dixon (1988, p. 15) puts it when warning of this danger, rather than be radical changes in thinking. If children are to become competent in using and understanding genres other than those they meet outside school, it will be through taking part in dialogue which brings them into the thinking patterns that the genre represents. The CLIS Project (Brook and Driver, 1986) is critical of whole class discussions which, they observe, usually involve children trying to guess what is in the teacher's mind and do not help the teacher to find out what the children's conceptions of any problem might be. They recommend asking individual pupils or small groups to work out answers to problems. The variety of answers can be collated on the board or on posters, and the comparisons and contrasts will highlight the different ground rules being employed.

White (1988, p. 20), again with science lessons in mind, similarly suggests that teachers should listen attentively to the way children talk about the subject matter, as a way of gaining insight into their existing ways of thinking about it. She also suggests that they should discuss with their pupils why some styles are less effective than others for expressing observations, hypotheses, explanations and so on, thereby introducing them explicitly to expected ways of reporting in the subject:

Although the expression of meaning in science has to do with discipline and training, the processes by which such meanings are made are creative and imaginative.

(White, 1988, p. 35)

This seems to be good advice, though it is not clear how effective it is to discuss with pupils how they talk. While we can say with some confidence that reflection on writing is likely to help children to match what they write to their intentions, this is far less clearly true of speech. Much of our spoken language is outside our conscious control.

Christie recommends more oblique approaches to genre:

Teachers can learn to consider the various forms of 'content' they aim to teach, analysing the language patterns particular to these, and building an explicit sense of them into their own teaching behaviour . . . They can devise teaching/learning tasks in such a way that children will be assisted to learn the behaviour patterns, including the patterns of language behaviour, necessary to deal with those tasks.

(Christie, 1985, p. 32)

Even more oblique is Edwards and Mercer's demonstration (1987) that in the course of lessons teachers often communicate interactively the appropriate patterns of working and thinking to their pupils. That is, by working together with a skilful teacher pupils learn without being explicitly told. Their examples include practical know-how about modelling in clay, and – a much more abstract kind of understanding – how to vary one dimension while holding the others constant. By taking part in discussion with the teacher, pupils begin to take over not just the language he or she uses, but also the concepts and the intellectual strategies that they need. It seems probable that this tacit learning needs to be supported by explicit discussion of the topic, so that pupils can develop conscious knowledge too. It will not have escaped the reader that what is being recommended here is the discussion of the ideas and processes, and only indirectly the discussion of the language to be used in expressing them.

In the following extract from a lower sixth form chemistry lesson, the teacher can be heard carefully introducing students both to new ideas and to unfamiliar terminology. Earlier that day the group had visited an industrial plant and seen a demonstration of the industrial use of high performance chromatography (HPLC). In this extract, the teacher is helping the students to relate what they had seen to their existing knowledge of chemistry:

PUPIL 1: What was HPLC?
TEACHER: Well, what does the last bit, word mean?

PUPIL 2: The chr . . .

PUPIL 3: Chromatography.

TEACHER: Yeah. Well, what does chromatography mean to me? You just told me what chromatography is, it's splitting . . .

PUPIL 1: Find out what's in there.

PUPIL 1/2: (*Together: not transcribable*)

TEACHER: Yes, in other words, you're . . . What are you separating?

PUPIL 1: The mixture.

TEACHER: Mixtures, yes.

PUPIL 1: Into different substances.

TEACHER: Into different substances. He injected things in there and heated it up . . . What did he inject and heat up in it today?

PUPIL 1: Liquid.

PUPIL 2: It's like a solution. He made it into a solution.

TEACHER: Yes. 'HP' means 'high performance'; in other words, they're . . . You see, we're using the way you see it on GCSE papers, things like that: we've got a mixture of colours, and you saw a little split, didn't you, on the paper? You've got what's known as a thin layer column. And lo and behold . . .

PUPIL 1: (*Too quiet to transcribe*)

TEACHER: If you've got what's known as a thin layer column . . . (*omission*) instead of using paper you can use what's known as silica gel. There's the silica gel. (*pointing*) It seems all faded, but what we did, we got – how many, eight Smarties, nine Smarties? – we got the different coloured Smarties on here, and then you put some water and different solvents . . .

This exchange is of particular interest because the teacher is primarily concerned to elicit the students' existing knowledge in order to help them to understand what they have seen; his interest in teaching appropriate language has a much lower priority. His own style of talk is very unlike the written language that is associated with formal science reporting. He deliberately uses everyday ideas and language – 'things', 'splitting', 'heat up', 'different colours', 'Smarties', 'all faded' – in order to build up the networks of meaning which constitute complex concepts such as chromatography. He places some reliance on existing concepts that he knows the students are familiar with and, because of this, is able to use the shorthand of technical terms such as 'substance', 'mixture', and 'solvent'; indeed, it is one of the students who introduces 'solution' into the discussion. The teacher marks his presentation of each *new* technical term with the phrase 'what's known as', but he does this only for 'silica gel' and 'thin layer column', both of which are being explained and exemplified in the course of the discussion. Probably his only use of a technical term that is not part of the essential conceptual structures that he is teaching is 'inject', which stands out because it is unlike the rest in not being strictly necessary.

We quote this exchange in order to show how a skilful teacher, aware of what his students are and are not familiar with, can carefully build up conceptual structures, explicitly associating them with new technical terms as they become necessary, thus taking the responsibility for inducting them into the linked concepts/terminology that they will need in their advanced studies.

Do we need to accept passively these demands for particular genres? Christie hopes that as a result of increased awareness of genre:

> Teachers will become more responsive to, and tolerant of, ways of meaning among their children which differ from their own . . . They will be caused to reconsider much conventional teacher/student interaction. Out of the need to demystify the ways of meaning of schooling, they will be caused to abandon some, and to make others more explicit and accessible. They will become much more actively collaborationist in the structuring of tasks and hence in the definition of the kinds of genres actually required for successful learning. Language will become no longer the hidden curriculum of schooling.
>
> (Christie, 1985)

What is needed is the active involvement of pupils in learning: they need to be given opportunities in all subjects to formulate ideas, to question, to hypothesise, and to plan, all in the interest of reshaping their understanding. And because their teachers recognise, support and join in this, they will gradually take over both the language and the meanings of the genres they need.

Genres are sometimes represented by the Australian theorists as far more rigid and homogeneous than they actually are, at least in the world outside schools (see Dixon and Stratta, 1992). When we move from talking to a colleague about our work to an enquiry about his or her family, is it a sharp 'switch' to a different genre or a vague series of slight adjustments of various kinds? May not the whole idea of genre misrepresent what happens in talk? There may be conventional ways of raising a point in a committee meeting, for example, but it is perfectly possible to break the convention and yet succeed in communicating, sometimes all the more effectively. We also know that in research science there exist informal as well as formal discourse modes. Teachers should beware of presenting genres as sets of rules to be followed without question, but should help their pupils to look at them critically so that they learn when it is appropriate to use, to transcend or to reject them.

Acknowledgement

We would like to thank Brian Teeley, Chafford School, Havering for the Chemistry transcript.

References

BARNES, D. AND TODD, F. (1976) *Communicating and Learning in Small Groups*. London: Routledge.

BROOK, A. AND DRIVER, R. (1986) 'The Construction of Meaning and Conceptual Change in Classroom Settings: case study on energy', Children's Learning in Science Project (CLSP), Centre for Studies in Science and Mathematics Education, University of Leeds.

CHRISTIE, F. (1985) 'Language and Schooling', in Tchudi, S. (ed.) *Language, Schooling and Society*. Portsmouth, NH: Boynton-Cook.

CHRISTIE, F. (1988) 'Genres as Choice', in Reid, I (ed.) (1988) *The Place of Genre in Learning: Current Debates*. Geelong, Vic.: Deakin University.

DIXON, J. (1988) 'The Question of Genres' in Reid (1988), op.cit.

DIXON, J. AND STRATTA, L. (1992) 'New Demands on the Model for Writing in Education: – What does genre theory offer?' in Hayhoe, M. and Parker, S. (eds) (forthcoming) *Language and Literacy*. Milton Keynes: Open University Press.

EDWARDS, D. AND MERCER, N. (1987) *Common Knowledge*. London and New York: Methuen.

HIRST, P. H. AND PETERS, R. S. (1970) *The Logic of Education*. London: Routledge and Kegan Paul.

MERCER, N. AND EDWARDS, D. (1981) 'Ground Rules for Mutual Understanding: a social psychological approach to classroom knowledge', in Mercer, N. (ed.) (1981) *Language in School and Community*. London: Edward Arnold.

SHEERAN, Y. AND BARNES, D. (1991) *School Writing: Discovering the Ground Rules*. Milton Keynes: Open University Press.

WHITE, J. (1988) *The Language of Science*. London: Assessment of Performance Unit, Department of Education and Science.

2.6

Towards a Multilingual Pedagogy

MARY MORRISON

AND

PERMINDER SANDHU

More than half the world's population can speak more than one language. In many countries, to be bilingual or multilingual is the norm, and the process of becoming bilingual is not experienced as stressful or confusing. Multilingual people can move readily from one language to another to suit their purposes and the social context. Typical of many Bradford pupils is Safiya, aged fourteen, whose scripts we represent below. They were written swiftly, while she was explaining to a small group her own oral language history. She had been in England for eighteen months and used her written competence in Gujerati, Urdu, English and Hindi to display the languages she could speak.

In *Curriculum Guidance 3, The Whole Curriculum* (NCC, 1990), seven out of nine statements of curricular dimensions concern access and opportunity for bilingual students. The first states:

> Dimensions such as a commitment to providing equal opportunities for all pupils and a recognition that preparation for life in a multicultural society is relevant to all pupils, should permeate every aspect of the curriculum.

In this article, we wish to explore what this should mean for the many bilingual children in British schools, how access to the National Curriculum can be made a reality for them, and what the implications are for teachers and monolingual pupils as well. We shall be drawing on our work with bilingual children in Bradford to illustrate what learning is like for them, because we believe that at the heart of any successful curriculum must lie an awareness of children's perceptions of themselves and their achievements in learning.

Tove Skutnabb-Kangas's definition of bilingualism (1988) seems to come closest to our working aims:

> A speaker is bilingual who is able to function in two (or more) languages, either in monolingual or bilingual communities, in accordance with the socio-cultural demands made on an individual's communicative competence by these communities and by the individual herself, at the same level as native speakers, and who is able positively to identify with both (or all) language groups and cultures or parts of them.
>
> (p. 22)

This definition, acknowledging the socio-cultural as well as linguistic demands placed on bilingual speakers, has far-reaching implications for educational practice and entitlement. In Bradford, bilingual teachers who shared first languages with the children in their classes, collected, recorded and analysed the conversations of many children in first and middle schools to gain an insight into bilingualism. They found that the two languages of a bilingual person were not two isolated entities, but had a strong interdependence. Children were drawing on both languages to enliven and express their meanings and intentions; mixing and matching, borrowing and creating new forms.

Bilingual children switch skilfully between their two languages, according to the context, audience and purpose of the dialogue. Code-switching, as this is called, can involve the insertion of a word, a phrase, a sentence or a number of sentences. Grosjean (1982) defines it as 'the alternate use of two or more languages in the same utterance or conversation' (p. 45).

Code-switching has become of interest to teachers both as a creative style of communication and as a window into the nature of language. A similar strategy can be found in the range of language varieties used in monolingual conversations. People normally switch from one mode to another unconsciously and spontaneously, adopting more formal or more dialectal discourse to suit the occasion.

Teachers who are themselves bilingual provide strong and positive role models for pupils, and their presence validates the use of other languages in school. Bilingual teachers are also able to recognise bilingual pupils' learning and achievement and to build on their bicultural and bilingual skills in ways that are difficult for monolingual teachers. This can enhance the self-esteem and confidence of pupils. The work of the bilingual teachers who observed, recorded and analysed transcripts of pupils' learning has resulted in dynamic multilingual approaches in some Bradford schools. They have monitored dual language use and identified the contexts within which these uses occur: when more, when less, with whom and for what purpose. Such information illuminates the ways in which use of two languages contributes to pupils' learning and can be used by teachers to develop the environments which most facilitate this learning. The curriculum has tended to become more global in outlook, rooting itself in the cultures and consciousnesses the children bring to school, and has drawn much more on the rich resources of the neighbouring communities.

By creating rich contexts for languages in these schools, bilingual teachers have helped their monolingual colleagues to recognise the cognitive ability of bilingual children and the ways in which differences in vocabulary affect the ways in which concepts are formed. Even very young children seem able to appreciate the differences between meanings in two languages and can move between them, thinking divergently and being aware of different sets of cultural or social norms. One example, of the way a Reception class of bilingual children struggled for expression in their new language, may help to reveal this awareness. Developing a story together in Panjabi about a scarecrow, they gave the following ideas in English:

> All the sparrows will fly away.
> All the birds will fly away.
> It will scare them away.
> Then the pigeons will run or go away.
> The scarecrow is looking at the pigeons.
> The pigeons will get frightened and go away.

Their bilingual teacher analysed an excerpt from their conversation and translated it from Panjabi to English to show monolingual colleagues the richness of allusion and connotation to which the children had access in their first language:

TEACHER: What will he (*the scarecrow*) do in the fields?

CHILD 1: It will be a kind scarecrow.

TEACHER: What if this scarecrow became alive – where will it go?

CHILD 2: It will only go anywhere if it has legs.

CHILD 3: If it has no legs, it will not be able to walk. If it has no legs or feet, it will not be able to walk.

CHILD 4: Then it will walk on its knees and it will collapse.

CHILD 5: If it goes on the road, it will collapse and cars will run over it. It will fall down. Then the ambulance will come. They will take him to the hospital in an ambulance. They will give him injections but it will die.

TEACHER: What will happen then?

CHILD 6: They will take him to Pakistan.

TEACHER: Why will they take him to Pakistan?

CHILD 7: They will bury him there. They will cover him with a sheet. Then they will cover it with soil and bury it.

CHILD 5: Then there will be a funeral.

CHILD 6: If it dies, all the girls will cry.

TEACHER: Will the men not cry?

CHILD 6: No, not the men. Men will be performing the funeral rites.

CHILD 4: If Miss S is not here and this (*pointing to the scarecrow in the classroom*) scarecrow dies . . .

CHILD 6: We will perform the funeral rites. Then everyone will come here and cry.

TEACHER: If it happens in school, who will be here?

CHILD 6: Then the girls and the men . . . my dad . . . and everybody's dad . . . and our mums, will come.

In answer to the teacher's first question, the first child shows some sympathy with the scarecrow, reacting against the slightly harsh image of it developed during the brainstorm of ideas in English. In answer to the teacher's next question, the next three children begin to hypothesise in an extended and logical way as they focus on the practicalities of a scarecrow 'walking', each building on the others' suggestions. Finally, the skilful questioning of the teacher links significant discussion of death and funeral rites to English school processes, bridging adeptly the range of cultural and social contexts the story is developing.

It is important that use of both languages for learning is maintained throughout a bilingual pupil's schooling. Older bilingual pupils, who visited a first school to study the younger children's language acquisition as part of a storytelling project, were amazed to discover that the younger children were often more fluent in their first language than the older pupils were. Telling parents about their work in the first school helped some of them to recognise the importance of keeping both their languages going. 'I couldn't say the words in my own language at first and that was really difficult, but I got it through in the end,' one student confessed. It shocked her to realise she was losing touch with her own language and made her more determined to keep it going. 'It could help me in my work, when I leave school, in a hospital, if I am travelling or at the office.' Another student, who had recently begun Gujerati classes in her upper school, said, 'I never knew what a beautiful language Gujerati is before I started studying it. It's a really beautiful language.'

Working on multilingual narrative, drama and poetry as part of their English work has given pupils rich opportunities to make translations and literary comparisons. These pupils have made important connections across languages and have developed more explicit understanding of the ways in which different language systems work through setting first language texts and English texts side by side. For example, the use of the 'doha' in Urdu was compared with the rhyming couplet in English. Asian and Caribbean writers have visited to share their writing and language experiences with pupils. They have looked at the ways in which their knowledge of varieties of English from different parts of the globe can extend awareness of 'identity' within texts, 'voice' within narrative form, and the effect of these on a text's structure and meaning.

Once the validity of all the languages spoken by students is accepted, they become very positive about themselves as language users and their self-esteem as learners flourishes. However, this has implications for the many schools without, as yet, bilingual teachers on their staffs. Will the potential of bilingual learners in their care be fully developed? How can those of us who are monolingual teachers have access to children's cognitive ability if the children do not yet know sufficient English to explain it to us?

For bilingual children, the monolingual teacher is a symbol of the majority group. The way a monolingual teacher acknowledges a child's first language is of crucial importance. Teachers who have taken steps to learn at least a few words or sentences of children's first languages have gained a new-found respect and status in the children's eyes. These teachers no longer feel insecure, threatened or isolated from the children but are rewarded by this mutual participation. An acting headteacher, who is keenly interested in supporting bilingualism in her school, invited children to come to her room if they wanted to do any work in Panjabi or Urdu at lunchtime. She learned Panjabi from the children in that time, as well as going to evening classes for further tuition. The response was tremendous. One day a little girl came to this teacher and said, 'Miss, can I join your Panjabi club?'

What else can teachers do in schools where the support of bilingual colleagues is not readily available? Teachers working in the Bradford Oracy Project have identified the following strategies to be those they find the most helpful:

- improving their own knowledge about their pupils' languages;

- creating a language-rich environment where pupils feel comfortable to use their first language and to code-switch;

- involving parents and the local community wherever possible;

- placing children in various groupings to encourage the modelling of, and listening to, second language (English), as well as ensuring help from language partners for translations;

- using workshop approaches to give pupils full access to the curriculum whatever their stage of learning English, with resources (for example, word processing, dictionaries) to support this;

- having reference points within the curriculum which recognise pupil's cultures and histories and which build on their intercultural skills.

The attitudes of monolingual children are also of great importance. All children need to be aware of linguistic diversity in order to appreciate the skills of their bilingual peers. Work on knowledge about language can help children to explore how languages work and the purposes for which we use them. Bilingual children are often reluctant to speak in their first languages in the presence of monolingual peers, and much pioneering work is currently being done to improve this situation.

While this work has been proceeding in Bradford, the National Curriculum has been introduced. There is a real tension between the requirements of a curriculum, whose content and assessment is founded in the culture and language of the majority group, and the need to ensure that bilingual students have the equality of opportunity that is their right. Teachers are particularly concerned that their bilingual pupils should have the level of support which can ensure full access to the curriculum and fair methods of assessment.

A major concern of teachers is that they may fail to recognise the cognitive ability of their bilingual pupils if the assessment arrangements do not allow for adequate bilingual partnership teaching, or recognition of the value of code-switching. They feel that more resources need to be placed here so that time can be spent with their students helping to establish the 'bridges' or intercultural links into the curriculum and developing the appropriate social contexts for assessment. Entitlement for bilingual students requires systems, resources and processes which will help them to achieve success.

What language rights do bilingual pupils have within the National Curriculum, where English is so clearly denoted as the dominant discourse? Bilingual teachers and their pupils see clear links between their first language and their identity and self-esteem, viewing access to their first language as a human right. Yet nowhere has this been placed centrally or recognised as implicit within the National Curriculum. Bourne and Cameron (1989) have taken this notion of linguistic rights further, arguing that Welsh students could be seen to be receiving preferential treatment, but that the rationale for this is that they 'own' territorial rights in ways that other minority language groups do not. The authors state that 'it is a discourse of national boundaries rather than one of minority rights (as we can see very clearly from the fact that individuals travelling beyond the Welsh borders could not take their language rights with them)' (p. 17).

In many of our schools, multilingual pupils have felt empowered by the recognition given to their language, identity and culture. Their teachers have developed strategies which have helped them to locate and articulate the reasons for the differential status accorded to different language groups, as well as the processes by which these arise. Empowering pupils in this way helps them, in turn, to deal more positively with the difficulties and racism of the world outside when they leave school. A sixth former described her feelings on leaving school like this:

> I know this school is a special place, it protects me, encourages me and I feel secure. I am not alone here. I know that the world of work will be very different, but I will always be able to look back on my time here in this school to help me face the difficulties. I know that goodness is possible.

The struggle for educational and linguistic rights for our bilingual pupils focuses directly on the links between languages and learning. The principles of the emerging multilingual pedagogy are congruent with those of the National Oracy Project. They are 'transformational' for all learners, within the sense of the model of learning suggested by Reid, Forrestal and Cook:

> If teachers want students to understand what they teach, they must give them the opportunity to personalise knowledge. Teachers cannot give students knowledge, they can only help them to come to know by

providing structures within which students can develop their own understandings.

(Reid, Forrestal and Cook, 1989, p. 15)

The work of Bradford's bilingual teachers shows that teachers need to be alerted to the realities of bilingual children's lives in order that they can be reflected through the teaching and learning strategies of the National Curriculum. Effective learning for bilingual children should lead to effective assessment, but their achievement will be dependent on the opportunities they are given to use their bilingual and bicultural experiences. It is clear that many more bilingual adults will be needed for this to be realised in every school. Those of us who are monolingual have learned, by listening to our bilingual colleagues, how much the status of the dominant discourse of English affects and sometimes excludes the learning and status of other groups living in this country. What we have learned from our colleagues' reflections and analyses has helped us to develop our commitment to multilingual ways of working. We see it as a way of looking to the future or, as Aronowitz and Giroux (1985) have put it, 'a language of possibility.'

Acknowledgements

We would like to thank the teachers and pupils from Margaret Macmillan First School, Belle Vue Girls Upper School, Grange Upper School and Byron First School, all in Bradford LEA.

References

ARONOWITZ, S. AND GIROUX, H. (1985) *Education Under Siege*. South Hadley, Mass: Bergin and Garvey.

CAMERON, D. AND BOURNE, J. (1989) 'Grammar, Nation and Citizenship' Occasional paper, Department of English and Media Studies. London Institute of Education.

GROSJEAN, J. (1982) *Life With Two Languages*. Cambridge, MA: Harvard University Press.

NCC (1990). *Curriculum Guidance 3: The Whole Curriculum*. York: NCC.

REID, J., FORRESTAL, P. AND COOK, J. (1989) *Small Group Learning in the Classroom*. Perth: Chalkface Press. (Also (1991) London: English and Media Centre.)

SKUTNABB-KANGAS, T. AND CUMMINS, J. (1988) *Minority Education from Shame to Struggle*. Clevedon Philadelphia: Multilingual Matters Ltd.

As Near to Life as Possible?

HILARY KEMENY

All our spoken language is 'gendered', in the sense that the gender of the speaker and listener is always a significant factor, overtly or covertly, in the exchange. The words we use, our body language, our readiness to interrupt or to be interrupted, the percentage of total time we spend speaking and listening during the exchange, are all affected to some extent at least by our gender. We have expectations embedded in us about appropriate speech behaviours and patterns from the time we begin to speak. Take these two examples from an Oracy Project classroom:

> I don't like working in a group where there's only . . . most boys and no girls, just me.
>
> (seven year old girl)

> Girls have got girls' ideas, and they just scream.
>
> (seven year old boy)

Stereotyped behaviours are often seen as 'only natural' – boys, after all, will be boys, and girls must, if they wish to participate more fully, become more assertive. But even the stereotypes may be inaccurate. Dale Spender (1988) has pointed out that:

> Women don't talk as much as men in mixed company, and girls don't

talk as much as boys in mixed classrooms. These facts, which have been proved by numerous research findings, appear to conflict with a stereotyped image of the female as an excessive talker.

(p. 148)

In this article, I want to explore how the part of a pupil's cultural identity which is to do with his or her gender affects the learning experiences he or she has in the classroom. As Tony Edwards suggests earlier in this section, 'Knowing how to manage unequal relationships, to choose the "right" forms and do the "right" things, is an important part of being communicatively competent.'

Much of the work of the National Oracy Project has focused on small group work in the classroom, and teachers have explored ways of planning, organising and managing this work more effectively. In a mixed school, if groups are chosen by the pupils, they will usually be friendship-based. Almost universally, they will be single-sex too. This is in conflict with the feeling many teachers have that mixed groups are somehow more 'natural' and therefore to be encouraged. In a discussion about gender and oracy, a small (mixed) group of teachers began by talking about gender issues in small group work. One suggested that classrooms should reflect society – 'shouldn't we make the classroom as near to life as possible?' Another responded, 'But if we make it as near to life as possible, men will dominate.' Here, it seems, is the crux of the problem – as Connell et al. (1982) point out, gender is 'not just a matter of the existence of two categories of people, male and female, but primarily a pattern of relations among people. It is an extensive and complex pattern, woven through all the institutions they live in – families, schools, workplaces – and shapes their lives at every level from public affairs to basic psychological make up.' (p. 33–34)

Co-education is an organising principle for secondary education which was extended greatly in England and Wales in the secondary phase as a largely unintended by-product of the move to comprehensive schools (Benn and Simon, 1972). In the primary phase, too, the 'naturalness' of co-education remains largely unchallenged. Implicit in many teachers' views of co-education is a vague notion about the transformative potential of boys and girls working together. And yet, as Nancy Jenkins (1990) shows in her work on oral assessment, the outcomes tell a rather different story. She focused on interpersonal skills in mixed groups doing GCSE English oral assessments and found that girls demonstrated superior interpersonal skills, while boys tended more to demonstrate poor listening skills and a lack of awareness of the importance of collaborative work in conversation. She found that 'teachers still hold largely stereotypical views of the roles boys and girls should play in conversation' (p. 27). She also found that girls did not gain much advantage in terms of marks awarded from their better interpersonal skills and that they were penalised more heavily than boys if they failed to play a sustaining, encouraging role in discussion. On the other hand, teachers were most appreciative of the boys who did play a sustaining role.

In fact, there has been a growing awareness of the unequal share girls have of classroom talk, as Swann and Graddol (1989) have pointed out:

> What we observe in the classroom is a consensus, a manageable and stable state arrived at through the combined efforts of girls, boys and class teacher. This consensus is one where an unequal distribution of talk is seen as normal. In particular, girls seem to have learned to expect a lower participation level than boys and boys seem to have learned that their fair share is a larger one.

This view of classroom talk seems to be depressingly accurate; however, it is also quite helpful, as it assumes an active, rather than a passive role for the participants in its creation, which in turn implies the potential for change. Recognition of the unequal share enjoyed by girls and young women in talk in mixed groups has led many teachers to devise strategies for enabling them to become more assertive, for example by encouraging them to work in single-sex groups, and to formulate their ideas and to develop confidence in their abilities as speakers. However, this approach can simply result in an 'interruption' of the classroom situation described by Swann and Graddol above, not a permanent solution to it. Also, if the girls are working in single-sex groups in a mixed classroom, the boys must be as well. What skills should they be encouraged to acquire and develop?

A more equal share of the 'turns' does not always result in a more satisfactory exchange, as the following short transcript from part of a Year 10 Personal and Social Education lesson illustrates rather well. Two girls and two boys, aged fourteen or fifteen, are discussing the likely life-style and achievements of a woman of 30. They have been given some basic facts about her as a school leaver, and have already discussed what her life might be like at seventeen.

GIRL 2: Important events . . . I reckon trying to get . . .
BOY 2: ⌈Marriage.
GIRL 2: ⌊Promotion
BOY 2: And a baby.
GIRL 1: And kids . . .
BOY 2: And a baby, she'd have a baby.
GIRL 2: And so, what was that? Promotion?

BOY 2: Have a baby. Commotion?

GIRL 2: **Promotion**, like when you go up in a job, sort of . . .

BOY 2: Oh . . . marriage.

GIRL 2: (*laughs*) Having children. (*writing it down*)

BOY 2: Getting married, marriage . . .

GIRL 2: What else would there be?

BOY 2: Visiting her, her grandma.

GIRL 2: She could do that every week, so . . .

BOY 1: Passing her car test.

BOY 2: Yeah, (*turns to Boy 1 and addresses him*) or her **motorbike** test! (*laughs*)

GIRL 1: Yeah, driving test . . .

GIRL 2: But she could have done that much earlier in her life.

BOY 2: Or she might have done loads and loads and loads and only just passed it.

Although Girl 2 and Boy 2 enjoy a fairly equal 'share' of the talk here, their talk also exhibits more negative characteristics:

- short 'turns' which do not build on, and sometimes completely ignore or contradict previous ones;

- a 'stance' which is often repetitive and combative;

- a patronising attitude to women (by Boy 2).

This brief example is extracted early on from an extended sequence of work where the teacher used a range of strategies to help all her pupils overcome these sorts of problems. It seems unlikely that merely grouping girls and boys together will result in much of a change in the pattern of social relationships in the classroom. An alternative starting point could be to consider why it is that, when given the choice, girls and boys will almost always self-select into single-sex groups. 'Real life' outside the classroom is highly gendered, with most of us spending a great deal of our work and leisure time in single-sex groups, engaged in stereotyped activities. Perhaps it should come as no surprise that pupils see same-sex groups as the most comfortable way of working for them. Girls and boys will also readily recognise different sex-specific language patterns and modes. Single-sex groups of Year 10 pupils, when asked to reflect on boys' and girls' talk, came up with the following:

Girls (by girls)	*Girls (by boys)*
Talk quietly	Talk sensibly
Listen to others' ideas	Don't get ideas
Listen when boys talk	Don't shout
Pay attention to teachers	Listen

Boys (by girls)	*Boys (by boys)*
Talk too much	Get more ideas
Don't listen to girls when they talk	Get more attention from teachers
Listen to each other	Don't listen enough
Interrupt	Talk noisily

If teachers are able to build on pupils' extensive, but often implicit, knowledge about gender and language use, then considerable improvements can be brought about. The following extract contains some reflections during a whole class discussion of earlier small group work on *Macbeth* which had been carried out by some class members and observed by others in a Year 10 English class. Yvonne has been asked to observe several groups at work and to focus on a specific issue.

YVONNE: I had to do which sex dominates, boy or girl – and out of the five groups I found that in four of them it was a boy, and just one of them it was a girl. Most of the four ones were hard to decide because the girls out of them ones were the ones who were contributing and talking. But as (*i.e. for example*) in one of the groups; . . . I found that the three girls were doing most of the talking and writing it down, whereas whenever Sam (*the boy in the group*) had a point to say he came in and took over.

TEACHER: How did he do that?

YVONNE: He just sat there and then as soon as he had a point to say, he just went straight in, no matter what they were talking about. He just sort of took over. Sorry, Sam. Between one, I thought it was between Sam and Jennifer, but I felt that Sam dominated more because he made the final decision.

JENNIFER: Yeah, I didn't tend to argue, I don't know. I wasn't in the mood.

TEACHER: So you weren't in an argumentative mood?

JENNIFER: No. I just thought I had my own points of view and I just kept them to myself, a lot of the time though I did say them and they sort of said what they thought so . . .

SAM: Yeah, I love a good argument – there's nothing against it.

JENNIFER: I let them get on with it.

TEACHER: So, Sam, did he resolve the argument at the end, or sum it up?

YVONNE: He just made a decision.

SAM: No. I made my decision. I didn't make a decision for other people – no.

TEACHER: So you thought you were making a personal decision, on what you thought?

YVONNE: . . . And thought he was making the whole group's decision.

SAM: Oh, that's just my loud voice.

YVONNE: But also the one where the girl was dominating was the one where it was four girls and Keith, and it was Alexa who was dominating because everything Keith went to say, to try to overrule whatever Alexa was saying, Alexa always had a piece of evidence to back up what she was saying so she rightfully dominated that group because she was backing up everything she said.

TEACHER: She had better argumentative skills, better . . .

YVONNE: Yeah, she just won that group. But as soon as it came to talking in the class discussion Keith talked for her group and yet it was Alexa who had contributed everything.

TEACHER: Right, why did Keith talk for your group? Did you elect Keith to do the talking? They all pointed at you? Right.

The teacher commented on the whole lesson: 'the discussion around the issues observed lasted for two and a half hours and involved much reflective talk. Pupils who had previously not spoken in whole class discussion became involved.'

Several points are worth making in relation to this extract:

- Explicitly focusing on talk in the learning process, and talking about it, can be a powerful way of increasing pupils' awareness about gender and talk and of how to extend/change their language use and roles in groups.

- A large part of the teacher's role is to create a supportive classroom atmosphere of tolerance and frankness.

- Although girls frequently adopt what appears to be a passive role, they may well have made a conscious and active decision to do so (Jennifer illustrates this very well in this example). Anyon (1983) has suggested that girls and women are constantly making conscious decisions between 'accommodation' (what Jennifer chooses to do on this occasion) and 'resistance' (the response chosen by Alexa).

- Boys can be encouraged, by reflecting on their own roles within groups, to listen and respond more actively. His teacher felt that seeing himself on video, and participating in discussions like the one quoted above, had helped Sam to become less dominating.

Earlier in this article, I quoted Edwards' observation about developing communicative competence: it is possible that, for girls and boys to achieve this, they will each need to do less of the 'right' things in traditionally gender-stereotyped terms, and to do more of the 'wrong' ones. In helping them to reflect on their gendered language use, teachers can make this a positive and empowering experience.

Acknowledgements

I would like to thank: Lynne Johnson, Chafford School, Havering; Sue Keeble, Crestwood School, Hampshire; and Inge Cramer and Mary Morrison from the Bradford Oracy Project, who have all helped me by providing classroom material for this article.

Thanks are also due to teachers from the Waltham Forest, Havering and Essex Oracy Project for allowing me to reproduce part of their discussion.

References

ANYON, J. (1983) 'Intersections of Gender and Class: Accommodation and Resistance by Working Class and Affluent Females to Contradictory Sex-Role Ideologies' in Walker, S. and Barton, L. (eds.) (1983) *Gender, Class and Education*. Lewes: Falmer Press.

BENN, C. AND SIMON, B. (1972) *Half Way There*. London: Penguin.

CONNELL, R. W., ASHENDEN, D. J., KESSLER, S. AND DOWSETT, G. W. (1982) *Making the Difference: Schools, Families and Social Division*. Sydney: George Allen and Unwin.

JENKINS, N. (1990) 'Oral Assessment' in *Language Matters*, 1990, No.1, Centre for Language in Primary Education (CLPE), London Borough of Southwark.

SPENDER, D. (1988) 'Talking in Class' in Spender, D. and Sarah, E.(1988) *Learning to Lose: Sexism and Education*. London: The Women's Press.

SWANN, J. AND GRADDOL, D. (1989) 'Gender Inequalities in Classroom Talk', in *Gnosis*, Issue 14, LDA, London.

'As Near to Life as Possible' – A Response

GEMMA MOSS

Teachers are often uneasy about manifestations of gender difference in the classroom. Oracy is no different from other areas of the curriculum in this respect, and Hilary Kemeny's article draws attention to some of the ways in which this unease finds its expression. Where girls' and boys' behaviour notably diverges, teachers feel obliged to search for neutral ground. In oral work this has led teachers to emphasise mixed sex groups, and to find ways of increasing girls' participation in whole class discussion, so that their contributions can match the boys'. But, as Hilary's article makes clear, the more we learn about the ways in which talk happens in the classroom, the less these seem like the only or even the best approaches.

In the past, much of the concern about gender and oracy has stemmed from an analysis of whole class discussion, where boys dominate the public forum. This problem has been discussed in terms of boys' assertiveness and girls' lack of confidence. However, there are difficulties with this analysis. It deflects attention away from the context for speech to the individual speaker. How girls behave is seen to be a product of their personal qualities, not a consequence of the way in which the social setting is organised. Such an approach has not proved useful to girls. They become responsible for changing themselves rather than changing the situation. If we were less worried about giving girls chances to be confident, we might spend more time experimenting with other settings for talk. After all, if boys unfairly dominate whole class discussion, is this the best way of organising learning in our classes?

By labelling what girls do in terms of negative personality traits (lack of confidence, lack of self-esteem), we effectively stop any further enquiry. Girls' behaviour is seen as being simply deficient, rather than interesting in its own right. Fortunately, this is now beginning to change. One of the greatest benefits of the National Oracy Project is that it has encouraged teachers to pay close attention to speech in all kinds of settings. This has meant that, for the first time, teachers are beginning to build a much more complex picture of the way in which gender is inflected in talk. (For a fuller discussion of these issues, see *Talk*, No. 4, Summer 1991.)

Part of what has happened here is a change of focus from whole class to small group discussion. In whole class discussion, where turn-taking is largely controlled by the teacher, it makes sense to concentrate on the length of contribution made and the number of turns taken by boys versus girls. In small group talk, however, we need a more complex analysis, one which allows us to see how one speaker follows another, how the group collaborates to function as a whole, and to see the importance of listening as well as talking. It is at this level of detail that the most interesting insights are emerging. We are beginning to document the ways in which particular conversational strategies are used differently by girls and boys. For example, there are significant differences in the use of questions, interruptions, minimal responses, in fact, the whole way in which conversations are built and sustained (Jarmany, 1991; Jenkins, 1990; Johnson 1991). Indeed, it is precisely these kinds of differences in style which may make mixed-sex groupings so awkward for participants. If girls and boys are using different ground rules, who gets to decide which set of rules is most appropriate?

Analysis which focuses on the differences between girls' and boys' linguistic behaviours in small groups stresses the importance of understanding talk as a collaborative performance. The strategies which are used mean what they do in relation to the other participants in the discussion. They mean comparatively little in the abstract. Take minimal responses, for instance. Murmurs of agreement – 'uh huh', 'mmm' – are associated with women's talk, rather than men's. But to use minimal responses in an all-female group, where the conversational style is more supportive of individual participants, has a very different effect from trying to use them in a group dominated by men, where speakers are competing to take and hold the floor. We can't therefore convert our more subtle understanding of different conversational strategies into a new and ever more refined checklist of skills with which to equip students. Nor should we expect that all speakers will have equal access to them. For any account of the differences between girls' and boys' talk inevitably reminds us of the close links between speech and specific social setting.

Explicitly addressing the differences between girls' and boys' talk in our classes can be a fruitful form of inquiry. The kinds of investigation and observation that Hilary Kemeny records are important. They can lead pupils to reflect on language itself, and on the political consequences of the ways in which it is used. They can lead teachers to reconsider how they organise talk in the classroom and whose interests are being served by the current set-up.

References

JARMANY, K. (1991) 'Considering Gender Differences', *Talk*, the journal of the National Oracy Project, No. 4 Summer 1991.

JENKINS, N. (1990) 'Oral Assessment' in *Language Matters*, 1990, No. 1, Centre for Language in Primary Education (CLPE), London Borough of Southwark.

JOHNSON, L. (1991) 'Paula or Paul – Listening to the Evidence', *Talk*, the journal of the National Oracy Project, No. 4, Summer 1991.

Learning Through Talk
– Children Together

3

Introduction

This section explores the complex relationship between spoken language and learning, with a focus primarily on children learning together. One of the fundamental concerns of the National Oracy Project was to establish that pupils could learn effectively through well organised collaborative group work. This required close attention not only to planning, but to what actually happened as pupils engaged in 'learning talk'.

Douglas Barnes's article, 'The Role of Talk in Learning', sets the scene by tracing the roots of social constructivist theories of learning. It signals some of the ways in which both children and adults can 'work on understanding' using talk, 'because the flexibility of speech makes it easy for us to try out new ways of arranging what we know, and easy too to change them if they seem inadequate'.

To illustrate this, Jenny Des-Fountain and Alan Howe draw on examples from Project teachers' classrooms where children are talking and learning together without an adult present in the group. Their commentaries explore in some detail what happens when pupils are 'working together on understanding'. They end with a useful summary on the nature of pupil/pupil talk.

Terry Phillips argues for a close examination of the tasks and purposes created by teachers to promote discussion in school, in

'Why? The Neglected Question in Planning for Small Group Discussion'. He suggests that 'What matters is that students develop an expectation that principles for "doing" group discussion can be elicited by interrogating the task', thereby giving students ownership of the task and focusing attention on the curriculum as an 'object of reflection at the centre of the learning process'.

The section closes with Peter Forrestal's reflective account of the ways in which he and colleagues in Western Australia developed a model of learning which can help teachers in 'Structuring The Learning Experience'. The model builds on the principle that:

> Learners need not only a sense of direction but also a sense that they are learning – that is, that there has been a change, a growth in their understanding of the world and their place in it. This is something that teachers have to prepare and plan for explicitly and deliberately.

The Role of Talk in Learning

DOUGLAS BARNES

To explain the importance of talk in learning, we have to consider both what the learner does, and how he or she relates and interacts with other people. There are two traditions in psychological theory which emphasise each of these, typically represented by Piaget and Vygotsky. However, we shall follow Bruner in attempting to reconcile the two, since both are necessary for a full understanding of the learning that goes on in schools:

> Teaching is vastly facilitated by the medium of language, which ends by being not only the medium of exchange but the instrument the learner can use himself in bringing order into the environment.
>
> (Bruner, 1966)

We shall begin with the tradition of thought about learning that is nowadays called 'constructivism'. Its central contention is that each of us can only learn by making sense of what happens to us, through actively constructing a world for ourselves. (The word 'actively' will receive a commentary later in this article.) Most learning does not happen suddenly: we do not one moment fail to understand something and then the next moment grasp it entirely. To take an example, compare the conception of electricity you had as a child with your understanding of it now. As a child you used the word correctly, no doubt, but you lacked the ability to analyse and explain as well as to make links with those purposes and implications which make electricity important. The difference between the two will be even more marked for those who have studied physics. Most of our systems of ideas – call them schemes, frames, models, or concepts – go through a history of development in our minds, some of them changing continually throughout our lives.

One implication of this is that learning is seldom a simple matter of adding bits of information to an existing store of knowledge – though some adults have received this idea of learning from their own schooling. Most of our important learning, in school or out, is a matter of constructing models of the world, finding how far they work by using them, and then reshaping them in the light of what happens. Each new model or scheme potentially changes how we experience some aspect of the world, and therefore how we act on it. Information that finds no place in our existing schemes is quickly forgotten. That is why some pupils seem to forget so easily from one lesson to the next: the material that was presented to them has made no connection with their pictures of the world.

New learning, therefore, depends crucially on what the learner already knows. When we are told something, we can only make sense of it in terms of our existing schemes. A child who has had no experience of blowing up balloons or pumping up bicycle tyres will make much less sense of a lesson on air pressure, however clearly it is presented, than will a child who has had such experience.

Retrieving and transforming what we already know is a crucial part of learning. It was Piaget who pointed out that some knowledge and experience can be assimilated because it fits comfortably into our existing schemes for understanding the world, and that other new ideas, because they do not fit, force us to accommodate them by changing our schemes. Some new ideas, experiences or information require a radical revision, and this we sometimes resist. For example, when a teacher passed a beaker of cold water through a bunsen flame, many of his pupils thought the droplets of water that appeared on it had either condensed or spilt over the edge, these being both familiar ideas. It required a major accommodation of their ideas about the relationship of water and burning when they discovered that these droplets were a chemical product of the burning of the coal gas.

Whatever teaching methods a teacher chooses – question and answer, guided discovery, demonstration, or another – it will always be the pupil who has to do the learning. He or she will make sense of the lessons only by using the new ideas, experiences, or ways of thinking in order to reorganise his or her existing pictures of the world and how they can be acted upon. It is useful to think about this aspect of learning as a matter of the learner 'working on understanding'. Working on understanding is, in essence, the reshaping of old knowledge in the light of new ways of seeing things. (Of course, 'seeing' here is a metaphor for various ways of symbolising, not just visual ones.) And, in this reshaping, the pupils' 'old' knowledge is as important as the new experiences that are to challenge it. It is this challenge that provides the dynamic for the 'accommodation', the changing of previous ways of understanding for new ones. This change is often resisted, and not only by children: it can be uncomfortable to change our ideas about how things are and how we should behave.

At the centre of working on understanding is the idea of 'trying out' new ways of thinking and understanding some part of the world: the trying out enables us to see how far a new idea will take us, what it will or will not explain, where it contradicts our other beliefs, and where it opens up new possibilities:

> Much of growth starts out by our turning around on our own traces and recoding in new forms, with the aid of adult tutors, what we have been doing or seeing, then going on to new modes of organisation with the new products that have been formed by these recodings.
>
> (Bruner, 1966)

Bruner here places considerable stress on the role of the adult tutor, yet in the National Oracy Project we have been impressed by the way in which groups of children can work on understanding (or 'recode', as Bruner puts it) without an adult being present. However, adults, even if temporarily absent, have crucial roles to play in talking for learning, and these are discussed in the next section.

There are various ways of 'working on understanding'. Teachers often ask pupils to talk or write in order to encourage this, but drawings and diagrams, numerical calculations, manipulation of objects, and silent thought may also provide means of trying out new ways of understanding. When I referred to learning 'actively' (p. 123), I was meaning 'working on understanding': 'active' does not imply moving about the room or manipulating objects (though either of these might be involved) but rather the attempt to interrelate, to reinterpret, to understand new experiences and ideas.

The readiest way of working on understanding is often through talk, because the flexibility of speech makes it easy for us to try out new ways of arranging what we know, and easy too to change them if they seem inadequate. Of particular importance is the fact that we can talk to one another, collaborating and trying out our new ways of thinking. This will provide the focus for the second part of this article.

Not all kinds of talking (or writing) are likely to contribute equally to working on understanding. For example, a great deal of the writing that goes on in school is mainly a matter of imitating what other people have said or written, and the same is true of at least part of the talk. It is useful to distinguish two functions of talk, according to whether the speaker's attention is primarily focused on the needs of an audience, or whether he or she is more concerned with sorting out his or her own thoughts. These two functions can be called 'presentational' and 'exploratory'. Exploratory talk is often hesitant and incomplete; it enables the speaker to try out ideas, to hear how they sound, to see what others make of them, to arrange information and ideas into different patterns. Exploratory talk provides an important means of working on understanding, but learners are unlikely to embark on it unless they feel relatively at ease, free from the danger of being aggressively contradicted or made fun of. Presentational talk, on the other hand, offers a 'final draft' for display and evaluation: it is often focused more on the expectations of an audience than on the speaker's ideas. Presentational talk frequently occurs in response to teachers' questions when they are testing pupils' understanding of a topic already taught. It also occurs when anyone, child or adult, is speaking to a large or unfamiliar audience. Such situations discourage exploration: they persuade the speaker to focus on 'getting it right', that is, on appropriate speech and the expected information ('right answers').

Much of the talk which teachers invite from pupils is presentational in nature, and it is not our intention to deny the value to learners of having to order ideas and present them explicitly to an audience, even one that may be critical. Teachers should, however, consider at what point in the sequence of learning this should take place. In the earlier stages of a new topic, it is likely to be exploratory talking and writing that will contribute more to the inter-relating of old ways of thinking and new possibilities: in other words, to working on understanding. (Peter Forrestal develops the idea of the 'sequence of learning' in his article later in this section.) Both presentational and exploratory talk are important in learning. Teachers need to be sensitive to the differences between them and to ensure a balance of opportunities. (See the following article by Jenny Des-Fountain and Alan Howe for a fuller development of the relationship between exploratory and presentational talk.)

It is useful to make another distinction. Sometimes what people say is deeply embedded in what they are doing, as when two children are using scientific apparatus together. Because purposes are shared and the relevant objects are in front of them, the talk is highly inexplicit. Much of the talk is of the nature of 'Put that there'. Not only are objects left unnamed, but reasons for actions are often assumed to be obvious. On other occasions, what is said is independent of any objects or activities except the talk itself, as in storytelling, or when we reflect aloud on the implications of a decision that has to be made. Some learning in schools appears to take place at first tacitly. Bruner (1986) wrote that we can reach conscious control only after we have achieved unreflective mastery. Edwards and Mercer (1987) illustrated how primary school teachers involve their pupils in activities and talk about them in such a way as to direct attention to the crucial features that they will need to be aware of in order to participate in similar activities. It seems important that such learning should later be reflected on and made explicit. It is when we have laid out clearly what we believe to be the case that we can look critically at our assumptions and determine whether we wish to stand by them. Reflection, including the reflection that is enabled by talk *outside the event*, seems to be an essential prerequisite for critical thinking and the modification of what we believe. (Terry Phillips, in the third article of this section, makes a strong case for the need for pupils to 'interrogate the task'.)

At this point, we need to turn to an alternative tradition in the psychology of learning which represents learners as essentially social beings who are being inducted into cultural practices and ways of seeing the world that exist in the groups to which they belong. Learners must indeed 'construct' models of the world, but the models they construct are not arbitrary; the experiences on which they are based do not come from nowhere. They are responses to activities and talk that they have shared with other, usually older, members of the community. This tradition provides a useful complement to what we have written from the more individualistic (or Piagetian) perspective. Exploratory talk does not provide new information. When we talk of learners 'constructing' meanings, we refer to them manipulating what is already available to them from various sources (including first-hand experience), exploring its possibilities, and seeing what can and cannot be done with it.

Vygotsky was one of the first psychologists to stress the role of talk in organising our understanding of the world: he would not have dissented from what has since come to be called the social constructivist view of learning. He insisted that our ability to talk and think is in the first instance social and only later becomes individual:

Human learning presupposes a specific social nature and a process by which children grow into the intellectual life of those around them.
(Vygotsky, quoted by Edwards and Mercer, 1987)

By participating in activities and talk we internalise both the categories and the ways of going about things that are essential to our social environment. Central to what we learn in this way is our speech – not just the forms of words and sentences that are used but, more importantly, the meanings and purposes which they represent, and the social relationships in which they are embedded. We learn to participate not only in activities but also in the meanings which inform them.

This brings us to an ambiguity that underlies all deliberate teaching. Our culture offers to young learners powerful new ways of understanding and influencing the world, so that much learning is a matter of 'getting inside' an adult way of looking at the world, in order to use it for thinking and acting. Each student needs to deal with those new experiences that challenge existing schemes or pictures of the world. However, only he or she has access to the particular preconceptions and misunderstandings which he or she needs to reflect upon and modify. Young people are more likely to struggle to make sense of new experiences when these are important in their own lives. One of the challenges that faces all teachers is how to help their pupils to try out new ways of thinking that may be disturbingly different from what they are used to and at the same time to give more responsibility to those learners to explore their own dilemmas.

References

BRUNER, J. S. (1966) *Toward a Theory of Instruction*. Harvard: Belknap Press.
EDWARDS, D. AND MERCER, N. (1987) *Common Knowledge*. London: Methuen.

Pupils Working Together on Understanding

JENNY DES-FOUNTAIN

AND

ALAN HOWE

In the previous article, Douglas Barnes has outlined the role of talk in learning. He also states: '. . . in the National Oracy Project we have been impressed by the ways in which groups of children can work on understanding . . . without an adult being present.' In this article, we illustrate this view of learning by examining in detail some examples of pupils working together in classrooms.

The assertion that children can learn in this way is not a new one. Barnes and Todd (1976) demonstrated the learning potential of small group talk, and the Bullock Report (1975) put considerable emphasis on group talk. The programmes of study and non-statutory guidance for English and other subjects in the National Curriculum emphasise the value of collaborative work. However, research suggests that, while the theory has for some time been in place, a gap still exists between theory and practice. For example, David Wood (1988) writes:

> . . . studies inspire confidence in the idea that teachers may be able to exploit child-child interactions to help facilitate learning. However, systematic observations of children working in groups in the classroom suggest that the pay-offs often found in laboratory studies appear rarely in schools.

(p. 226)

And Neville Bennett (1984) states:

> Boydell (1975) and Galton et al. (1980) both report similar findings
> with other primary age children. They found that most of the talk in
> groups was not related to the task, that conversations were not sustained,
> and that boys tended to talk only to boys, and girls to girls. Boydell thus
> argued that seating children in groups is no guarantee that they will talk
> freely about anything, let alone their work.
>
> (p. 153)

We believe that there are two related reasons for these disappointing
findings. The first is that too few teachers understand, or know how to
organise, true collaborative work. Bennett himself, in a more recent
finding (1990), indicates that 'where a demand for co-operation was
made by the teacher, co-operative endeavour and on-task behaviour
increased to a high level. It was also established that there was a
relationship between interaction in the group and pupils' understanding of the task' (p. 63). The second reason is that there has been a
surprising lack of close attention to, and evidence of, the complex
ways in which talk between children supports learning. We still
encounter a prevailing view among many teachers that, while talk
may help pupils to 'get the job done' and be a pleasant lubricant to
classroom work, it doesn't have a significant effect on their knowledge
or understanding. This article challenges that view by providing
evidence of 'thinking voices' at work.

We offer five contrasting examples of pupils working on
understanding. We also use different styles of commentary, reinforcing the message that there is no one 'right' way to describe
talk.

Roman coins

A pair of Year 1 pupils has been asked to discuss some Roman coins.
They know that another pair of five and six year olds from their class
will join them later, and that they will need to offer the new pair their
observations on the coins. Here they observe, construct a hypothesis,
develop it into narrative and reflect on their own degree of interest in
archaeology. Their explanations draw on previous experiences and
understandings, relating those to this new experience. We see each
one test out how far his/her current explanation will stretch. They
interrogate and rework meanings, sometimes seeming to echo others'

voices, sometimes moving towards a new way of expressing their ideas.

There is a degree of tension, however, even in this sustained, successful collaborative talk. Daniel (six years and two months) draws on his knowledge of fossils and archaeology; he conveys his enthusiasm but also makes a subtle claim for the authority of the 'scientist's' voice. Laura (five years and eight months) returns to narrative and pragmatically resists Daniel's claim to the more expert role. Might we be seeing here the beginnings of attitudes to knowledge and to differences in talk which result from and contribute to gender differences? We are reminded of the way that social, communicative and cognitive aspects of talk are inter-linked.

Daniel and Laura are learning about collaboration, about negotiating an expert role, about claiming and resisting an authoritative voice at the same time as they are working on their understanding of their historical investigation, of what it is to work as an historian:

Commentary

1 TEACHER: Look at those now; remember what you're thinking about. Are they old? What does it tell us about the people?

LAURA: What's that number, Mrs Loader?

5 TEACHER: – E 90 21. (*teacher leaves*)

LAURA: E 90 21? That's very . . .

DANIEL: 90 21 – oh, man! . . .

LAURA: 90 21 . . .

DANIEL: Look at this coin. These are all

10 dirty.

LAURA: Yes, because they've been underneath the sand.

DANIEL: Yeah, they've been under . . . these . . . This one has been underneath

15 sand; you can see all the sand pattern on it, can't you?

LAURA: This has been underneath sand, yeah, and it's been right down, ⌈ yeah?

DANIEL: ⌊ I know,

20 I know . . .

LAURA: And there've been mud under there, right under the sand, yeah? And that's where it's been, it's been really precious to other people that they've lost it.

1–3 Their teacher reminds them of two of the historical questions she modelled when she 'thought aloud' her observations about a genuine and a replica Roman lamp with the whole class.

4–8 Daniel and Laura had noticed the museum's catalogue numbers on the first in the series of three sets of artefacts. They had begun to develop a hypothesis that the numbers were dates. The reverence and excitement in their voices indicate that they realise that the numbers may convey important information. However, as they continue to examine the coins, the decoding of the numbers is left to one side.

11–12 Laura offers an explanation for Daniel's observation. She initiates a pattern of response which signals the way one listens and builds on the other's ideas with 'yes', or 'yeah', or 'I know' or 'guess what'.

13–20 Daniel agrees, repeats the idea, reinforcing the hypothesis with an additional observation. His tag question, 'can't you?', invites Laura's agreement. They both continue to use this device ('yeah?', 'right?', 'eh?', 'aren't they?') to seek the other's active listening, to check that they are moving towards a joint understanding.

21–24 Whose voice can we hear in Laura's words here? Her teacher's? An adult who uses a metal detector to treasure hunt? She begins the 'lost coins' narrative.

25 DANIEL: I know, it's like . . . like . . .
   like – when . . . erm . . . people die because
   they are very, very old, they die on
   the ground and then the tide comes in
   and washes another load . . . when
30 they die, ⌈right? . . .
   LAURA: ⌊Yeah, yeah, and all the water
   comes and it makes things come out their
   hand like one of these might've come out
   their   ⌈hand, yeah?
35 DANIEL: ⌊Now, guess what? Guess what?
   They died holding all these coins, right,
   on the seaside, and then the water came
   in and flushed another load of sand on
   top of them. Then people . . . then
40 the tide ⌈came in . . .
   LAURA: ⌊That's . . .
   DANIEL: . . . then the tide came in again
   and washed all the sand away and people
   found them. They didn't find the people,
45 but they found the coins, eh?
   LAURA: And this one is a Indian, yeah?
   That Indian was born, yes.
   DANIEL: Hold on. Look, look. It's got a
   Roman helmet on!
50 LAURA: I know.
   DANIEL: Can't you see . . . it's got that
   there. That's Roman.
   LAURA: I know that.
   DANIEL: These are all Roman, aren't they?
55 LAURA: Yeah, they've all came from
   Roman. That proves they are very old.
   If you look at that, that's very, very old.
   See, that's very dirty, that's a horse, and
   that's a boy trying to climb on to
60 the horse.⌈They're very old.
   DANIEL: ⌊I know. Can't, can't you see what
   I . . . Laura? I've got fossils at home, right,
   and they're over 70 million years ago which
   are older than these.
65 LAURA: Why don't you bring them in
   then, in the bag?

Commentary:

25–30 Daniel begins to draw on his understandings of archaeology: 'it's like . . .'

31–34 Laura's contribution to the joint text returns to the idea of lost treasure.

35–45 Daniel moves into another gear: 'Now, guess what?' and constructs a vivid narrative, in the past tense, to develop their hypothesis and to describe the enterprise of archaeology.

46–47 Laura moves on to a new topic. She interprets the rather spiky representation of a laurel wreath as a North American Indian headdress.
48–53 A helpful challenge? Daniel corrects Laura, perhaps drawing on his experience of other work with artefacts. He invites her to observe the coins more closely and reminds her that they are looking at Roman artefacts. He may be drawing on his conversations with his elder brother at home – or referring back to the information the teacher gave them in her introduction to the activity.

54 He invites her to agree, checking their joint understanding of the task.
55–60 Laura reassures Daniel and opens a new round of observation, explanation and narration.

61–64 Daniel returns to his archaeological theme and indicates something of his developing sense of chronology.

65 A challenge? A genuine enquiry?

DANIEL: I'm not allowed, 'cause all the naughty children would go into my bag, see them and they'd end up breaking
70 them. They're very, very precious. They're fossils! I've got a dinosaur bone, and I've got fossils of dinosaurs.
LAURA: I know that. I'm into Turtle drawings 'n' dinosaurs.
75 DANIEL: I know. I'm into both. I want . . . I want to grow up ⌈and be a scientist.
LAURA: ⌊How d'you t . . . I'm going to turn it off. (*she turns off the tape recorder*)

73–79 Laura's resistance to Daniel's claim to a more expert role? Does she decide he's off task? Or has she just had enough of the coins?

Molluscs

The Year 6 pupils quoted below were on a field trip in France. Their teacher had organised their seashore investigations in a 'jigsaw' structure. Four 'expert' groups had focused their observations on the molluscs, the seaweeds, the rocks and the animals they found on the seashore. The 'expert' groups also consulted information texts, talked together to rework their initial observations and decided on priorities for their presentations.

In this short extract, Paul, the molluscs expert, tells Christopher, John and Neil what he knows about molluscs as part of the session where each expert reported back to the 'home' group:

PAUL: This is a dog whelk, it's single shelled, but it's not a   1
   vegetarian . . . it eats barnacles. See that little tube there . . .
CHRISTOPHER: Yeah.
PAUL: That one there . . .
CHRISTOPHER: Yes.   5
PAUL: Right, it sticks the little tube inside of the top of the
   barnacles and it sucks all the little fleshy juicy bits out . . .
   that's how it eats . . .

JOHN: Repulsive things . . .

CHRISTOPHER: Someone says it's got more than a thousand teeth. 10

PAUL: Some of them have bi-hinged . . . that's a bi-hinged shell cos it's got two shells and it opens up like a hinge . . . that's the beak – that bit there.

NEIL: So, what's inside it? . . . just like a . . .

PAUL: Just like a snail . . . 15

NEIL: Slug . . .

PAUL: Yeah.

JOHN: Like an oyster?

PAUL: Yeah.

NEIL: Slimy. 20

PAUL: Somewhere in the beak it's got a little hole.

NEIL: Will that be dead now? . . .

PAUL: It opens up. It waits for something. No, no . . . it waits for something to swim by . . . it opens up and the water rushes in and it like sucks whatever is swimming by out . . . in . . . 25 (*laughs*) and then it pushes the water through this little hole . . . and it's got whatever it caught to eat . . . Right . . . Say there is three of these, they have different ways of breathing . . . that's lowest . . . towards the tide, right? And when the tide comes in . . . this is under the water, so it has gills and it can just like 30 breathe under the water . . . And when the tide's out and it's not under the water . . . it traps water under its shell like that . . . and it just breathes through the water . . . cos if it didn't have any water it would suffocate . . . This one has got half, it's got both lungs and gills . . . so that it can stay out of the water 35 and in, because it's half way up the beach . . . and it's like . . . it can be out of the water from anything up to to two hours . . . he can be up, like, six, six in and six out . . .

CHRISTOPHER: Twelve.

PAUL: . . . and this one has got lungs . . . cos he's out of the water 40 nearly all the time . . . cos the water comes in and he's only in the water for about . . . two hours . . . and he can be out for up to er . . . twelve hours . . . so he's just got lungs, and the tide comes in over the top and he traps air under his shell and he just breathes that air. (*pause*) Tom . . . Dick and Harry I call 45 them . . . These bi-hinged shells . . . they move around like . . . you know how they suck the water in and they've got a little hole in the beak there . . . they push it out really hard . . . as hard as they can, and it uses like a jet and pushes it along like that.
50

CHRISTOPHER: Jet propelled.

PAUL: Yeah . . . I don't think I know anything else.

Commentary

The writers of this article discussed the transcript. Part of their discussion went like this:

— Douglas Barnes suggests that there is a kind of talk we can call 'presentational' – where the speaker's attention is directed towards an audience. This seems to be a particularly good example of this kind of talk. But I wonder if 'presentational' is a helpful term to describe this?

— There's a big difference between the sort of presentation that children are asked to make to a large group and the quality of interaction built into presentation to a small group.

— Yes, notice how Neil asks, 'So what's inside it, just like a . . .', and Paul responds, 'Just like a snail', following Neil's contribution, 'Slug' and John's, 'Like an oyster?'. Paul's exposition is 'fuelled' by the quality of attention his listeners provide – perhaps because they've all been asked to be both 'experts' in one field and 'listeners' to others' expertise. They are aware of the reciprocal nature of the talk, even though Paul holds the reins.

— I'm struck by the way that Christopher, John and Neil all feel able to interject, for example at line 39. When Christopher interjects, 'Twelve', this suggests that active listening is taking place and that Paul is making sense. Later on Christopher interjects again, 'Jet propelled'. He seems to be supplementing Paul's description of the bivalve shells using the sucked-in water 'like a jet'.

— Paul's in expert role, but his biology isn't quite accurate, is it? He calls the molluscs 'bi-hinged' (line 11) when he means that they are bivalves, and later on (line 35) he states that molluscs have lungs – they don't!

— No, but what is interesting is where those 'mistakes' come from and what they tell us about Paul as a learner. Paul is working on understanding here, and in his search for the 'correct' term to describe the shells (bivalves) lands instead on his invented term 'bi-hinged' which focuses on their hinged construction. I'd guess that he's drawing on his experiences of looking at empty shells, there.

— Yes, and when he suggests that molluscs have lungs, he's probably over-generalising from his knowledge that land creatures have lungs and water creatures have gills. He's in the process of reorganising his thinking: this presentation catches his understanding at a particular point in its development. It'll be his subsequent experiences that'll challenge this working hypothesis. I wonder if that challenge came elsewhere in the sequence of work?

– Douglas Barnes says, 'retrieving and transforming what we know is a crucial part of learning'. What we're arguing for is the value of saying what 'you know' out loud and testing it against the response of others. It's not just consolidating . . .

– . . . It's part of the active process, what I suppose we could call 'deploying' understanding. In the actual act of using language to explain to someone else, you clarify it for yourself too.

– Yes, look how he organises the ideas for the others, moving from description to explanation (if you're interested in this as a text, note the use of qualifying clauses such as 'when the tide comes in' and 'cos if it didn't have any water it would' . . .).

– It's another really good example of a 'press' on language working in favour of the child. Remember he's only eleven, yet there's a marine biologist talking here!

– That's right. And yet he seems to be able to draw the others into the enterprise of marine biology. He's bringing his language and experience closer to theirs: it's very much more difficult for adults to do this.

Reactivity

The next account attempts to put a particular example of small group talk into its wider educational context, and, in so doing, to illuminate ways in which the talk contributed to the pupils' scientific understanding.

A Year 10 class taking 'double science' at GCSE was working on the topic of metals. In a previous lesson, small groups had conducted a series of experiments to test the reactivity of various metals (magnesium, copper, iron, lead, zinc) in acid and when burned in air. Each group had noted and then discussed the different reactions produced. At the start of this (75 minute) lesson, the teacher asked groups to 'double up' and to compare, check and discuss their results. Most of the original groups of fifteen year olds were single sex groups; when they 'doubled up', some mixed groups were formed. A group of six (three boys, three girls) met around one of the workbenches and began to carry out the task set, by discussing each metal in turn and comparing results. The talk is characterised by short, overlapping utterances as information is exchanged, but there is little evidence of any extension of the pupils' understanding.

Gavin moves the group on by asking, 'Zinc?' 'Hydrogen and bubbling a little,' replies Emma. Gavin agrees, 'Yeah, hydrogen; our's was bubbling very rapidly actually.' Sharon intervenes with, 'Our's wasn't bubbling all that much', to which Gavin responds, 'It should really bubble a lot.' This is a different kind of comment – Gavin has introduced a different frame of reference from the simple swapping of observations and is implying that the girls have got the wrong result. His comment is challenged with, 'Why? Why?' from Emma and June, to which he replies, 'Because it's high up in the reactivity series', at which point Michael comes in to support Gavin by repeating, 'Reactivity table, yeah.'

There are a number of interesting points here. The boys bring in a reference to the reactivity series, referring to an authority beyond their own evidence to justify their results and implicitly to criticise the girls' result. The girls are 'reduced' to asking questions – a role that then continues throughout their discussion – and thereby invests the group of boys with a degree of authority. A little later in the talk, when another of the girls' results is questioned, again by Gavin, who says, 'It shouldn't really be as fast as zinc, cos it's lower down in the reactivity series', Sharon is forced to complain, 'Well, some of us haven't got those things!', referring to a reactivity table.

We might seem to be rather critical of this example, but we don't think that the talk was completely counter-productive. The sharing of results and the anomalies that arose enabled the issue of the reasoning behind the experiment to be talked out. The girls were able to challenge Gavin to justify his statement in a way that they might have found difficult to do to a teacher. A little later on in the discussion, another example of this occurs.

Gavin (still invested within the group with the 'expert' role) says, 'We'll go on to the acids now', and is immediately asked by Emma, 'Why are you going on to the acids?' to which he replies: 'Well, it was a more controlled experiment really, because the metals didn't melt, did they? . . . See, it depended on the melting point of the metal to the success of the air experiment . . .' There is some evidence that the three girls are prevented from articulating their own understanding, and are limited by the boys' apparently more authoritative grasp of the scientific understanding. However, this would, in our view, only become a major drawback if this were the only context for talk provided by the teacher. The direction the lesson took opened up an opportunity for Emma, Jane and Sharon to 'try out ideas for size' in a way that didn't happen in this example.

Each group was asked, in the light of its observations, to produce its own reactivity series for the metals studied and to write a group statement giving reasons for the group's decision. Group statements were read out to the whole class and briefly discussed and commented on by the teacher. He then introduced a new experiment (conducted as a demonstration to the class) which, he said, 'leads us on from this'. He told the class that he was going to leave them 'with a little problem to solve at the end'. He then placed a mixture (in powdered form) of iron oxide and aluminium in a crucible with some magnesium powder as a 'fuse' to 'kick the reaction off'. A brief, bright white flare followed, leaving a hard metallic lump and a sprinkling of white powder. The teacher then told the class that he wanted them to 'try to work out a little hypothesis – that means a sort of scientific theory about what's happened . . .' Emma, Jane and Sharon returned to work together as a group and began to tackle the task.

What is immediately apparent is the very different nature of their talk in comparison with the previous discussion in the mixed group. They begin by searching for analogies which might help to explain their observations:

EMMA: Like, sort of gold dust.
SHARON: Like, um . . .
JANE: Gold dust!?
SHARON: Oh, what's dad do at home . . .? We've got a model, dad's made a model out of something like this.

A little later on, Jane introduces a different analogy, 'like air bubbles in it', which prompts a period of discussion during which this idea is extended as the group search for ways of explaining how air bubbles could become trapped in the metal:

EMMA: Why has it got air bubbles in it?
SHARON: Because, when it was mixed . . . you know, when heat expands . . .
EMMA: You could but, the mixing gave air bubbles like you mix a cake.

We can see, through the talk, what Douglas Barnes is referring to when he writes, '. . . most of our systems of ideas . . . go through a history of development in our minds'.

The group speculates that the shape and form of the substance remaining after the experiment might be 'like gold dust', 'like glitter', 'like air bubbles'; that the iron oxide and aluminium powder 'stick together', 'fused together', then 'fused and melted together', 'melted together by the heat'; that the metal 'expanded', 'cooked . . . and set' – a development of an hypothesis which is finally summarised by Jane (who is trying to note down the ideas as they occur) as, 'I've got "the powders could have melted and fused together because of the heat . . . mixing left air bubbles . . . when heated, the air expanded and when cooled the metal formed around the cold . . . leaving just spaces in the middle."'

This is a reconstruction of just a small portion of the group's talk, but we consider that it provides enough evidence of Douglas Barnes's account of pupils 'working on understanding'. We cannot claim that Emma, Sharon or Jane reach new understanding as they talk. Douglas Barnes writes, 'most learning doesn't happen suddenly: we do not one moment fail to understand something and then the next moment grasp it entirely.' We would argue that the talk in which the three girls are engaged as they attempt to make sense of the new experience (the experiment and its product) is an example of the reordering of information and experience which they already possess. They do this in the light of experience from outside school, as well as by drawing on work which they have recently done in science. Perhaps it is not without significance that culinary metaphors begin to emerge.

The story doesn't (and shouldn't) end here, of course. Once groups had formulated a working hypothesis, the teacher reconvened the whole class and asked representatives from each group to put the theory into words for everyone to hear. Interestingly, other groups had also produced explanations that, in part, tracked the same territory as Emma's group. Another group had two unresolved ideas, one of which proved to be closest to the 'correct' scientific explanation (the transfer of oxygen from the iron oxide, forming aluminium oxide – the white powder). All ideas were received, and groups were then asked to return to their discussion, briefly, to see if anyone else's ideas could help. At this point, the teacher decided to summarise for the class the science of what had happened, putting it into the context of previous work.

We would argue that it was through the opportunities created for talk that the pupils developed a 'readiness to learn'. Having to grapple with a difficult 'new' experience had 'loosened the cement' of previously formed ideas enough for the teacher's explanation to be accommodated far more successfully than might have been the case had they had little chance to see what they thought for themselves. We would even go so far as to argue that the various opportunities for talk, and the way that the ideas which emerged were treated by the teacher as being of value – worthy of serious consideration – meant that the pupils could begin to make sense of the information on their own terms.

Let us end with the teacher's own reflections on how the talk was contributing to the girls' understanding:

> I think they found it very difficult, I think their perception of chemical reactivity is pretty well nil . . . I don't think they thought there was any reaction at all, they just think the heat just sort of melted it all together and it's just a big mess . . . I don't really think that they perceived the idea of a chemical reaction at all. Not to start off with anyway, and then they began to grasp that towards the end of the lesson . . .

> As far as I am concerned, oracy is where a person actually uses talk as a way of examining his or her world, the ideas about his or her world, to

try and put into actual words the things that are perhaps going on in his or her mind . . . I think it provides another way of getting the kids to think about their learning, it provides one with a way of getting them to actually get inside the problems I set them in science.

There is a tendency in some accounts of talk to portray the group as another, smaller and safer, forum for solo talkers and listeners, whose individual contributions can, albeit with some difficulty, be unravelled. Our experience, allied to our reading, suggests that to try to do this may be to misrepresent much interactive educational group talk. We have learned a lot from recent studies which draw on Vygotsky's pioneering work in stressing the social, interactive nature of learning through talk. For example, evidence from Edwards and Mercer (1987) and, more recently, from studies conducted by Janet Maybin (1990) alert us to the way that conversation is essentially 'dialogic' in nature. Participants finish off each others' utterances, build on each others' ideas, support and extend what the other is trying to say, create dual, and at times even ambiguously shifting patterns of meaning (what Maybin calls 'provisional' meanings), to the extent that it is possibly closer to the truth to talk about the construction of *joint utterance* and *joint meaning*. In the example quoted above, the construction of a working hypothesis about the science experiment is shared between the three girls. We would be hard put to extricate any one pupil's contribution and identify it as the source of the idea. Equally, any attempt to unravel one pupil's spoken thread and regard it as a solo 'text' is doomed to failure. The meanings being worked on often hover uncertainly between the participants – part of a spoken text being worked on collaboratively by three authors.

At this point, we would like to introduce two examples of a particular type of 'co-construction of meaning', in which, as a result of a challenge from one or more of the participants, others in the group are able to reformulate their understanding, to 'refocus' it or, to continue the analogy with writing, to start to 'redraft', moving from rough verbal 'jottings' towards a first attempt to organise and extend ideas. The *responsibility* for the work on understanding is still shared, but, unlike the more equally shared 'duetting' discussed above, these examples show pupils adopting different roles – the one prompting the other(s) to 'rework' an idea.

Whim Jim

In a Year 10 History class, fifteen year old pupils were studying the topic of the development of the mining industry in the nineteenth century. Small groups identified a particular aspect of mining which resulted in technological change and researched it, using a variety of source materials and reference texts. Having completed this stage, each group was asked to prepare, using overhead transparencies, a short 'presentation' of its findings for the rest of the class. Prior to the presentation, one member of each group went as an 'envoy' to another group to explain the group's ideas. Those remaining in their groups and receiving an 'envoy' were asked to question their visitor and seek clarification. The teacher was thus creating an opportunity for the rehearsal and reformulation of ideas as a prelude to the presentation to the class. Lynn has been sent as an envoy to join Simon, Paul and Jason. Her group has been researching developments in the systems used to bring coal up to the surface. In the short transcript which follows, Lynn confidently launches into an explanation, dealing successfully and with good humour with the interjections of the group of boys, whose contributions and questions appear in brackets:

> LYNN: In some of 'em, the people had to carry the coal out of the mine in . . . in baskets and on their head, right? (Yeah.) Then people got more brainy, OK? (Yeah.) So, their systems got more brainy too. And this is how they got the people up (You've got a picture of a train track.), they got the people up and down and the coal, OK? And it was just like a pulley system when they turn it, and they can take people up and down and things and everything. (Yeah.) And then as they got even more brainy, their schemes got more brainy, too, right? This is called Whim Jim, OK? (A what?) It's called a Whim Jim. (A Whim Jim?) I don't think up the names, so don't blame me, OK? (A Whim Jim?) A horse – this is a horse, OK? (A horse?) Pauline drew this horse, this is a horse, right? (Right.) The horse walks round and round this . . . the horse walks round which moves the drum which goes round and round, right? (Yep.) which turns the pulleys which makes the vertical spindles go round, which in turn makes the ropes go up and down the mine which takes the coal and people up and down the mine, OK? And that's as far as we got.

We are struck by the register adopted by Lynn here – she manages to combine explanation ('the horse walks round which moves the drum which goes round and round . . .') with an appropriate degree of colloquialism ('so their systems got more brainy, too') and also incorporates the boys' responses – which could be seen as an attempt to dislodge Lynn's poise as much as a genuine quest after knowledge! – into her 'text', so that she retains the communicative impetus ('I don't think up the names, so don't blame me, OK?').

As mentioned earlier, Douglas Barnes argues for two types of talk in school – the 'exploratory' and the 'presentational'. While we find the distinction a useful one, reminding us of the need to promote opportunities for talk which serve the talkers' purposes first, as well as for talk which communicates to others, we don't regard the distinction as a hard and fast one. In fact, we would suggest that in this extract, Lynn is moving between the exploratory and the presentational, and that this shifting focus (which we might characterise as the speaker both listening to herself and beginning to have to take account of her listeners' needs and level of understanding) is of particular benefit to her. She is, under the 'challenge' offered by the context, testing out her own thinking in a situation which has placed a greater external demand on her language within the relative security of the small group.

Paper Boats

The second short example comes from a Year 3/4 classroom where pairs of pupils (aged between eight and nine) were planning, carrying out and then reviewing two different problem-solving activities, each involving making something. One group of pairs had to construct a mobile to hang above Mr. Grinling's bed (Mr. Grinling is the lighthouse keeper in Ronda and David Armitage's book *The Lighthouse Keeper's Catastrophe*) to help him to sleep; the other group were constructing a boat out of newspaper to hold afloat twenty marbles. The pupils are in a class that is used to planning, conducting and reviewing an activity through talk (finding out what others did and making positive comments) – as is shown in the way that they cross-question each other when reviewing in groups of four (a pair from each activity), prior to carrying out the parallel activity themselves:

HELEN: What did you do, what's your task?   1
SYLVIA: Our task . . .
MANZEER: We had to make a boat out of newspaper.
MOLLY: And what happened to yours?
SYLVIA: It kept on sinking, and the newspaper, it kept on . . .   5
MANZEER: Leaking.
SYLVIA: Breaking.
HELEN: Did you put masking tape on it?
SYLVIA: Yeah.
HELEN: All the masking tape came off?   10
SYLVIA: Yeah.
MANZEER: We put card on it, and then we cutted the
   newspaper . . .
SYLVIA: And the newspaper kept on coming off?

MANZEER: Yeah, it kept on coming off.   15
HELEN: What happened to it in the end – it just got broke up?
MANZEER: The first time, you should have seen it, it looked like a
   bit of food, it was all cut up, like, cut up.
SYLVIA: And there was masking tape everywhere!
MANZEER: All in the water . . .   20
MOLLY: . . . how did you make – did you put the news . . . did you
   make a newspaper boat first and then made it out of card?
SYLVIA: Well, we thought that we'd fill it with cardboard because
   newspaper, when you put it in water, it wouldn't really . . . It
   would sink and then the newspaper would go everywhere and   25
   then it would tear up, so we put card.
MOLLY: Did you do a flat bottom, or was it, triangle sort of . . .?
SYLVIA: Sort of like upwards. (*demonstrates*)
MOLLY: So, it was going from there, upwards? (*demonstrates*)
SYLVIA: Yeah.   30
MOLLY: Do you think you should have done a flat bottom?
SYLVIA: Yes.
HELEN: But then water might get over it more easily.
MOLLY: But you could have a flat bottom, stick card or newspaper
   underneath, and then, just stick it on from underneath, then,
   make the curves, curve up, the sides sort of come upwards.   35
   (*demonstrates the shape with her hands*)

We notice how Helen and Molly gradually, sensitively, find out from
Sylvia and Manzeer the source of their difficulty. Their first strategy,
after discovering that the boat 'kept on sinking', is to find out
whether binding it together with masking tape would have helped to
strengthen it to prevent it 'leaking' and 'breaking'. Manzeer
introduces the materials ('We put card on it'); the following
interchange elaborates on the disaster which occurred despite all the
masking tape. Then Molly comes back to materials (line 21), which gives
Sylvia a chance to talk about the relative strength of card and newspaper.
Molly then returns to ask about the design itself. So, with Molly and
Helen's support, Sylvia and Manzeer are required to reflect on:

a) the materials used to bind the first model;
b) the relative strength of the two materials;
c) the design of the hull itself.

The process which is helping Sylvia and Manzeer to reflect on what
went wrong with their boat is also laying the ground for Helen and
Molly when they embark on their own boat design. It is this
reciprocity which infuses this interchange and proves to be so helpful
to both pairs. The pupils who ask the questions are clearly doing some
thinking themselves. Although Molly seems to act a little bit like a

mini-teacher, we would argue that the power relationship is crucially different. Genuine questions are asked, and genuine interchange occurs; Sylvia and Manzeer don't feel quizzed; Molly and Helen are genuinely trying to be helpful, and are being challenged themselves. This is another example of 'thoughtfulness' being valued over and above succeeding, failing, or just carrying out a task.

If, as we and others in this volume wish to argue, this kind of occasion is crucial for pupils in the challenge it presents to their thinking – the need to refashion ideas as a response to genuine questions – then teachers need to consider how best this can be built into classroom work. This requires a sensitivity to questions about the stage in a learning process when interactive talk will develop thinking, rather than simply accompany action. The talk in most of these examples is, to some extent, separated from the activity; in 'Whim Jim', for instance, it acts as a rehearsal for an oral presentation; in 'Paper Boats' it both looks back to work already carried out, but also contains within it the seeds of future thinking. While we have deliberately focused on the interactions between pupils, it is essential to state that these episodes 'worked' because the teachers involved had not only established a 'climate for talk' but had carefully planned these activities to use talk to support thinking.

Conclusion

In commenting on these extracts, we have tried to develop our own understanding about the nature of pupil-pupil talk and its connections with learning. Douglas Barnes says that speech is 'flexible', and we can sum up this characteristic, as it affects learning, as follows.

Talk is shared, social, and interactive (usually), in which the following things can happen:

- A readiness to learn can be created because:

  - pupils can, through talk, recall and review what they already know and define what more they want to know about a topic;

  - pupils have already contributed their own ideas and therefore have a greater stake in the learning;

  - the input from teacher, text or other resources can be matched more accurately to the pupils' current understandings;

- pupils who are struggling with literacy can use talk to work on their understanding and to gain access to new areas of knowledge.

- Pupils can work on ideas together because:
  - talk 'loosens the cement' of previously established ways of thinking;
  - ideas can be tried out to see how they 'sound', how far they'll stretch ('How do I know what I mean until I hear what I say?');
  - 'provisional' meanings are likely to be made as a group feels its way towards some shared understanding;
  - tentativeness can be valued and supported, and judgement can be deferred;
  - because pupils are more likely to say 'I don't understand.'

- Opportunity can be created for pupils:
  - to make sense of new information;
  - to renegotiate ways of handling a topic, allowing their own voices and 'other voices' (text, teacher, parent, friend, etc.) to be tried on for size;
  - to share their own set of cultural references, into which ideas can be accommodated;
  - to learn in the variety of English or the community language which best suits their needs and purposes.

- Pupils working together provide social support for the learning process because:
  - they can provide each other with an authentic audience;
  - there is the possibility of an immediate and engaged response;
  - there can be a sympathetic, but not sentimental valuing of each other's contributions;
  - there can be a tolerance of the need to take time out (involving social talk, or silence) which can actually enhance their ability to return to the task after some 'thinking time'.

- Tentatively expressed thoughts can become clearer in well-structured group activities because:
  - pupils are more likely to interrogate peers than their teacher;

- one person's ideas can be interpreted and expanded by others;

- group talk can place pupils where they represent and make explicit their thinking to others;

- encouraging pupils to cross question each other about their work may result in a clearer definition of meanings;

- pupils will take longer 'turns' in expert role, providing opportunities to clarify and consolidate their own understandings.

Learning and knowing are often about knowing enough for a particular purpose at a given time. Pupils' purposes may differ from adults'; we need to have faith in pupils' ability to carry out the process in their own terms, rather than to expect their talk to replicate directly the teacher's understandings. Talk isn't simply a more sociable way for pupils to arrive at a point previously decided by the teacher.

Learning through talk is often a long process, the 'completion' of which may resist attempts to marshal it into a timetabled space. Because it is social and collaborative it will often appear 'untidy'. But those who accept the case that we argue in this article will enable it to happen. We believe that the benefits of a clearer curriculum content, which the National Curriculum has achieved, will be seriously diminished for all pupils if they are not given worthwhile opportunities to work together in small groups, making meaning through talk, supported and challenged by their peers.

Acknowledgements

We would like to thank Pauline Loader, Glebe Infants School, Rayleigh, Essex; Jim McManners, Durham Oracy Project and pupils from Cassop Primary School, Cassop, St Wilfred's Primary School, Bishop Auckland and St Joseph's Primary School, Bishop Auckland; Tony Cole, Wootton Bassett School, Wiltshire; Jo Dalton-Leggett, Castledown School, Ludgershall, Wiltshire; Sally Livesey, May Park Primary School, Bristol, Avon; and the many colleagues who, in discussion of the ideas in this article, have helped us clarify and consolidate our thinking.

References

ARMITAGE, R. AND D. (1986) *The Lighthouse Keeper's Catastrophe*. London: Oliver and Boyd.

BARNES, D. AND TODD, F. (1976) *Communicating and Learning in Small Groups*. London: Routledge and Kegan Paul.

BENNETT, N., DESFORGES, C., COCKBURN, A. AND WILKINSON, B. (1984) *The Quality of Pupil Learning Experiences*. London: Lawrence Erlbaum.

BENNETT, N. AND DUNNE, E. (1990) 'Implementing Co-operative Groupwork in Classrooms' in Lee, V. (ed.) (1990) *Children's Learning in School*. Sevenoaks: Hodder and Stoughton.

DES (1975). *A Language for Life (the Bullock Report)*. London: HMSO.

EDWARDS, D. AND MERCER, N. (1987) *Common Knowledge: The Development of Understanding in the Classroom*. London: University Paperbacks, Methuen.

MAYBIN, J. (1990) *Children's Informal Talk and the Construction of Meaning*. CLAC Occasional Papers in Communication, Number 25, November 1990, Open University School of Education.

WOOD, D. (1988) *How Children Think and Learn*. Oxford: Basil Blackwell.

Why? The Neglected Question in Planning for Small Group Discussion

TERRY PHILLIPS

'Why are we doing this?'

An important curriculum planning challenge in the context of the National Curriculum is how to give pupils ownership of the learning agenda. The statutory curriculum is not negotiable; it comes from 'out there' and has to be followed. Good teachers are able to design approaches that match known pupil interests to prescribed curriculum content, but pupils themselves have little direct say in deciding what they will learn. The danger is that they will come to see themselves as passive receivers of education rather than as active partners in it. Anything that can be done to encourage pupils to take an initiating role will be a valuable protection against this potentially destructive trend. This is a good enough reason for encouraging pupils to develop the habit of 'interrogating the task', that is, asking 'Why are we doing this?' and, on the strength of the answer(s), deciding the most appropriate way of doing it. For the interrogation of tasks can set up an habitual 'argumentativeness' which is the very antithesis of passivity. In this article, I am going to look specifically at the application of this principle to small group discussion.

When pupils are asked to use discussion as part of a learning activity, they bring to the task their previous experiences of classroom discussion and their intuitive familiarity with the 'ground rules' for doing certain classroom tasks. For instance, pupils who have learned from experience that what counts in doing a practical task is the successful achievement of an outcome in the shortest possible time will focus primarily on the operational as they endeavour to avoid disagreement and finish quickly. On the other hand, pupils whose experience suggests that there is merit in planning the activity together and testing ideas out on each other before beginning the activity proper tend to be more speculative and to adopt a problem-solving focus. And those pupils who regularly receive mixed messages from their experience – and there are quite a number – vacillate between approaches, in a pragmatic attempt to achieve several aims simultaneously. When any of these groups faces a task which demands something 'surprising', however, they will be rendered incompetent if their experiential learning is unreflective. To cope with the unexpected, it is necessary to be able to examine experience and develop out of it principles which can be applied in novel situations.

In setting up an activity involving discussion, a teacher may have several, overlapping purposes. One of these is, of course, the ostensible purpose in the job or task – what the pupils have been actually asked to do. This is likely to be from a scheme of work based on the requirements of the National Curriculum in the curriculum area(s) involved. In addition, there are the particular oracy purposes specified in the Speaking and Listening attainment target and in the curricula for other subjects. Because the National Curriculum looks on talk as both a set of skills to be acquired and developed and also a medium through which a pupil's stock of information and concepts will be gained, group discussions are bound to have one or other of these focuses. The teacher may also have specific purposes relating to assessment, and classroom social and management purposes. Finally, there is the larger educational purpose of increasing individual and/or corporate understanding.

There is clearly a responsibility for teachers to make their purposes as explicit as possible, but the transfer of ownership requires that pupils sort out in their own minds what the true purpose of a discussion is, and learn how to achieve it, even when it is complex and multi-faceted. This means that pupils must be encouraged to ask the theoretical question, 'Why are we doing this?' in order to begin to formulate principles for deciding the answer to the practical question, 'What is the most appropriate way of doing it?'

It would be wrong to assume, however, that asking 'Why are we doing this?' will render discussion unproblematic. Discussions, like tasks, are inherently multi-functional. People are always doing more than one thing when they are talking together. The development of a set of strategies for making principled decisions about the most appropriate way of doing a task does not guarantee that the task becomes easier. Appropriateness is a socially constructed quality and changes as knowledge becomes more sophisticated, so it is quite possible that pupils, as they become more adept at recognising the variety and range of possible reasons for doing a specific task, may decide that the most appropriate response to it is a highly complex one. What matters is that they become involved in the decision-making process. Systematic interrogation of the task – asking 'Why are we doing this?' – will lead to the collaborative establishment of principles for making informed choices, and to an expectation that educational activities are principled rather than arbitrary. Because this can lead in turn to the establishment of genuine learner-independence it is clearly a worthwhile educational activity in its own right.

'But why precisely are we doing this?'

Having considered the effect of asking 'Why ...?' on pupil perceptions of their role in the learning process, let us look at the part it can play in helping their understanding of a task. Although it is undoubtedly helpful to ask 'Why are we doing this?', it is certainly not sufficient to ask it only once. If the intention behind interrogating classroom tasks is to help children decide how best to 'do' them, and in particular how to 'do' the related discussion, then the response to the single question is unlikely to provide precise enough information. As tasks always have a range of purposes, pupils have to identify the purposes which have priority on a given occasion. Only *intensive interrogation* of the task – i.e. asking frequently and systematically, 'But why precisely are we doing this?' – will enable step-by-step movement from an impressionistic understanding of what they have to do to greater clarity.

Intensive interrogation may sound to some like an activity which could be seen as challenging and potentially offensive in a classroom context. At its simplest, however, it may involve nothing more contentious than close inspection of the metalanguage of talk-mediated tasks. Helping pupils differentiate the often subtle nuances in meaning carried by words like 'explain', 'discuss', 'persuade', and 'argue', can increase their learning autonomy. By asking 'What does this word mean exactly?' they are in fact asking 'But why precisely are we doing this?' They will discover, for instance, that task words like 'discuss' are used in such a general way that it is impossible to know precisely what is intended by them. They will find that there are words about talk – such as 'argument' – that have several meanings, and that these are sometimes opposites. They will also find that words such as 'persuade' are not meant to be taken literally but applied in a special classroom sense. (See below for more detail about these examples.) As students reiterate their 'Why?' question, they and their teachers will become engaged in language study itself, not as an empty exercise but for a real purpose with an actual outcome.

Becoming 'argumentative' as a way of doing discussion

We can illustrate some of the claims made so far in this article by looking at several examples of classroom discussion. Since it has been suggested already that the development of an 'argumentative' frame of mind through the intensive interrogation of the task is a worthwhile educational activity in itself, and that much of the metalanguage associated with 'argument' lacks clarity, it seems appropriate to choose examples of 'argumentative' group discussion for this purpose. Before moving to the examples, however, a word about 'argumentative' talk.

For my purposes, 'argumentative' discussion is group talk in which speakers set out to challenge their own or someone else's ideas, values, understanding, attitudes or opinions. 'Persuasion', 'discussion', 'debate' and 'argument' are all words associated with being 'argumentative', and are often regarded as synonymous even though practice shows that they are in fact often applied differently. Some people consider 'good' argumentative talk to be debate that persuades by strength of rational argument expressed in terms of cause and effect, in which the pros and cons of a case are presented succinctly without deviation from the main topic, and the proposals are set out in the language of logic (if . . . then; it will . . . because; consequently . . .; etc). The emphasis for them is on persuasion. However, although argument may result in some people changing their views by the end of the discussion, such a change is not essential for successful 'argumentative' discussion. Exploratory discussion expressed in a less explicitly logical language, and discourse to play with ideas rather than persuade, are also forms of argument.

Debate and persuasion are predicated on the notion of one point of view winning out over another. They focus on decisions and outcomes; high-profile activities in business and management. Discussion and discourse, on the other hand, are more about exploring possibilities and alternatives than reaching decisions. They focus on the process itself, delaying the decision-taking and emphasising the decision-making activity. A legitimate outcome of discourse and discussion would be an agreement to look further at some unresolved issues, and an acknowledgement that others could not – maybe even need not – be resolved. This sort of outcome, in contrast to the outcome of debate and persuasion, can be inconvenient from a classroom management perspective because it asks that decisions be delayed, that closure be avoided for as long as possible. In schooling terms, it is educationally desirable but administratively difficult to have a curriculum founded on the notion that discussion is as much about the exploration of opinions, ideas, concepts, values (even, perhaps, facts) for the sake of learning that a range of alternatives exist, as it is about deciding which idea, etc. should take precedence. In political terms it might be embarrassing to have a generation who habitually looked for ways to keep open for exploration alternative views of the world.

Why some 'problem-solving' tasks are a problem

We can now examine an actual pupil discussion and the participants' comments about it. We will note first the way the pupils' previous experience seems to affect their discussion. Then we will speculate about how intensive interrogation of the task may have helped them handle these tasks differently. Finally, we will consider some of the implications.

The first extract is taken from a lesson in which twelve year olds were asked to choose a set of objects for storing in a 'hypothetical' time capsule.

> PUPIL A: We've got to start selecting which ones we want now, so let's have yours.
> PUPIL B: A Mars bar definitely . . . clothes . . . this is the sixth one now that we're going to have.
> PUPIL A : Right, six . . . now we'll all keep the same so we send them clothes . . . number one.
> PUPIL B: I'm only going to send them some chocolate, cos they know . . .
> PUPIL A: What?
> PUPIL B: They might not have things like that.
> PUPIL A: Yeah, all right, then . . . number two.

PUPIL B: Number two . . . chocolate.
PUPIL A: Right, just a minute.
PUPIL B: Photos is a good idea.
PUPIL A: Yeah, cos then they know what you look like.
PUPIL B: Yeah.
PUPIL A: Right, let's have a look at yours.

Both the extract and the full discussion suggest that the pupils perceive the task as a practical and highly concrete one. For them, it was about drawing up a written list. They reached decisions over what should be included in the list, largely on the basis of 'weight-of-support' – how many agreed and how forcefully – rather than on the quality of reasoning.

The pupils' reason for doing the task was, in their own words, 'because we were asked to discuss it'. It had no obvious purpose beyond complying with that instruction to 'discuss' and, consequently, nothing much was at stake. They were prepared to leave explanations of their choices implicit simply because they saw the activity as one requiring nothing more than completion of an apparently arbitrary list. Indeed, why justify the choice of items to put in a time capsule, when more rapid completion of the list can be achieved by a kind of bartering – one of mine for one of yours? And why bother to ask for a 'better' reason in response to a 'poor' one when in the end the case being put is of no real significance to you?

It is significant that the teacher who set the task intended the group of pupils to persuade each other 'properly' of the value of the particular items they suggested for inclusion. She hoped individuals would give well-reasoned justifications for their proposals, and wanted the group to explore the validity of those justifications. She was disappointed in the quality of the discussion.

We can speculate that if the pupils had felt able to interrogate the task, and had begun with the highly specific question, 'What exactly do you mean by "discuss"?', they would have found that they were supposed to 'persuade' each other. If they had gone on to ask, 'What exactly do you mean by "persuade"?', they may have discovered that persuasion in this case was to be done through presentation and exploration of reasoned proposals. Further interrogation would almost certainly have raised the question, 'But why do we need to convince each other about something that has no consequence?', and an honest answer might well have resulted in the task being seen for what it was, an empty exercise.

The second extract is from a discussion between two six year olds who are discussing the adventure game, Concept Kate, while playing it on the computer.

PUPIL A: You've gone the wrong way . . . go there.

PUPIL B: Oh, all right. (*presses key*)

PUPIL A: Now it's press . . . now press 'walk away' . . . no, not that one . . . look what this says.

PUPIL B: 'Towards', 'walk away', 'towards' . . . that's 'walk away', and that's 'towards'.

PUPIL A: I'll do this bit.

PUPIL B: I know . . . I love this bit.

PUPIL A: I'm going up that path.

PUPIL B: (*presses key*) I'm going up the short one, okay?

PUPIL A: Yeah.

PUPIL B: I'll go up the first one and you go up the second.

PUPIL A: Okay.

As the extract shows, the children found ways of quickly getting through the obstacles within the game path with minimal 'discussion'. They used their speech to direct each other, to respond to what happened on the screen when the instructions were carried out and to share their excitement when a 'way through' was discovered. They rarely offered justification for their instructions, although one of them would occasionally mention their short-term (i.e. immediate) plan of action. In the later stages of the game playing, the children began to intersperse the predominantly procedural talk with sporadic comments about the adventure story narrative and its characters' fortunes in a way characteristic of spontaneous response to crafted texts such as story and film.

In this instance, it is not the teacher's instruction but the task set by the computer which could have been interrogated. This particular adventure game task is intended to encourage the children to solve problems and learn to make choices. Instead, they frame their conversation as a series of closure-marked exchanges, plan short-term, and engage superficially with the narrative component of the adventure.

Interrogation of this task would have led to the realisation that the intended purpose is in conflict with the design. The emphasis in the game on 'jumping hurdles', and on solving the problem rather than analysing the problem, leads inexorably to short exchanges and closure rather than to exploration. There is, indeed, a positive disincentive to getting involved in reasoned discussion of alternative solutions, and a pressure to push a key on the computer keyboard to test out a 'hypothesis in action'. If children and teacher together had interrogated the task, they may have decided that, because the precise reason for doing it was to promote understanding of problem-solving, whenever a new problem presented itself it should be talked through away from the keyboard. On the other hand, they might have agreed that it was not an appropriate programme for achieving the intended spoken language aim.

The educational implications

Both discussion and thinking would benefit from the creation of a classroom climate in which 'argumentativeness' and criticality were regular events. On the one hand, it would help to give pupils both 'ownership' and understanding of tasks; on the other, it would make the curriculum itself an object of reflection at the centre of the learning process. Intensive interrogation of tasks provides a simple strategy for encouraging the development of principles and procedures for critical discussion.

Acknowledgements

The examples are taken from two projects that the author co-directed and whose participating teachers and students he wishes to acknowledge with thanks. They are: The Becoming Argumentative Project, funded by University of East Anglia and Norfolk LEA, and The Spoken Language and New Technology Project, funded by the Economic and Social Research Council.

Thanks in particular to North Walsham High School and Bowthorpe Clover Hill First School for permission to use transcripts.

3.4

Structuring the Learning Experience

PETER FORRESTAL

In his article, 'The Role of Talk in Learning', Douglas Barnes explains that pupils need to build on what they already know in order to assimilate or accommodate new information. They need to interact actively with new ideas to reorganise their existing pictures of the world. Anyone who accepts this view of learning is likely to consider that what currently takes place in many classrooms is inadequate for this purpose. Pupils need to be more active and engaged – to have more opportunities to think, to talk and to write in ways that develop new understanding.

The role which most teachers adopt in the classroom is also likely to be challenged. If they are to allow their pupils to interact actively with new information, teachers need to talk less. Rather than being responsible for telling pupils what they need to know, teachers need to adopt the role of organising and monitoring the learning experience of their pupils. Explicit teaching will still be a necessary part of classroom activity, but it will be only one of a range of responsibilities that teachers undertake.

With Jo-Anne Reid and Jonathon Cook, I published a book in 1989, in which we suggested a model of learning which helps teachers plan lessons or units of work. This model, through which pupils move from information towards understanding, sees the learning process as involving several stages. The present article explores some of the issues raised by myself and my colleagues in attempting to find ways of translating these ideals into classroom practice and, in particular, to developing an approach to learning in small groups.

The Geraldton Talk Project

While head of a high school English Department in the country town of Geraldton, Western Australia during 1978, I directed a project which looked at the role of talk in learning. This was funded by the Federal Government and involved twelve teachers from six schools covering Years 1 to 12, including secondary teachers of English, Social Studies and Science. With the grant money, we were able to tape pupil talk and have it transcribed.

Having read and discussed the works of Douglas Barnes (1976), James Britton (1970) and Nancy Martin (Martin *et al.*, 1976), we were committed to allowing pupils more space in which to talk in the classroom. We met fortnightly throughout a year and talked about what was happening in our classrooms. We shared the transcripts of our pupils talking and rejoiced when the transcribed talk showed signs of their developing understanding. Our major focus involved asking how we could ensure that pupil talk would be purposeful at all times: and we gradually became more interested in planning, as we saw this as vital to keeping pupils on task.

Planning a talking classroom

Our starting point was the work of Douglas Barnes (1976) who suggested the following learning sequence to make small groups operate more effectively and to keep pupils on task.

Focusing Stage
Topic presented in full class. Teacher focuses upon the topic, encourages pupils to verbalise necessary preliminary knowledge, and, if appropriate, makes a demonstration to form the basis for group work.

Exploratory Stage
Pupils carry out necessary manipulations of materials and talk about issues which their attention has been directed towards.

Reorganising Stage
Teacher refocuses attention and tells groups how they will be reporting back, and how long they have to prepare for it.

Public Stage
Groups present their findings to one another, and this leads to further discussion.

Barnes suggested that for effective learning in small groups, it was essential that:

- pupils have access to the same information or materials;

- the teacher had to focus pupils' attention on the task;

- pupils needed the opportunity to make public their findings to an interested yet critical audience.

Our initial adaptation of Barnes's ideas involved a four stage model:

Input
Exploration
Preparation for Presentation
Presentation

This became a five stage model of learning which is explained in detail in *Small Group Learning in the Classroom* (1989):

Engagement
Exploration
Transformation
Presentation
Reflection

The shifts in our thinking which led to these changes mirror our developing understanding about the theory and practice of using small groups as a central classroom strategy.

Setting the scene

The term 'Input', used to describe the first stage of the learning process, turned out to be quite problematic. In Geraldton, we used the term to emphasise the need for pupils to have 'common ground', in particular, access to the same information.

Later, in writing *Small Group Work in the Classroom* (1982), Jo-Anne Reid, Jonathon Cook and I had other agendas to address. We wanted to confront the criticism of small group work – that it encouraged pupils to 'share ignorance'. This, we believed, was a product of the kind of teaching which invited pupils to move into groups to discuss their opinions of capital punishment. We wanted to stress to English teachers the need to provide pupils with information and to reassure the teachers of subjects like science, mathematics and social studies that the approach we were using was very much concerned with pupils processing information. However, for many teachers, the term seemed to imply that this is a rather passive stage for the learners – a time when they are confronted with information, or information is made available to them. This was not our intention, nor our practice. The term itself was a problem.

The suggestion for a new name for this first stage of the learning process (Engagement) came in an article by Bill Green and Jo-Anne Reid (1989). They made it clear that this stage should involve more than the teacher merely providing pupils with new content material. For the pupils to become engaged in an activity, they need to understand why they are examining a particular topic, text, information or material. They also need to understand how a particular lesson, or unit of work, fits in with what they have done before and what they will study in the future. Learners need not only a sense of direction but also a sense that they are learning – that is, that there has been a change, a growth in their understanding of the world and their place in it. This is something that teachers have to prepare and plan for explicitly and deliberately. It should never be a case of teacher and pupils simply growing old together.

Pupils generally become engaged, or their intention to learn is aroused, when they become curious or puzzled about what they are to learn. They need to recognise the problematic and want to solve their puzzlement. What they learn must, therefore, matter to them as well as to their teacher. This may involve starting from a sharing of the pupils' own knowledge and experience of a topic.

By the end of the Engagement stage, pupils need to have charted the territory they are to explore and to have a clear sense of the required outcomes. Further, they should be conscious of ways in which their learning path is going to achieve these outcomes. Clearly, the teacher has responsibility for providing this direction, but the more the pupils contribute to the process the better.

This clearer spelling out of the theory and re-naming of the first stage has not solved all problems. Some of our colleagues remain concerned about the use of the term 'Engagement', believing that pupils only become engaged in learning as they become more involved.

Exploratory talk

We had little trouble in encouraging exploratory talk and making it a normal part of classroom practice. Our pupils realised that we were serious about giving them opportunities to talk to clarify their thinking, and they used those opportunities purposefully. There may well have been a halo effect from our involvement in the project. The omnipresence of tape recorders, the occasional transcripts and our obvious interest in pupil talk could well have contributed to this.

We were convinced of the importance of exploratory talk by the difference it made to the engagement of our pupils in their learning. Some incidents stood out. I observed a Year 8 science lesson in which the teacher explained how levers worked and then asked his students to conduct an experiment. The group that I focused on had been totally uninterested during the teacher's explanation and continued to be uninvolved while they were conducting the experiment. During the second part of the 80-minute lesson, I asked the class to reflect on what they knew about levers. They were told they could reread their text books and talk about levers within their groups. The change in attitude of the group I was observing (and the class generally) was significant and immediate. For the first time in the lesson, they became involved.

When I interviewed Janine, one of the group, later, she said:

> Well, I sort of . . . when we are in class we are told and it doesn't really . . . sort of . . . doesn't enter my brain . . . but when I . . . sort of . . . talk myself and . . . sort of . . . read and discuss it with other kids in the class . . . I sort of . . . remember a lot about it.

In making the application for the grant, I gave the following as one of the reasons for wanting to transcribe pupil talk:

> As the teacher cannot always be present in small group talk and as it is necessary for pupils to be engaged in talk situations among their learning peers as well as with teachers, having transcripts of tapes available will enable the teacher to see what stage of understanding the pupil has reached and to reveal any inadequacies in understanding or gaps in knowledge which are often not revealed in writing or in talk in the presence of the teacher.

Although the examination of transcripts of pupil talk became the most important source of discussion for the project, it proved to be totally unrealistic to expect that they could be used to monitor pupil learning. Even if the transcripts could have been prepared quickly enough, the teachers could not have found the time to examine them and check on how their pupils were processing new information. Consequently, we had to find other strategies for monitoring what was happening in each group.

We learned to watch pupils' faces, to note their engagement in the task, to listen to what was being said without appearing to be listening, to move around the classroom observing the developing understanding of several groups rather than being caught up in one group's discussion. We learned to listen to what our pupils said – and to question whether we had really listened to pupil talk before.

In all likelihood what was happening was that there had been significant changes in the kind of exchanges that were occurring in the classroom. Previously, most pupil talk had been in response to questions from us. And these were scarcely genuine questions: we already knew the answers and were only asking them to see if the pupils could give us the answers we expected.

Our view of the learning process shifted and we became increasingly interested in structuring learning experiences so that pupils could develop their own understandings. Exploratory talk, and occasionally exploratory writing, allowed pupils to become involved in the learning process by relating new information to their past experiences and by giving them opportunities to clarify their initial thoughts. Being able to monitor what they were saying sometimes gave us windows into their thinking.

One science teacher who was revising the topic of 'Respiration' with a Year 9 class was stunned to see one pupil's exploratory writing about the difference between respiration and breathing:

> The difference between breathing is where you breathe by yourself.
> Respiration is where you need somebody to help you breathe.
>
> Breathing happens when you inhale.
> Respiration happens when somebody is unable to breath by the self.

The non-threatening instruction, 'Make some notes for yourself', had given the pupil the freedom to write for herself and, consequently, the teacher was able to understand just what misunderstanding had occurred in her mind.

We found that pupils had no trouble staying on task when given time for exploration. They had a clear task – to think aloud, to talk in order to clarify their initial thoughts – a limited time and (usually) written material on which to focus. The short structured time for exploration became a normal part of classroom activity. Because the teachers believed that pupil talk was important, pupils came to see it as significant in the learning process. We were even able to identify groups of pupils who could be relied upon to produce interesting examples of exploratory talk whenever we needed it. This was to prove useful when we wanted to document our work on video and film.

The main activity

During the time of the Geraldton Project, we referred to the third stage of the learning process as 'Preparation for Presentation'. As this suggests, our focus of attention was on the fourth stage: Presentation, enabling pupils to present their findings to others. We were concerned primarily with finding ways of putting a press on their language, with making sure that they would remain on task whenever they were given an opportunity to talk. This worked admirably, as the Presentation stage focused pupils' attention and their talk became increasingly purposeful.

As we became more interested in the issue of planning, we came to see that one of the important keys to successful learning was the activity in which pupils were asked to engage. Instead of this stage merely being Preparation for Presentation, we saw it as increasingly important. The decision about what the activity would be became a vital matter for the teacher's professional judgement.

At first, we referred to this stage as Reshaping, and our emphasis was clearly on how information would be reshaped during this stage:

> The learner is required to work with new information in some way . . .
> to enable him or her to move closer to understanding.

Later, however, we placed more emphasis on the activity itself, and the wider term Transformation was used. The focus was on how the activity might help pupils to achieve their goals and those of their teacher.

> The choice of activities will be determined by the aims of the teacher's programme and will be crucial to the results and quality of pupil learning. Any text or piece of information is susceptible of a wide range of possible transformations, all of which could involve learners in potentially profitable activity, but only some of which will lead pupils

towards an understanding of the material most appropriate to a particular teaching context.

The Transformation stage came increasingly to be seen as the starting point for planning. Most teachers begin to plan by asking what their aims are. We found that addressing the following questions provided a useful framework to begin planning for a lesson or, as we came to prefer, a series of lessons:

- What are my aims?

- What activity (or activities) will best enable pupils to achieve these aims? (This would become the activity at the Transformation Stage.)

- What information will the pupils need to fulfil these aims and carry out the activity? (This would determine what was used at the Engagement stage.)

Once teachers are clear on the answers to these questions, they are in a position to plan.

Presentation

The Presentation stage has not seemed problematic to us and our thinking about it has not altered greatly with experience. The rationale remains:

> Having to present the results of the activity to a critical and interested audience in Sharing Groups should give pupils a sense of urgency and purpose. Explaining their developing understanding to others plays an important part in the process of assimilating new information.

Our greatest efforts have revolved around practical issues, such as exploiting the possibilities for variety which we believed the model of learning offered and deciding what terminology would be most helpful to teachers interested in using small group work.

Influenced by our Canadian colleagues, especially Mark Brubacher and Judy Clarke (Clarke *et al.*, 1990), we differentiated between Home Groups (their Base Groups), in which the pupil generally worked, and Sharing Groups, which were specifically constituted for the Presentation stage. We found that the work of Brubacher and Clarke made explicit many of the functions for which groups operate at different times. They talk about Informal Groups, which provide an immediate forum for discussion at different stages in the learning process, a role which, for us, was taken by Home Groups. For them, representative groups (consisting of one person from each group in the class) provide a way for groups to report on their progress to the whole class. Clarke and Brubacher differentiate between Combined and Reconstituted Groups whereas, for us, these are just different types of Shared Groups. We tended to favour Reconstituted Groups because Combined Groups (two groups combining) were generally too large.

Similarly, they have used the terms (Jigsaw and Snowballing) from the American Co-operative Learning Movement, and although our strategies (developed separately) were identical, we chose not to use these labels. At the Transformation Stage, all Home Groups could work either: on the *same* information and take their findings to Sharing Groups (Snowballing); or on *different* material and pool their findings in Sharing Groups (Jigsaw). The decision about which approach to use depended on what was most appropriate for achieving the aims of this activity.

With further experience, we have shifted ground on the value of whole class discussion, and see it as a useful strategy following the Presentation stage – so that the teacher can draw threads together, clarify any points and allow pupils to share any major discoveries with the whole class. As well as this, we are convinced of the value of giving the Shared Group a specific task, once they have exchanged their findings. The group is likely to work more effectively together if they have to do more than just share.

Reflection

A major development in our thinking about learning in small groups has been the addition of a Reflection Stage to our model. This was not something that occurred to us while we were involved as teachers in the Geraldton Project but came later as we worked with teachers who were interested in using small groups in their classroom. Jon Cook, consultant to the project and a key figure in the follow-up teacher development work, insisted that:

> Reflection has a significant part to play in the learning process, if teachers are concerned with pupils accommodating new information into what they already know. Reflecting on what they have learned and the way in which they have handled the learning process will help pupils deepen their understanding of the product and the process of learning.

Addressing the problematic

Because we are dealing with the complex business of individuals' learning, a model such as this is not without its problems. It is one way to describe the learning process. As I have explained, the terms we have used to describe the stages of the process may cause problems for some people because of the connotation of those words. What we have tried to do is to suggest that learning involves several steps and that one way of looking at it involves five stages. What those stages are called is largely a political matter, depending on what those who label (or those who adapt) the model want to stress or promote. I am tempted now to think of talking about:

Setting the Scene
Exploration
The Main Activity
Presentation
Reflection

Other problems include the question of overlap and the apparently sequential nature of the model of learning. Of course, there may well be overlap between the stages – for example, exploratory talk or reflection occurring at any stage of the learning process. The model was intended to provide a structure to help teachers to plan rather than as a strict formula which needs to be rigidly followed.

As a general rule, we believe that there are some things which should be sequential. But we do not see this as a linear model. For example, we believe that:

- Whenever pupils are confronted with or exposed to new information, they should be given an opportunity for exploratory talk or writing. Exploration should therefore follow Engagement.

- It may be necessary for input to occur at different stages in the learning process – not just at the beginning. There is no reason why there should not be more than one Engagement stage.

- Logically, Presentation should follow Transformation. However, there is no reason why there could not be more than one activity before the groups are re-formed for Presentation.

- Reflection might come at any time during the learning process. It may well become the starting point for a new cycle of learning.

A flexible approach

What I have described here is a flexible approach to planning to enable effective learning to take place. Exactly what is planned for a particular class at a particular time will depend on the kind of factors with which teachers are used to dealing: the needs of the individual class, the available resources, local conditions, the specific aims of the teacher and the information with which the pupils are engaged. It is important that pupils are given some choice over what, when and how they learn.

There will be occasions when the most careful planning needs to be changed in the hurly-burly of classroom life: the class may need to listen to some additional input from the teacher, or groups might be called on to make an interim report to the class. The more thorough a teacher's planning, the less likely it is that this will occur. The better the teacher's understanding of the theory that lies behind the planning, the more effective pupil learning is likely to be.

References

BARNES, D. (1976) *From Communication to Curriculum.* Harmondsworth: Penguin.

BRITTON, J. (1970) *Language and Learning.* Harmondsworth: Penguin.

BRUBACHER, M., PAYNE, R. AND RICKETT, K. (1990) *Perspective on Small Group Learning.* Oakville, Ontario: Rubicon.

CLARKE, J., WIDEMAN, R. AND EADIE, S. (1990) *Together We Learn.* Scarborough, Ontario: Prentice-Hall.

GREEN, W. AND REID, J. (1989) 'A curriculum framework: teaching for powerful learning', *Australian Journal of Reading,* Melbourne, Vol. 12, No. 3.

MARTIN, N. et al. (1976) *Working and Learning Across the Curriculum 11–16.* London: Ward Lock.

REID, J., FORRESTAL, P. AND COOK, J. (1989) *Small Group Learning in the Classroom.* Perth: Chalkface Press. Also (1991) London: the English and Media Centre.

REID, J., FORRESTAL, P. AND COOK, J.(1982) *Small Group Work in the Classroom.* Perth: Education Department of Western Australia.

Learning Through Talk
– Teachers and Children

4

Introduction

In this section the focus shifts from pupil with pupil to pupil with teacher. But the question remains the same: 'How does this interaction help pupils to learn?' Teachers' own talk was not the initial focus for most local projects, but it was one that grew in importance as teachers reflected on their practice and listened to themselves and their pupils. They quickly recognized the enormous impact of their interventions and utterances on pupils' talk and learning.

Many teachers in the National Oracy Project had to resolve a genuine dilemma. They accepted from research and from the evidence of their own tapes that teachers usually talk too much, don't listen carefully to pupils and are not good at getting pupils to contribute their own thinking. Acceptance of the advantages of group work, demonstrated in the previous section, combined with an awareness of the effect of their own presence, seemed to argue for minimal intervention in groups, for cutting down on whole class teaching, for taking a more facilitating and observational role. But they were employed as teachers, they had knowledge, experience and expertise which their pupils did not have, and, concurrently with the phasing of the Project, they had responsibility to implement the National Curriculum.

One complicating factor in the debates in the Project around this issue was that it made a significant difference to a teacher's view whether he or she had a primary or secondary background. To oversimplify, primary and nursery teachers expressed a concern that the nature and quality of teacher interventions were in part responsible for the fact that 'child-centred' practice, while giving many opportunities for the exploration of ideas in a supportive climate, was not realising the full learning potential of these situations and was not sufficiently differentiated or challenging. Secondary teachers, on the other hand, were more concerned to question the 'transmission' model, which they saw as too didactic and unresponsive to pupil needs. All teachers, however, were quite clear that there was a body of knowledge and understanding that it was their job to help pupils learn: their concerns were with the manner in which this could most effectively be done.

The articles in this section offer some ways of resolving this dilemma and provide some answers to the question: 'How can teachers "teach" in ways that help, rather than hinder, pupils' "learning"?'

One answer lies in the appropriateness and flexibility of the teacher role. Roy Corden's article, 'The Role of the Teacher', presents a range of contrasting examples of helpful teacher intervention. We see skilful teachers responding 'contingently' to children's learning needs in ways which not only improve pupils' knowledge and understanding of the task in hand but also their understanding of, and control over, the learning process itself.

The work of Vygotsky, and Bruner's interpretation and development of his theories, is crucially important in reassessing the role of the teacher. In the next article, '"Scaffolding" Learning in the Classroom', Janet Maybin, Neil Mercer and Barry Stierer examine the concept of 'scaffolding' – the process by which a 'mentor' helps a learner not only to do something but to know how to do it, and thus be able to do it in future. The concept of scaffolding is particularly relevant to this volume and its title, because talk is the means through which the mentor draws attention to the significant features of the activity which the child internalises as thought.

In 'Surprisingly Disciplined Squads', Harold Gardiner looks at the other end of the spectrum – where teachers temporarily abdicate the role of expert and transfer it to the pupil. From his experience, particularly with low-attaining pupils, he makes a strong case for the transforming effect on pupils' spoken language of an interested but less informed adult listener.

It is highly significant that, in the examples of teachers' talk reproduced in the articles above, the discourse patterns are very different from those that research in this area might lead us to expect. The teachers ask few questions; they more frequently offer suggestions, 'think aloud', respond to pupil questions, give information or advice. Pupil contributions are extended, thoughtful, often challenging, and they ask many questions. The next two articles look more closely at what teachers actually say, or don't say, and particularly pick up the issue of teacher questions – what function they serve and whether there are preferable alternatives. David Wood's article, 'Teaching Talk', makes a strong research-based case against teachers' over-use of questions, arguing that they have a detrimental effect on pupils' talk and thus on their thinking. He offers alternative strategies which have been shown to work in classrooms.

Neil Mercer's main recommendation in 'Talk for Teaching-and-Learning' is that teachers should make explicit to children the point and purpose of what they are doing. He is less critical than David Wood of teachers' use of questions to fulfil the function of marking 'some knowledge and experience as significant': 'What is crucial is the quality of teachers' communications with children.'

In 'No, We Ask You Questions', a group of teachers from the Oracy Project respond to issues raised by David Wood and Neil Mercer with short accounts of their own practice. They reflect on complex issues such as: 'In what circumstances is it acceptable to "pretend" not to know in order to get pupils to think?'

And, in the final article in this section, 'Teacher Talk and Pupil Competence', Tony Edwards comments on the previous articles and makes his own contribution to the debate. He suggests that all this 'displays a much higher level of professional skill than the traditionalist notion of teacher expertise'.

The Role of the Teacher

ROY CORDEN

Teachers involved in the National Oracy Project in Staffordshire, with whom I worked as co-ordinator, explored the premise that teachers should 'present to the child a variety of appropriate audiences'. Teachers often do this intuitively; we found it helpful to make these intuitive strategies explicit. As Dave Wood, a Project teacher, reflected:

> Successful teachers have a fairly wide repertoire in the way that they deal with children, and they don't deal with all children or all situations in the same way. I think that the main thing the Project has done for me is it's allowed me to move from an implicit, intuitive understanding of that to an explicit theory where we've attempted to draw out an audience model ... some suggestions of what these roles might be, and I've found that very useful for my own teaching. I think that when you're clearly aware ... when you have the explicit knowledge, you can apply it more sensitively and more knowingly to the individual needs of the pupil.

In a later article in this section, Harold Gardiner shows what can happen when the transmission teaching model is turned on its head and the relationship and linguistic interchange between children and teachers undergo a complete revolutionary turn. Between the traditional teaching role (with the teacher as expert) and Gardiner's model (with the child as expert) there is a whole range of potential teacher-pupil relationships.

These relationships come into being when the teacher responds contingently to children's learning needs (Wells, 1988). As children's needs are diverse and dependent on their stage in the learning process, the appropriate role at any particular time will vary. Acting contingently also means being respectful of the knowledge and experiences which children bring to the learning situation.

This preparedness to act contingently is central in determining how successfully the teacher is able to enter into different kinds of interactional dialogue. The following examples were chosen to highlight some differing types of contingent response, although in practice a teacher will find himself or herself moving in and out of different roles in a fluid and dynamic way. They are offered as snapshots taken from a whole, and much richer, interactional process of teaching and learning.

Responding to children's expertise

In the following extract, eight year olds are beginning a topic on building and buildings. They are examining a variety of building materials and artefacts. At this point, the teacher feels that she possesses more knowledge than the children and she assumes the role of expert. She begins by asking direct questions to which she already knows the answers:

> TEACHER: Do you know what this is?
> JANE: Pebbledash . . . pebbledash.
> TEACHER: No . . . do you know where we use this?
> SARAH: No.
> PETER: On the floor . . . on the floor.
> TEACHER: Yes . . . why?

The children respond by attempting to get as close as possible to what they believe is the correct, or acceptable, answer (to enter into the teacher's frame of reference). When a child's attempt is well wide of the mark (outside the teacher's frame of reference), she responds with a direct evaluation such as 'no'. If the answer is just wide of the mark, she responds with a prompt such as 'not quite':

> TEACHER: Do you know what we call these?
> PETER: Ermm . . . Rafters.
> TEACHER: Not quite . . .

Alternatively, the teacher provides a starter such as 'So what do we call it ... it's a corner ...?' encouraging the child to fill in the missing word.

TEACHER: So this is a corner ... ?
PETER: Of the ... err ...
JANE: Someone's house.
TEACHER: Co ... so what do we call it? ... It's a corner ...?
JANE: Slab.
TEACHER: Slab?
PETER: Corner tile.
TEACHER: Corner tile.

Some of the children clearly possess a great deal of first-hand experience of the subject, which they begin to display:

SARAH: Mrs Naylor ... my uncle was getting this window out, and you could see it like ... there was like two layers of bricks ...
TEACHER: Yes.
SARAH: What's like that (*indicates with hands*) and then a build up to the top and then there was a gap and then there was another two.
TEACHER: And what was that ... what was he doing?

Having recognised that the children are bringing more knowledge to the situation than she had at first realised, the teacher responds by moving out of the expert role. She encourages Sarah to continue with a supportive 'yes' and follows this with a genuine question. Consequently, the discourse pattern changes from being teacher-initiated to a more fluid and interactive discussion in which children are allowed to draw upon their existing experiences as they construct new meanings.

SARAH: He was putting a new window in ... he took the window out completely.
TEACHER: Yes.
SARAH: And all you could see was a gap in the middle ... of the wall.
PETER: Oh, ... it was ... it was ... must've had two windows ... a split thing and two windows.
JANE: Mrs Naylor?
TEACHER: Yes, Jane.
JANE: This is ... me grandad ... he was using some of this and he had ... he took about a quarter of an hour to fit it on cos it was like ... heavy and he had to put all the tiles to get completely on it.
JOHN: When me grandad and dad were building a porch at my house we ... we first ... first we had to mix the cement first ... and then we got the bricks and we put some cement down and put the bricks on top ... then we got the spirit level ... made sure it was level and ... then we put some ... some cement on the top and put

more bricks on and then made sure that was level again . . . but ermm . . . before we moved on to another layer we had a string across . . . to make sure that we were building it level then we had the spirit level to make sure it was level and err . . . we kept on going up and then we came to the window frame and we just put the window frame in and built by the side of it.

TEACHER: Mark was talking to me this morning about this . . . Mark, would you like to tell the children?

MARK: Well, you get three shovels of sand . . . one shovel of cement and mix it with water . . . and . . . and then you mix it . . . around until it comes into cement.

(*John is clearly not happy with this*)

TEACHER: Have you got something you would like to add, John?

JOHN: Well, err . . . when Mark said that you erm . . . what he said . . . I think he said it wrong because . . .

TEACHER: Come and put us straight then.

The teacher reflected on this experience:

It was astonishing really. John is normally such a quiet boy who hardly says a word. I was amazed at just how much some of the children already knew about building and buildings.

Responding as a working group member

In the following extract, a teacher joins a small group of Year 10 (fifteen year old) pupils who are discussing Wilfred Owen's poem, 'Dulce et Decorum Est'. The poem is unfamiliar to the pupils, and the teacher wants them to explore and question its form and possible meanings. He does not want his presence to impose an authorised interpretation upon them:

NINA: 'Towards our distant rest' . . .

LOUISE: Instead of retreating, we thought they were going to die. We thought they are walking into death . . . turning their backs on life, and the only thing they are thinking of is death.

TEACHER: That's incredible . . . I'd never thought of that.

LOUISE: That's what we think.

KATE: They won't have any rest in the war . . . like the only rest they are going to get now is when they die.

LOUISE: And they are walking into it.

NINA: Just trudging along.

TEACHER: I think lots of men had that view . . . just a question of time.

NINA: Like they are walking along all curled up like tramps . . . coughing.

KATE: I love that verse where he can't get his mask on . . . 'stumbling' . . . 'fumbling'.

LOUISE: He's got his mask on and he can see it all.

DEB: Yeah, he can't do anything to help him . . . if he did, he'd die.

NINA: I think it's good in Latin at the end, because if it was in English you'd just read it straightaway.

The teacher quickly establishes the open, exploratory learning climate by showing his appreciation of the pupils' views. His own contribution, prefixed with the marker 'I think', indicates tentativeness and suggests it is an offering that is open to evaluation and critical appraisal. It is the teacher who moves into the pupils' frame of reference, when he contributes to, rather than challenges, the group's initial interpretation. He is also modelling for his pupils an appropriate discourse for this kind of learning activity.

Responding as a neutral chairperson

The children's needs are somewhat different in the following situation, where a group of eleven year olds are discussing the siting of a new road. Each pupil has adopted a role and is arguing the case from a particular viewpoint:

MARCIA: I want route A.

STEVE: Well, I don't, I want route C, cos . . .

MARCIA: I don't care what you want.

STEVE: Route A will destroy my golf course.

TERRY: And what about Elkin Hall? . . . It'll . . .

TRACY: What about the people who live in Lawstown . . . the kids having to cross the road?

MARCIA: What about it . . . it's falling down anyway.

STEVE: You're not coming through my golf course and that's that.

MARCIA: Oh yeah . . . we'll see about that . . . we're having route A.

TEACHER: Perhaps Marcia would give us her reasons for so strongly supporting route A?

TERRY: There aren't any, she's just being awkward.

TEACHER: I think we should listen to what Marcia has to say in favour of route A and then put forward any questions or queries or worries that we have.

MARCIA: Route A is the cheapest . . . it doesn't go through the town so it won't be a danger or a nuisance to the residents of Lawstown . . . and it won't mean having to destroy an area of beauty where there's lots of wildlife.

STEVE: Yeah, route A has some good things about it . . . but the golf
. . . the golf course provides for lots . . . of people . . . their
recreation.
TRACY: But couldn't the golf course be rebuilt . . . I mean it's better
to build a golf course than to have a busy road through the middle
of the town.
TERRY: Yeah, but Elkin Hall . . . I know it's old but that's the point,
isn't it? . . . You could take it down and move it . . . rebuild it, but
it wouldn't be the same . . . it wouldn't be like for real any more,
would it?

Without fuss or undue imposition of authority, the teacher skilfully
intervenes in this discussion to steer the social interaction and to focus
attention on the relevant issues. In adopting the role of neutral
chairperson, she is able to help the children overcome a potential
impasse and to bring them to a point where they are able to continue
with their debate. The teacher has, in this instance, recognised that
the most appropriate response is for her to take a directive role.
Having established a productive work pattern through minimal but
significant intervention, she withdraws from the group.

'Scaffolding' learning

In the following extract, nine year olds have been looking at methods
of seed dispersal. One girl has made a model parachute using paper,
string and a crab apple. However, the model has not been entirely
successful:

TEACHER: How's the experiment going then?
RAINA: Well . . . it's O.K. but, well, . . . I can't work out why this one
isn't working very well.
TEACHER: You're not entirely happy with this one?
RAINA: No, cos . . . it's not right . . . it's falling too much.
TEACHER: Tell me about it.
RAINA: Right, well, . . . it looks OK, doesn't it? . . . I mean, . . . you
know, it looks like it'd work . . . float down and that . . . but when
you throw it up . . . eroooom plop . . .
TEACHER: Shall we try it . . . oh yes, . . . plop . . . I see what you
mean.
RAINA: Something needs changing.
TEACHER: Yes, you're right . . . have you had any thoughts?
RAINA: I thought maybe . . . to change the apple . . . use a bit smaller
one.
TEACHER: That's a good idea, yes . . . to lighten the load a bit.

RAINA: Yeah, lighten the load, that's first.

TEACHER: Yes.

RAINA: Mmm . . . and then if that doesn't do it . . . doesn't work.

TEACHER: We'd need to look elsewhere then, I think . . . mm . . . to make changes somewhere else perhaps.

RAINA: Well, all these . . . I might have too many strings . . . you know . . . if I had a few less strings.

TEACHER: To make it lighter, yes . . .

RAINA: And, yeah, and cos they're pulling it all in too tight . . . too much.

TEACHER: Oh, I see, . . . right . . . it needs to catch enough air, doesn't it, to stop it . . . plopping?

RAINA: Yeah to stop it doing a plop dive . . . that's the main thing that is . . . catching . . . spreading out flat to catch the air . . . I think that's the main problem, the strings are pulling the paper down too much . . . like too tight.

TEACHER: Mmmm . . . I'm wondering what we can do about it.

RAINA: Change the apple for a littler one . . . take some of the strings off, and then shall I test it?

TEACHER: Yes, give me a shout, and I'll come with you.

Rather than simply telling Raina what to do or using direct questions, the teacher helps Raina to clarify her own understanding. The teacher's interjections ('Tell me about it', 'Have you had any thoughts?') encourage Raina to identify the problem and offer solutions herself. But it is far from simply a supporting role. Through selection and rewording of the child's suggestions, the teacher sensitively draws attention to significant features – 'to make it lighter, yes', 'it needs to catch enough air'. The parting utterance from the teacher epitomises the relationship and indicates that she is offering her help as an interested adult, not an evaluator. This extract seems to be a fine example of 'scaffolding learning'. (See the following article for a fuller discussion of the concept of 'scaffolding'.)

Responding as a source of information

Teachers are one source of information on which pupils may draw. As such, they can aid pupils' learning in a way that allows them to retain ownership of the process. In the following extract, Year 10 (fifteen year old) pupils are working on a GCSE module concerned with global economy. They are examining the concept of underdevelopment and are confused by what they see as conflicting information regarding the level of nourishment and the life expectancy in China:

RACHEL: I don't get that . . . I think we should . . .

JENNY: Shout Mrs Wilding.

LINDA: I thought Brazil traded well though . . . like.

RACHEL: Yeah, let's shout Mrs Wilding.

ALL: Mrs Wilding . . . Mrs Wilding . . . she's ignoring us.

(*Mrs Wilding eventually joins the group*)

RACHEL: Well . . . what . . . what we're doing, right . . .

LINDA: We've got the first three . . . we're on number four and we can't decide which . . .

JENNY: Cos it says . . .

RACHEL: Cos we don't understand this . . .right . . . because China . . . it says here that China . . . their life expectancy is between 60 and 70 years . . . which is pretty good.

LESLEY: But they don't get enough food.

TEACHER: Right.

LESLEY: But they're undernourished . . . here . . .

LINDA: So how come?

LESLEY: How come they live so long . . . if they haven't got enough food?

RACHEL: When they're undernourished.

JENNY: When some countries that are undernourished only last less than 40 years.

TEACHER: What's the measurement of undernourished, though . . .?

JENNY: Oh yeah.

TEACHER: How are they measuring undernourishment?

RACHEL: Calories.

TEACHER: Right . . . now, if we say that a woman on a diet in this country goes to about 1,500 a day . . . you can live off that . . . but we tend on average to live off something like 3,500 and be very greedy . . . yes?

LINDA: Yeah . . . so why is 2,500 undernourishment, then?

TEACHER: Right . . . it's the perception of what you actually need.

ALL: Mmmm . . . yeah.

TEACHER: So, in actual fact we tend to do categories like this in a book on what we value and need as nourishment.

ALL: Yeah.

TEACHER: So, by our standards they're undernourished.

RACHEL: Mmm, I was getting worried then . . . I thought I was undernourished.

TEACHER: Oh you look it, Rachel . . . you look it.

RACHEL: Thanks.

TEACHER: OK?

LINDA: I think Brazil's next.

LESLEY: Yeah.

RACHEL: I do.

TEACHER: Oh . . . right . . . I've been dismissed . . . I can tell.

RACHEL: You have . . . you've been dismissed.

JENNY: Brazil . . . right . . . next one.

It is the pupils who explicitly call upon the teacher as a learning resource to supplement the texts which are not meeting their needs at this point. The teacher responds first of all by listening carefully to what the pupils have to say. Her use of the word 'right' indicates her genuine interest, and invites the pupils to elaborate and to fully explain the problem. She then identifies the source of confusion and helps to clarify the issue by providing sufficient information to enable the pupils to continue with their investigation. Realising that she has served her purpose, the teacher then leaves the group. The remark made by the teacher on leaving, and the response this elicits, is significant. It denotes the existence of a shared understanding of working relationships and an established learning climate.

Responding as an equal

Role-play offers teachers the opportunity to engage with children in ways that may otherwise be difficult because of their relative social and political positions within the educational system and the school as an institution. In the following extract, a very reserved nine year old boy was expected to work with a partner in developing a story from a storyboard of cartoons selected from a computer. As the child's partner was absent, the teacher elected to take his place. The dialogue began in a restrained manner with the teacher having to provide most of the initiative. However, this pattern changed significantly when the teacher and child entered into role-play.

> SIMON: Right . . . what's that noise . . . I think the coffin lid's opening.
> TEACHER: Get away . . . don't be so daft . . . hey . . . you're right.
> SIMON: I'm hiding behind the door . . . you find a place to hide.
> TEACHER: Too late, it's opened . . . what is it?
> SIMON: I don't know . . . it looks to be a ghost.
> TEACHER: How do you know?
> SIMON: The shape of it . . . and it's white . . . quick, it's flying out of the window.
> TEACHER: Let's get out . . . which door?
> SIMON: We'll pick that one . . . creek . . . that definitely isn't it . . . huh!
> TEACHER: Hang on . . . let's think . . . think which one we came in.
> SIMON: When we came through the door it was the right . . . or was it the left?

Responding as a learning partner

The following extract shows a teacher and a nine year old child working together on a computer program. The work is part of a project based on the book, *The Jolly Postman*, and the task is to determine the most efficient delivery route for the postman to take. The teacher and child both have their attention focused on a town plan which is displayed on a computer screen. At this initial stage in the activity, ideas are being formed and no-one is controlling the keyboard.

The transcript is laid out in such a way as to illustrate what I would call a 'parallel' thinking process. This occurs when two people are engaged in the same activity and are 'thinking aloud'. The dialogue shows the concurrent nature of the utterances, with each line approximately displaying simultaneous utterances from the teacher and child. To gain an accurate representation of the discourse, two people should read this extract aloud, with Adnan beginning, 'Mmm . . . let me think' and the teacher coming in with, 'I bet the best way':

Adnan	*Teacher*
Mmm let me think . . . if we started there . . . yeah, at the edge of the estate maybe and went round that way . . . mmm a clockwise way . . . but we'd miss these two . . . It'd take us further to come back round than . . . than going there for start with . . . zig-zag . . . mmm across there . . . to that to that . . . that'll take more probably than if it's straight . . . or . . . or could go like that to them in the middle and then out up that street and back down and then up that one and again . . . yeah . . . so like . . . it's, yeah, a star shape . . . a star . . . shape.	I bet the best way is clockwise . . . starting on the edge of the estate and . . . mm . . . it's not quite that simple . . . I might have guessed . . . err . . . if we go down there in a zig-zag pattern that would mean we don't have to come all the way back to deliver to that little group . . . mmm, I don't know though . . . that doesn't seem very efficient either . . . how about . . . yes . . . working a way into the centre and operating from there . . . from the . . . yes . . . like the spokes of a wheel.

The computer program is unfamiliar to both the teacher and child. The teacher is interacting with Adnan as a learning partner, in the same way as he would with another adult in the same situation. There is a subliminal exchange of ideas as the teacher and child both feed and direct each other. Instead of issuing a string of questions or directives at Adnan, the teacher is working through the problem with him and providing the clear message that he doesn't know the answer either! The teacher is providing a model of learning. He is displaying explicitly, through his actions, that problems are solved through trial, exploration, hypothesis, mistakes, rethinking and reforming of ideas. He is showing that voicing one's thoughts and sharing them with a partner can help to solve problems and clarify issues.

Responding with minimal intervention

In order for children to be able to work alone, to wrestle internally with problems and to engage in personal inner dialogue, they need to feel free from constant interference from the teacher. Similarly, if we wish children to interact and to work collaboratively with their peers, they need to be given the time and the space in which to do so. The teacher must therefore be prepared to withdraw from the interaction, or to adopt, at least for a time, the principle of Minimal Teacher Intervention (Gregory, Wilding and Wood, 1990).

In this example, a group of seven year olds have read various adaptations of the story, *The Three Little Pigs*. They have been given the task of designing and building a model house made from straw. Throughout a very lengthy discussion and without any teacher intervention, the children successfully develop ideas and establish the ground rules for social interaction:

MICHAEL: But the windows are gonna have to be actually in the middle of it.

BRIAN: The straw's got to be there on all the other ones, but where's the door gonna be?

TRACY: And the door's here, like this . . . the straw's got to go round the window.

BRIAN: The windows are there and the door's there . . . but how far has the door got to be in, cos . . .

MICHAEL: Wait a minute . . . wait a minute . . . the door's gonna have to be say there or there . . .

TRACY: And the window's there

MICHAEL: Because the window's higher.

EMMA: The windows are going to be here.

MICHAEL: If we go by . . . if they go past the roof then we're gonna spoil it.
HELEN: What shall we do for the top anyway . . . what shall we do?
(*All children talk at once*)
MICHAEL: Just wait a minute and listen to David's advice.
DAVID: Well, the door'll have to be that high and then the window'll have to come about there.
BRIAN: No, but we've got to do the marks, haven't we? . . . We haven't done any marks at it.
DAVID: We're not going to have to draw it.
(*All children talk together*)
BRIAN: I can't hear anybody! There are too many people talking.
HELEN: Go on, what were you saying?

Only when the teacher senses that the children have reached a stage where her intervention could be productive does she join the group:

TEACHER: How are you doing now?
MICHAEL: We haven't started yet . . . we're still thinking about the door handle.
BRIAN: Because we don't know if it's card or wood.
HELEN: We could have a bit of tissue paper or straw.
MICHAEL: Just bungled up.
TEACHER: What do you think about a wooden door for a change?
DAVID: Oh, a wooden door . . . how'd we do that?
TEACHER: Do you want to have a look in the book?
ALL: Oh yeah.
TEACHER: Sit where you are and I'll bring it to you.

This timely intervention then leads to further fruitful discussion and to a resolution of the problem, as the children discover that, in the story books, the doors are made of wood. The teacher's refusal to intervene earlier, despite the temptation to do so when the discussion at times became heated, allowed the children the space to develop their own sense of control and to accept more responsibility for the learning.

Conclusion

Allowing children to express and to use their knowledge does not mean that teachers have to assume a role of ignorance, to abdicate their own position, or to enter into a series of pseudo-relationships. As one Oracy Project teacher, Sally Wilding, said:

I agree with allowing the child to become the expert whenever possible. But, in reality, the number of occasions I can do this is limited. The difference in our age, experience, education and training means that, for the most part, I invariably have a greater knowledge and level of expertise.

Rather than thinking in terms of teachers having to suppress their expertise, I believe it is more useful to think in terms of how teachers can best use this expertise in nurturing and developing that of the children. Being an expert is about more than possessing and transmitting information. It's about understanding how children learn, encouraging and creating effective learning climates, developing interpersonal relationships and knowing when and how to intervene productively.

Through interactions of the sort described in this article, teachers can not only extend children's existing knowledge in ways that increase understanding, but also teach them how to learn. Their interventions help pupils to internalise the processes of effective thinking, such as identifying problems, seeking alternative answers, referring to previous experience and considering other viewpoints. As Geoff Butt, ICI Education Liaison Manager, said at a conference in 1989:

> We don't want people who can just give us well rehearsed answers . . . we need people who can wrap their minds around problems . . . who can collaborate and negotiate issues.

Acknowledgements

I would like to thank all my teaching colleagues in the Staffordshire Oracy Project and also the following schools for permission to use transcript material: Weston Coyney Junior School, Stoke-on-Trent; St Margaret Ward High School, Stoke-on-Trent; Oldfields Hall Middle School, Uttoxeter, Staffs; Sir Thomas Boughey High School, Stoke-on-Trent; Ouston Junior School, Ouston, County Durham; St John's Primary School, Essington, Staffs; Newford Primary School, Stoke-on-Trent.

References

GREGORY, G., WILDING, S. AND WOOD, D. (1990). *Talk for Learning: An Audience Model for Classroom Practice*. Occasional Paper 10, Staffordshire Oracy Project.

WELLS, G. (1988) 'The literate potential of collaborative talk', in Maclure, M., Phillips, T. and Wilkinson, A. (eds) (1988) *Oracy Matters*. Milton Keynes: Open University Press.

'Scaffolding' Learning in the Classroom

JANET MAYBIN

NEIL MERCER

AND

BARRY STIERER

The concept of 'scaffolding'

Recent interest in talk and learning in the classroom has encouraged a new metaphorical use for the term 'scaffolding'. This term is increasingly used to describe certain kinds of support which learners receive in their interaction with parents, teachers and other 'mentors' as they move towards new skills, concepts or levels of understanding. It is a term which helps to portray the temporary, but essential, nature of the mentor's assistance as the learner advances in knowledge and understanding.

The term 'scaffolding' was originally used by Bruner as a metaphor for depicting the form and quality of the effective intervention by a 'learned' person in the learning of another person:

> If the child is enabled to advance by being under the tutelage of an adult or a more competent peer, then the tutor or the aiding peer serves the learner as a vicarious form of consciousness until such time as the learner is able to master his own action through his own consciousness and control. When the child achieves that conscious control over a new function or conceptual system, it is then that he is able to use it as a tool. Up to that point, the tutor in effect performs

the critical function of 'scaffolding' the learning task to make it possible for the child, in Vygotsky's words, to internalise external knowledge and convert it into a tool for conscious control.

(Bruner, 1985, pp. 24–5)

Bruner relates the term 'scaffolding' explicitly to Vygotsky's concept of 'the zone of proximal development' – that is, 'the distance between the actual developmental level as determined by independent problem solving and the level of potential development as determined through problem solving under adult guidance or in collaboration with more capable peers' (Vygotsky, 1978, p. 86). Bruner therefore uses the metaphor of 'scaffolding' to represent the special quality of this 'guidance' or 'collaboration'. Though its source is child psychology, the metaphor has become adopted in 'language in education' circles because of its emphasis on the role of language – and especially spoken language – in children's learning.

Along with many others who are interested in the role of talk in the process of teaching and learning, we find the metaphor of 'scaffolding' tremendously appealing in principle and at the same time elusive or, at least, problematic in practice. The appeal of the concept among teachers derives in part from the fact that it directs attention to the quality of their participation in the learning process, and does so in a way which emphasises that good teaching strategies are necessarily based on, and responsive to, the state of understanding achieved by particular learners. Teachers appreciate a model of the learning process which can accommodate the teacher as active participant (as opposed, for example, to a custodian of stimulating environments) and which, moreover, offers teachers a possible conceptual escape from the tired debate about 'traditional versus progressive' pedagogies.

At the same time, however, teachers have recognised that the scaffolding concept remains at an abstract level and is not easily translated into a practical classroom context. The familiar difficulty of aligning theory and practice without distorting either of them is especially problematic in this case, since the concept was originally developed by researchers investigating the linguistic and cognitive development of very young children, usually observed in one-to-one conversations with a parent or adult care-giver. Teacher-pupil relationships, and the discourse within them, are unlikely to be characterised by the same degree of emotional intimacy and intuitive understanding as parent-child relationships. One-to-one interactions in classrooms tend to be more truncated than interactions between parents and their children. Parents' utterances within such interactions tend to respond directly to, and to extend, the communicative intent of their children, whereas teachers' interventions may be more consciously informed by curriculum-related learning objectives. Moreover, discourse between a teacher and an individual pupil is usually contextualised by other discourse, whereby the pupil relates to the teacher as part of a group or whole class. Teacher-pupil discourse will inevitably be influenced by the institutional norms of schools and the peculiar power relations within classrooms.

What the notion of scaffolding offers, then, is a way of conceptualising the process whereby one person in the role of 'teacher' facilitates the progress of another person, the 'learner', by reducing the scope for failure in the task the learner is attempting. 'Scaffolding' is clearly a form of 'help'; but what kind of help is it? What are the specific features which distinguish scaffolding from other forms of assistance? We begin with the working hypothesis that it is not just any assistance which might help a learner accomplish a task. It is help which will enable learners to accomplish a task which they would not have been quite able to manage on their own, and it is help which is intended to bring learners closer to a state of competence which will enable them eventually to complete such a task on their own. Our use of the word 'task' here is not meant to imply that 'scaffolding' is only applicable if pupils are doing a certain kind of well-defined problem solving activity: we do, however, wish to retain the idea (covered in Bruner's original usage) that 'scaffolding' is help given in the pursuit of a specific learning activity, one which has finite goals. (We would not find it acceptable to make broad claims such as: 'Teacher X scaffolded pupil Y's progress in mathematics', though we might not object to the claim: 'Teacher X scaffolded pupil Y's work on a specific maths project'.)

Whether this distinction (between 'scaffolding' and other forms of help) is easy to apply in practice is an open question. To know whether or not some help counts as 'scaffolding', we would need to have at the very least some evidence of a teacher wishing to enable a child to develop a specific skill, grasp a particular concept or achieve a particular level of understanding. It might also be reasonable to expect some evidence, usually in the quality of the talk between learner and mentor, that the mentor had 'tuned in' to the learner's present state of ability or understanding. A more stringent criterion, but one which we would treat tentatively at this stage, would be to require some evidence of a learner successfully accomplishing the task with the teacher's help. We could speculate that an even more stringent interpretation would be to require some evidence of a learner having achieved some greater level of independent competence as a result of the scaffolding experience (that is, demonstrating his or her increased competence or improved level of understanding in dealing independently with some subsequent problem).

Some of these issues might be clarified by looking at examples of teaching and learning. We will consider two recorded sequences, one from a primary and one from a secondary classroom, and begin by looking at a fairly straightforward example of what might be categorised as 'scaffolding'.

Sequence 1: categorising seashells

This sequence took place in a primary school classroom where two eleven-year-old boys were engaged in an activity intended to develop their understanding of how scientific classification schemes work, by getting them to classify a collection of sea-shells into distinct categories on the basis of their physical features. The kind of hierarchical scheme they were expected to generate was that which in botany is called a 'key'. A botanic key (often to be found in the appendix to books on wild flowers, trees or other natural vegetation) enables the user to identify any plant specimen found in the world by answering a set of specific questions to which only yes/no answers can be given: 'Has it got leaves?', 'Are its leaves arranged in pairs?', 'Do its leaves have serrated edges?', and so on. The boys therefore had to write a series of questions which would enable other pupils to identify any specific shell in the collection.

As an educational activity, this task operates on more than one level. The notions of 'procedural' and 'principled' kinds of understanding (Edwards and Mercer, 1987, Chapter 6) are perhaps useful here. At a procedural level, the boys are meant to develop and practise their skill at sorting a set of objects of subtly different shapes and sizes. At a rather more abstract level, they are meant to generate a series of yes/no questions to identify shells in the collection. And at the most principled level, they are meant to grasp the essential logic and heuristic value of scientific systems of classification.

At the point at which the sequence begins, they are a bit 'stuck' and so have appealed to their teacher for help. (Note: **** = unintelligible speech.)

DAVID: I can't think of one to separate these two. I've got to separate some of these.
TEACHER: What's an obvious difference between them?

DAVID: They are cones.

GRAHAM: ****

TEACHER: All right. That would . . . So you would separate those two, but it wouldn't be a question that applies to those. Is there one difference between those two that is also a way you could group those? (*indicates different shells on the table*)

DAVID: Well, that's pointed . . .

TEACHER: Um . . .

DAVID: . . . and that one isn't.

TEACHER: I think, perhaps, think you are limiting your thoughts to shape at the moment. Think about some other things . . . some other variables that you could look at.

GRAHAM: Colour.

TEACHER: Try colour.

GRAHAM: Is it that sort of colour. Is it dark? That is dark ****

TEACHER: You are going to have problems. People would say, well compare . . . if someone said to you which is the dark one of those two, you would immediately point to that one. Now, this is where the difficulties arise, isn't it, because there is no doubt which is the dark one there.

BOTH: Yeah.

TEACHER: And at the first glance at the whole group there is no doubt which is the dark one there, but if that was the only shell you had, and someone said to you, 'Is that a dark shell?', what would be your answer?

DAVID: Yeah.

TEACHER: You would probably say, 'Yes'. Graham, you might say, 'No'. I mean, I think I would probably say, 'No, it isn't a dark shell'. But, I mean, I'm sure that if you went round the class you would find that half the class would probably say that was dark and half would say it was light. So it might not be a good question. Simply because people's judgement of what light and dark is varies. But, I mean, don't put that thought out of your mind. But that . . . that's the sort of question you need to ask yourself, you know, when you're making, when you are asking the question: 'Is there only one definite answer?'

DAVID: Maybe, 'Has it got more than two colours?' That's got brown, black and white. That would split those into that.

GRAHAM: **** Yeah. ****

DAVID: ****

TEACHER: What are you trying to say?

GRAHAM: Is it . . .?

DAVID: Has it got two, more than two colours?

TEACHER: All right. Delete the line and rewrite the question.

(Open University, 1991)

In this sequence, the teacher helps the pupils to make progress on a task in which they are already engaged and in which they have got 'stuck'. He tries to draw out from the boys ideas (for example, the variable of 'colour') which he knows will take them along productive paths to a solution. He gives them some feedback on their suggestions, pointing out weaknesses where they exist. He tries to help them adopt a suitably detached or 'decentred' perspective on the problem by pointing out that relative terms (like 'dark') won't work in the circumstances in which other people will use their 'key'. On this occasion, we see pupils making progress with teacher support: by the end of the sequence they have, with his help, discovered a way of distinguishing the shells in question. Our criterion of seeing pupils achieve a task with help which they had been unable to do on their own has then been satisfied. Our most stringent criterion, which requires evidence that the pupils are subsequently more competent at independent problem solving, is not met by anything contained within this short sequence. However, subsequent video-recording of their activities shows that Daniel and Graham went on to complete a satisfactory classification of the shells and generate a suitable series of questions. If we are prepared to take a longer time-scale into account, then, this criterion too may be satisfied (depending upon what 'level' of learning outcome we are prepared to accept for this task). That is, we have some fairly good reasons for identifying Sequence 1 as a piece of 'scaffolded' learning.

Sequence 2: a language autobiography

This next sequence comes from a secondary school classroom. It involves a conversation between one pupil and her teacher.

Samantha comes from a class of fifteen year olds who have been researching and writing about their own language development. She has discussed what she sees as key points in her own language history with friends in the class, and has written one and a half pages for the first draft of her language autobiography. She is now showing this to her teacher. The draft is a rather rambling piece of narrative about various events in Samantha's life, and her teacher wants to help her to focus the content of the writing more clearly on issues of language, and to develop the structure of the piece so that it conforms to the style required for 'narrative' and 'descriptive' writing for GCSE. Two short extracts from their conversation are transcribed below:

TEACHER: Right, Samantha could you, erm, tell me how far you've got and what problems you've had? Have you gone any further than ten?

SAMANTHA: Yeah, eleven, and, like, when I just come, like, left Beechside, my previous school, come to this school and where I met Angela again from where I met her up the hospital and that and . . . erm, then I met her friend, Sharon, now we're friends again.

TEACHER: And what language bit are you talking about there when you're meeting up with your new friends, with your old friends?

SAMANTHA: Well, I knew Angela from like when my nan used to go up the hospital and that and have checkups, but I didn't know Sharon until I come to this school and until Angela introduced me to her, that was when I was eleven.

TEACHER: So it's part of your language biography you've described there, your meeting up with those friends again. What points are you going to make after that? You're going to be looking at your vocabulary or looking at the way you talk with friends?

SAMANTHA: Yeah, in a way, in a way I acted in some of my lessons and that and how I acted against, erm, like books when I first come to this school cos I didn't really like them. (*pause*) I'm not sure if I've got enough from nought to one.

TEACHER: Right, OK. Can you just read the start there, and I'll listen to how it sounds, OK?

SAMANTHA: What to that bit?

TEACHER: Well, is that where your first paragraph's gonna come to an end?

SAMANTHA: Yeah. I think so, cos there's, like, what I'm talking about how, what about my mum and dad and that and my family and I go onto how I, how I learned to speak and that.

TEACHER: Right, OK. So test that out, see what it sounds like.

(*Samantha reads*)

TEACHER: Why are you so worried about putting that at the beginning, why would I think, do you think, that that is a good start?

SAMANTHA: I dunno, I think it's a bit of a mouthful in some ways.

TEACHER: Why is it important to, why have you decided to put all that in there about your mum and dad, what's that say about you?

SAMANTHA: It's sort of tell em why I'm a bit sort of cockney accent and that and shows, em, like what sort of background I've sort of had off of my parents.

(Open University, 1990)

This seems to be the sort of context in which the notion of scaffolding would apply. Samantha feels she is stuck with her piece of writing, and her teacher has specific teaching aims which he hopes to get across in the course of their conversation. The vicarious mental scaffold which he is attempting to hold for her includes the language agenda which needs to be made more explicit in her piece, and also the ground rules which apply to GCSE writing. He continually tries to relate what she has already written to these two sets of criteria. It is a one-to-one encounter, and the teacher tunes in very sensitively to Samantha's own ideas, trying to draw her on from these towards a content and structure which he knows will make for a more effective piece of writing. Notice, however, that Samantha persistently sidesteps her teacher's questions, answering them in a way which remains firmly within the boundaries of her own agenda. For example, when he asks her 'And what language bit are you talking about there when you're meeting up with your new friends, with your old friends?', Samantha answers by explaining when she met Angela, how she got to know Sharon, and so on. On the discourse level, this looks like a piece of attempted scaffolding which has failed.

However, in order to understand the nature of what is happening here, we need to look closely at the context. The teacher has a number of reasons for not giving Samantha more explicit directions about what to include, what to expand on, and how to structure her piece. First, since personal language development is so closely tied up with emerging personal and social identity, he has to be particularly sensitive in helping her to achieve a balance in the content of her writing between accounts of incidents in her life and drawing out relevant language issues. Secondly, he knows Samantha is very resistant to criticisms of her writing, and, if she becomes discouraged, will probably give up and do no further work to the draft. His own teaching style is to show clearly that he values his pupils' ideas and then to direct them to the kinds of decisions and choices they need to make in order to develop and refine those ideas, in a way which will conform to the appropriate ground rules. It is up to the pupils themselves to decide precisely how they will use their teacher's advice in redrafting their work.

In the event, this proved to be one of the best and most extended pieces of writing Samantha produced for her GCSE folder, although none of her pieces obtained a very high grade. She did write in parts of the autobiography about incidents in her life which had affected her deeply, without relating these to anything about language, and at these points the structure became more rambling. But she included enough appropriate content matter and structured her writing clearly enough overall, to produce a piece of work which was considerably stronger than her previous assignments. Thus the written outcome from this example does seem to suggest that her teacher successfully scaffolded Samantha's learning in this instance, in spite of the lack of evidence for this in the transcript example. She could not have produced such a finished draft without her teacher's help.

The fact that the work carried out, and the decisions taken, were very much Samantha's own would suggest that the notion of scaffolding should not be seen as giving all the power to the teacher. It is clear that pupils can take an active, creative role within the process and exert some influence over the nature and direction of the scaffolding.

Conclusions

We have tried to show in these two short analyses how the 'scaffolding' concept can be used as an analytical tool to help gain a greater understanding of teaching and learning. There are distinctive dimensions of the teaching and learning process, and each of them needs to be scrutinised separately in order to determine the essential features of the scaffolding phenomenon. That is to say, we must take account of the features of:

● the talk (for example, the kinds of questions asked by the teacher);

● the learning task (for example, skills, concepts, understanding);

● the teacher's intentions (for example, to respond to the learner's 'confusion', to introduce a new learning task);

● the learner's intentions (for example, to use the teacher as a resource);

● the context (for example, the quality of the mentor-learner relationship, the social and physical setting, the implicit understandings of teacher and learner about the activity);

● the outcome (for example, practical demonstration of new learning, tangible products, something in the talk).

These six dimensions have provided us with an analytical framework for examining classroom interaction. They have also enabled us to explore the practical implications of the scaffolding concept for the way we promote talk in the classroom and for the way we interact with individuals and groups. Nevertheless, much investigation and refinement remains to be done before we may confidently identify the essential features of scaffolding in a classroom setting, and distinguish it from other successful forms of teaching and learning.

Acknowledgements

Thanks to: Philip Stevenson and Class 7 of Icknield Primary School, Sawston, Cambridge for the talk in Sequence 1; Kit Thomas, Walthamstow School for Girls for Sequence 2.

References

BRUNER, J. (1985) 'Vygotsky: a historical and conceptual perspective' in Wertsch, J., V. (ed) (1985) *Culture, Communication and Cognition: Vygotskyan perspectives.* Cambridge: Cambridge University Press.

EDWARDS, D. AND MERCER, N. (1987) *Common Knowledge: the development of understanding in the classroom.* London: Methuen.

OPEN UNIVERSITY (1991) Video-cassette 2 of *EH232 – Computers and Learning.* Milton Keynes: Open University.

OPEN UNIVERSITY (1992) Video-cassette 4 of *E271 – Curriculum and Learning.* Milton Keynes: Open University.

VYGOTSKY, L. S. (1978) *Mind in Society.* London: Harvard University Press.

WELLS, G. (1985) 'Language and learning: an interactional perspective' in Wells, G. and Nicholls, J. (eds) (1985) *Language and Learning: an interactional perspective.* Barcombe: The Falmer Press.

4.3

Surprisingly Disciplined Squads

HAROLD GARDINER

It is no longer as simple as it once seemed to answer the two philosophic questions of education: 'What is teaching?' and 'What is learning?' When Gordon Wells wrote (1989) that 'all knowledge has to be actively constructed by the individual knower', he was summarising a view of learning which underlies the work of the National Oracy Project and which leads to a redefinition of the teacher's role.

This redefinition involves the replacement of a limited range of teaching behaviours – in which the teacher, as an authority who has knowledge, transmits it to learners who do not have it – by a wider but much less well defined range, the quality of which is judged against the criterion of whether the learner has 'actively constructed' the knowledge. Where teachers have been prepared, on occasion, to abdicate the role of 'authority', pupils have revealed unexpected abilities in language and control of ideas. This article is about those abilities; it will also suggest ways in which the roles adopted by the adults might have helped to make the pupils' achievements possible.

In the examples quoted, the pupils have a genuine stake in what is going on: they 'own' the task. The adults' role is to make a 'contingent response'; they are listening and watching, in order to interpolate in ways which confer value on the pupils' meaning and to help them to expand into appropriate modes of thinking and responding.

In this first example, a visitor, HG, was in the school library for a 'project' lesson with a class of fifteen year olds. One boy, David, claimed that he had left at home the books he needed, and could do nothing without them. His topic was fishing. He reluctantly agreed to record a seven minutes' conversation with HG about his fishing experiences and expertise. At first, he dealt in facts – the rod, the mechanism, the breaking strength of the line. Prompted by HG, he recalled landing his first tench. He talked of some of the pleasures and disappointments of his hobby. The conversation then took an interesting turn, prompted by a new question from HG:

HG: Don't you think you've got all – all the strengths on your side? I mean, you're a thinking creature, you can lay your plans, and so on . . .
DAVID: Well . . .
HG: And he's just . . . the fish is just behaving in an instinctive way . . .
DAVID: No . . .
HG: You . . . you respect . . .?
DAVID: Yes . . . they know what they're doing.
HG: Do they?
DAVID: Yes. You can catch fish . . . there's one fish I know . . . it's been hooked . . . thousands of times, and no-one's landed it . . .
HG: You . . . actually *know* a fish . . .?
DAVID: Yes . . .
HG: How do you know it?
DAVID: How? . . . You can go down and watch him . . . just stand there watching him. Plenty of people have hooked him, and they all think, 'I've got him.' And you get your net down, and next minute, whoosh, he's gone. In the end, when he feels like it, he just comes off, as if he's been playing you around.
HG: He's taking the mickey out of you?
DAVID: Yes.

That is a simple example of the interaction that can result when the conversational initiative is transferred. The extract is brief and may not be considered particularly profound, but David makes his point with some vigour. He knows what he is talking about, and the adult's role can be described as that of an interested and articulate learner.

The next piece of conversation shows a twelve year old handling a serious and complex issue. Keith offered to talk to a visitor, PE, about the problems of South Africa. He began with an uninterrupted 'long turn' of some seven minutes, without notes, on the historical background. This established the fact that he was 'in the chair'. PE sought clarification, in the light of the background, about some more recent events, and Keith referred to the education of the black population. These exchanges followed:

> KEITH: The black . . . there was . . . there are schools in the black homelands, but they're made of corrugated iron, and it's very hot in there . . .
>
> PE: The homelands that have been set up by the South African government for the blacks to live in? But aren't they where they have come from? It isn't their homeland, just a place for them to be . . .?
>
> KEITH: It's just a place for them to be . . . cos if you speak a certain language you have to go to a certain place . . . if you speak another language, you've got to go where . . .
>
> PE: Ah . . . the blacks don't all speak the same language (no) they don't all come from the same (tribe) . . . ah, I see, different tribes are they in their origin . . .?
>
> KEITH: Yes . . . and with the schools it's very crowded . . . it's about 87 children to one teacher . . . cos there's very few teachers . . . they have a few books . . . but not many . . .

The hesitancy is evident even in the words on the page, but it is being used to positive effect. This twelve year old is feeling for the significant features in South Africa today, as he talks – it is worth noting – to an adult he does not know. The occasion is one of some tension, but he is committed to communicate. And if the rest of the context is right – that is, if the questioning and listening are sympathetic, if there is time to be tentative, and a genuine respect for his offerings, then he will more than do himself justice. Before long, indeed, he is introducing the topics of religion, the Pass Laws, trade and sanctions and getting into the complexities of the South African problem.

When pupils have made or done something visible and even tangible, their language is capable of a sharp focus on the thing created, as the next two examples illustrate. When Stephen, who had helped to lay a concrete path, was asked to give a visitor an account of the processes and skills involved, this sharp focus was particularly notable:

> STEPHEN: . . . then you had to bang it down with this big plank of wood to let . . . and you had to bang it down harder at this end to make it come down at an angle so the water'd run off. We had to get some little planks of wood and put them on the concrete kerbs so that the wood we was laying over the top wouldn't touch the . . .

um . . . concrete . . . and then we had . . . as the planks were put around they've got some larger planks . . . and so they were supports . . . and where the lamp post is there was a special piece of wood with a hole cut out . . . we had to be extra careful cos we had to step on the support woods to get the other wood on properly . . .

We can gather from that brief extract how much concentration Stephen is devoting to the processes, and to the intentions that lay behind the results he was describing. It is a fascinating glimpse into the 'equipment of his mind' – equipment that was not brought into play in most of his school experience – as he incorporates his main and subordinate subject matter into utterance. He can do this because he is assured of his listener's interest and attention, so that he is free to give his own attention to the message he is working to convey. Like Keith earlier, he manages to operate in a context of some stress and importance for himself, and achieves success in those terms.

The next example shows greater evidence of interaction between the listener and the speaker than the previous one, but it reveals a firm structure of a different kind. A Year 11 boy, Len, is telling an English teacher, GC, about his engineering technology project, a fabric testing machine which they have in front of them as they talk. After more than ten minutes' conversation, he says, 'Looking at the finished product now, if I went back and started again, I think I could do better.' Here are some of the things he says in the next few minutes, with some of GC's enabling contributions:

GC: What would you do?
LEN: I don't know. It's because I've encountered so many problems on the way . . . it's the odd bearing or joint here and there you could tidy up and . . . er, you could make it . . . I don't know . . . a bit cheaper to build, I suppose, and sort of more economical when running.
GC: Looking at this now I can't imagine any other way to do it.
LEN: Well, it was . . . well, I think I've just added things like an extra wheel to slow it down . . . er, a guiding rail and the clamps. The fabric was going to be brought along the plate and folded under and I've had sort of . . . grand designs of springs and pulleys and levers underneath that would grip the fabric tight . . . and then I just came up with the cheapest and easiest way of doing it.
GC: There seems to be nothing here that could go very wrong, nothing that's just for the sake of it . . . it's very functional . . .
LEN: Yeah . . . well, everything I think has got a purpose . . . there's no pretty bits . . . no glamorous kind of . . . I don't know . . . I suppose it could be made to be a little more attractive but it does the job so that's . . . I'm quite pleased with it.
GC: I can see that it might be enclosed . . .

LEN: . . . Yeah, some kind of protective cover cos you've got your wheels whizzing around . . . you've got your belts and . . . um . . . originally there was 240 volts just hanging around in that brush so we had to take it down to 12, I think it is now.

GC: So you're using . . . that's a transformer, is it?

LEN: Yeah, that sort of box of tricks sort of takes it all down and plays with it a bit . . . I don't know anything about the electricity side of it.

In this extract, it is clear that GC shows interest in learning more about the project, probing and prompting Len to delve into detail – how the fabric is gripped, the lack of decorative features, the idea of a protective cover, and so to safety issues. Her friendly persistence causes his active mind to generate the words that shape his message. But whereas we noted that Stephen was occupied with the content and hardly notices his listener, Len is having to engage actively with GC's interjections. It is also worth noting the colloquial touches which indicate a more relaxed relationship than that of the previous example. Both, though, are substantial; both are orderly.

We who are referred to as 'teachers' should, it seems, more often stand outside the behaviour that is characteristic of our vocation. But we do not have to learn a whole new range of speaking parts, like actors, to do so. Rather, it is a matter of unlearning some accustomed routines, such as assuming that our chief function is to know what pupils do not know. When the reverse happens, when pupils know something that we do not know, or when their knowledge is fresher than ours, their words often come surprisingly naturally.

A final example illustrates precisely the roles of sympathetic adult and responsive young person. An English teacher, GC, talked for fully 25 minutes with Dawn about her work experience visits to a local hospital. About halfway through, there is a mention of the geriatric ward:

DAWN: . . . those people you have to do everything for . . . you have to feed them . . . everything . . .

GC: And could you have coped with that if you'd been there?

DAWN: Yes . . . I went there for a week . . . I didn't like it that much . . .

GC: It must be pretty depressing because . . . you know . . . people are only going down (yeah) . . . you know . . . but if someone's in hospital . . . and they've had an operation . . . you know they're going to . . . you see them getting better . . . and then they go out . . . and you know they're going to be alright . . .

DAWN: No, but this . . . the only week I went down there . . . they had a person die the night before . . . and apparently this was one of the ladies who could do something for herself . . . but she just slipped away in the night . . . (*pause*) . . . and there was another lady . . . my mum was home help for her . . . and the first week I was up there she was in a wheel chair . . . and the next week she was in bed . . . she just went down and down and down . . . the next time they had her in a hammock . . . just to stop her bed sores and things like that . . . she sort of kept looking up and getting better . . . and going back and getting better again, and then she just went . . . in the night.

GC: And could you cope with that?

DAWN: Yes. (*pause*) I didn't sort of . . . I didn't pay much attention to her in case it sort of hit me . . . I just sort of went and held her hand and gave her a drink . . . didn't give her much attention . . . nobody did . . . the only time we sort of paid attention to her was when she had an injection . . . that was to sort of numb her brain so she couldn't feel any pain . . . she had cancer . . . cancer all over her body. (*long pause*) It was . . . funny . . . at first . . . but I sort of took it in . . .

The shape and subtlety of this conversation repays attention and commands respect. First of all, Dawn explains why the geriatric ward is without hope; people can do nothing for themselves. That is why she did not like it there. She answers GC's questions about coping in two stages – first with two anecdotes, one that links back to the subject of helplessness ('one of the ladies who could do something for herself') and another that links forward to the personal association ('my mum was home help for her'). GC's next move hints at the difference between those who will leave the hospital restored, and those who are in the geriatric ward. Dawn 'reads' this move very sensitively; she shows she understands what GC is not making explicit. Her reply to the repeated, and modulated, question, 'And could you cope?' is precise and honest, 'a correct compassion'. It has two telling pauses, and the use of 'sort of' is not the sign of linguistic poverty that complainants about the state of language assert. This is, indeed, language of worth.

The Bullock Report, *A Language for Life*, referred to 'the degree to which learning and the acquisition of language are interlocked'. It is now clear that the quality of learning depends to a great extent on the nature of the language in which it takes place, and that relationships between people tend to influence the language they use. What this article has claimed is that young people have, among their 'strategies of meaning-making,' as Gordon Wells calls them, language resources which are available to make their learning effective. T.S. Eliot called words, 'undisciplined squads of emotion.' When young people are invited to talk seriously about something that they feel is important, to listeners who want to hear what they have to say and are prepared to value it as serious utterance, it is often surprising what linguistic resources they have at their command. The more often the kind of conversations illustrated here are replicated, the less of a surprise they become; but they never stop being a source of pleasure.

Acknowledgements

I would like to thank St John's School, Marlborough, Wiltshire; Castledown School, Ludgershall, Wiltshire; Hreod Parkway School, Swindon, Wiltshire.

References

DES (1975) *A Language for Life.* London: HMSO.
WELLS, G. (1989) 'Language in the Classroom: Literacy and Collaborative Talk', *Language and Education*, Vol 3, No 4, 1989.

Teaching Talk: How Modes of Teacher Talk Affect Pupil Participation

DAVID WOOD

The year 1976 was an important year for me. For the first time since I left school, I began working with teachers in their classrooms. I was drawn into this line of work, which I have pursued ever since, for two main reasons. The first was theoretical: an interest in the nature of instruction and tutoring. I had spent the preceding six years studying teaching and learning in the laboratory, confronting three to six year olds, to borrow Urie Bronfenbrenner's words, with 'strange tasks, in strange situations, with strange adults'. Working with Jerome Bruner and other colleagues in the USA, I was trying to articulate a concept which we had come to refer to as 'scaffolding'. The question was whether the ideas which underpinned this metaphor had any currency in the real world. Could any of the complex and difficult processes which teachers undertake each day of their professional lives be described and understood in the same sorts of terms that we had been using to analyse contrived teaching and learning processes in the lab? This, more practical question, provided the second impetus towards working in schools.

I began, in fact, working in three different educational settings; playgroups, nursery schools and schools/units for hearing-impaired children. I think it was largely through the differences and similarities I encountered in these contexts that I first began to see how some of our laboratory-inspired notions might supply a useful perspective on teachers and teaching. Since my brief here is to concentrate on the language of classrooms, I will try to illustrate some of these notions with reference to varieties of teaching talk and their immediate and long-term effects on pupil performance.

Questioning

Raising questions about the practice of questioning provides the best point of entry in the exploration of classroom talk. For one thing, questions are a pervasive and even dominant feature of teacher language. Indeed, Kerry (1987) estimates that a teacher will pose one and a half million questions during a typical professional lifetime! It seems likely, therefore, that, if we are going to discover any effects of styles of teacher talk on pupils' learning, questions are going to figure in the story.

Many studies in different parts of the world attest to the seeming universality of teacher questions. Two statistics illustrate their frequency in pedagogical discourse. The first comes from a North American study of social studies and science classrooms in which it was observed that teachers asked, on average, two questions per minute. Pupils, meanwhile, posed about two questions an hour – and that was the rate of questions for all pupils in the class, not the number raised by each and every child (Susskind, 1969). This preponderance of teacher questions, and this paucity of pupil questions, seems remarkably unaffected by the age or composition of the class. In a study of discussion sessions involving American sixteen-seventeen year olds, for instance, we found that teachers ended 44% of their speaking turns with a question. The figure we found in UK playgroups and nursery schools was 47% and, in schools for the deaf, 46%. Of all the conversational turns taken by the US college students, 8% included a question. The rate for British pre-schoolers and deaf children was 4% and 1% respectively (Wood and Wood, 1988).

Perhaps, you might protest, frequent questions are a 'good thing'. Many people, including both Socrates and Plato, have believed this to be the case. Questions often serve as expressions of interest and place the ears of the questioner at the disposal of the voice of the person questioned. Anthropologists have compared language use in several different cultures and suggested that, universally, questions serve as forms of politeness. But most questions in school cannot be classified in this way. Teachers, like policemen, doctors, and barristers, are licensed by society to pose questions in their professional lives in the expectation that they will be answered in particular ways. Teachers, unlike the person met casually on the street, can insist that their questions are honoured with a response. Furthermore, they can ask for a defence of any answer given, probing for reasons, justifications, or understanding. Classroom questions are quite different from those found in most other situations: they are far more powerful and potentially threatening.

OK, you might concede, classroom questions serve different purposes from those encountered in social chat. And, of course, children have to learn that a teacher's questions are based on social conventions, or ground rules, which differ from those operating in most other contexts. But the aim of pedagogical questions, as Socrates demonstrated, is to motivate, sustain and direct the thought processes of the pupil. Questions promote reflection, analysis, self-examination and enquiry. Great idea – but is it true?

Until quite recently, about thirty years ago, in fact, such 'great ideas' about questioning went untested and unchallenged. They were taken by many as being self-evident truths. What does the evidence have to say?

The first finding of considerable generality is that most questions posed in the classroom are not of a kind which might be expected to promote deep or searching intellectual activity (Dillon, 1982). Rather, they are so-called 'closed' questions which demand, and typically receive, short, factual responses: 'What colour are your new shoes?', 'What is the chemical symbol for gold?', 'What is the main product of Brazil?', and so forth. Such questions, to which the teacher usually knows the answer, not only fail to promote intellectual activity in pupils but serve, if anything, to inhibit it.

In the wake of the first observations which revealed the extent and frequency of such styles of questioning, a number of intervention and training studies have been premised on the assumption that, if teachers could only learn how to raise the level of 'cognitive demand' of their questions, the result would be more thoughtful and productive responses from their pupils. If, instead of asking closed, factual questions with known right answers, they posed questions which demanded, say, analysis, justification, reasoning, or integration of information, children could be led along more profitable lines of thought and helped to discover how to think for themselves.

While I remain personally convinced that this idea has some merit, intervention and training experiments designed to bring about such effects have not, in fact, worked (Dillon, op cit). More recently, however, other findings have emerged which draw attention not so much to the content or 'level' of questions as to what occurs after them: silence.

When questions are posed in everyday conversations, a response usually comes within less than a second of silence. This is also true of classroom questions. Teachers usually allow about a second for a reply and, if none is forthcoming, they take back the conversational floor. In a pioneering study, Swift and Gooding (1983), two North American researchers, recorded and analysed 40 middle school science lessons. They corroborated the fact that teachers usually leave just over a second of 'wait time' after posing questions but they went on to discover that where a longer silence was left – even one as short as three seconds – the quality and extent of pupils' responses improved dramatically. Answers were not only longer but also more thoughtful. Such findings are in accord with the results of controlled laboratory investigations. Briefly, these show that the more intellectually demanding a question is, the longer people take before starting to answer it, and the slower their rate of delivery once they start to talk (for example, Goldman-Eiser, 1968; Taylor, 1969; Levin *et al.*, 1967). With children, the time needed to think, to formulate a response and to put that response into words demands considerably more than a second's 'wait time' after a thought provoking question. But they rarely get the time they need. In follow-up studies, Swift, Gooding and their colleagues went on to show that teachers can be helped to increase wait time and that, when they do so, pupils' immediate responses improve in quality and quantity; in the longer term, indeed, academic achievements improve (Swift, Gooding and Swift, 1988).

It is not easy, however, to train oneself to modify what is a very 'deep' and entrenched feature of our conversational conventions. In everyday talk, where questions are often undemanding, calling for a personal response rather than a considered answer, we receive answers within a second. Imposing a new tempo on our interactions in the classroom is stressful and difficult to maintain. The teachers who worked with Swift and Gooding were helped to increase their silences by means of a piece of electronic gadgetry which enabled the researchers to provide 'bleeps' that were relayed to the teachers' ears to mark the end of the increased wait times. Even after such training, however, teachers found it extremely difficult to maintain the new tempo of talk.

These observations point to at least one reason why any attempt to promote the use of more intellectually demanding questions from teachers seems not to have worked. We would not expect such demands to bear fruit unless longer silences were also achieved and this, as we have seen, is extremely difficult to do. It may be that we need to look to alternatives to questioning if we are to find teaching tactics which can, in fact, be acted on in the classroom. Perhaps silences, time for thought, can best be found elsewhere.

Alternatives to questioning

In everyday talk, question sometimes meets question. For example, if I ask a friend, 'Are you driving to town?', he or she might be well advised to enquire, 'Why do you ask?' before answering. Such question-question sequences are a sign of relative equality in discourse. They signal the fact that the person questioned is negotiating the conditions under which they are prepared to respond and are working out the possible implications of any answer he or she might give. We have almost never encountered question-question sequences in teacher-pupil talk where the second question was posed by a pupil. More generally, I suggest that pupils do not ask questions of their teacher (as opposed to peers and parents) because they do not feel free to take control, since the questioner dictates how his or her listener will spend the next few moments of thought. The strong asymmetry of power in interactions between teachers and children thus creates a powerful barrier to the achievement of interactions in which children display initiative, curiosity or negotiation. However, if one compares teachers in terms of the way in which they exercise control and use their powers, one unearths some striking differences both in the content and structure of teacher language and also in pupil performance. Pupils can be encouraged to take the initiative but, as we shall see, this demands tipping the balance of control in the pupils' direction. And tipping that balance demands attention to a teacher's use of questions and alternative conversational tactics.

Consider the list of conversational 'move types' illustrated below:

---

1. Enforced repetition   ('Say "I have one at home"').
2. Two-choice question   ('Did you have a good time?').
3. Wh-type question   ('Where did you go yesterday?').
4. Personal contribution   ('I think sugar is bad for you').
5. Phatic   ('Oh, lovely').

Main types of moves in discourse

Imagine a teacher uttering a move of each type in turn. An enforced repetition dictates the content of what the next speaker will have to say – if he or she complies with the demands of the utterance. Pupils, we find, are almost invariably compliant, responding to the 'force' of the teacher's utterance if they are able to do so. After an enforced repetition, then, what a pupil might have to offer is fully dictated. The next move type, a closed or two-choice question, can be answered with a single word, often with a gesture. Pupils might be expected to add more information than this and some, in fact, do. However, whether they are prepared to do so depends upon the manner in which the teacher manages the interaction, as we shall soon see.

Wh- type questions, like enforced repetitions, and two-choice questions, exert control over where the discourse next moves. They specify the focus or topic of what a compliant pupil will think and talk about next: 'Who . . . ?', 'Where . . . ?', 'Why . . . ?', and so on. Here, too, it might be hoped that the pupil who responds will not only answer the question but be motivated to expand, elaborate or explain his or her response. In practice, however, this almost never occurs. Pupils do their best to provide an answer and then relapse into silence.

On the other hand, when a teacher tells the class something, makes a 'personal contribution', one might expect one of any number of things to happen. Pupils might simply acknowledge what has been said, offer a contribution of their own or discuss the teacher's contribution between themselves. They might even address a question to the teacher (a rare happening, as we have seen). Similarly, after an acknowledgment or 'phatic move' from the teacher pupils could offer an acknowledgment back, raise a new direction or topic of talk, contribute, question, or address each other. In many different classrooms, we have found that each of these eventualities occur. These 'low control' moves from teachers engender the widest range, longest and most animated responses from pupils (for example, Wood and Wood, 1983; Wood and Wood, 1984).

The distribution of these various types of teacher talk throughout a lesson or part of a lesson influences the whole atmosphere of the classroom. Teachers who employ most controlling moves (i.e. frequently resort to the first three move types) face pupils who:

a) give short responses;
b) ask few, if any, questions;
c) seldom elaborate on their answers to any questions addressed to them;

d) talk to their peers only infrequently;

e) seldom volunteer their own thoughts or ideas when opportunities are left for them to do so;

f) show most frequent signs of confusion or misunderstanding.

On the other hand, teachers who give their own thoughts and ideas, who speculate, suggest or surmise, inform, interpret or illustrate, or who simply listen and acknowledge what children have to say, create a classroom climate which produces the mirror-image of this pattern. Even with pre-school aged children, I have found that youngsters will respond to speculation with speculation, hypothesis with hypothesis and suggestion with interpretation. Questions are not the only, nor are they usually the best, means of engendering evidence of thought.

If the aim of a lesson or teacher-pupil interaction is simply to establish whether or not facts have been learned and committed to memory, then talk which is rich in teacher questions and high in control will probably achieve the result intended. If, however, the aim is to discover what pupils think, what they want to know, or what they are prepared to share with their peers, then such lessons will prove self-defeating. If you wish to know 'where the learner is at' or where they would like to go next, then avoid frequent questions.

I have worked with a number of teachers – some working with pre-schoolers, others with deaf children, and yet others charged with the education of children with moderate to severe learning difficulties – to see if they are both willing and able to modify their style of talk. Working with the same groups of children, they try, on different days, to create sessions high in each of the types of discourse move illustrated above. I record, transcribe and analyse the ensuing interactions. In every case to date (and others have tried the same experiment in other parts of the world with similar results), I have found both that teachers can modify their style and that, when they do so, their pupils respond as we would expect, becoming more or less loquacious, displaying few or many signs of initiative, depending upon the style adopted by the teacher.

The first teacher to work with me in these studies had the following things to say about her experiences (the children in this study were severe to profoundly deaf seven year olds). She began by recording her 'natural' style, about which she writes:

> In the original tapes, the conversations between teacher and children were brief in duration, dominated by the teacher asking questions, with the children in a passive, question-answering role, making short responses.

After recording and analysing a series of sessions in which she sought to offer more personal contributions, she concluded:

> . . . the transcripts indicate that the children were able to contribute interesting information, with events described in detail and in time sequence, without being constantly bombarded with questions. Indeed, some information was unusual and unexpected and would not have been given had the child merely been answering questions . . . it was the teacher's personal contributions which made an impact. Sometimes they prompted the child to begin asking a series of questions.
>
> (Lees, 1981, p. 262)

I present below a short extract from another classroom study in which a teacher sets out to concentrate on asking two-choice questions to a pair of (non-disabled) four-year-old girls.

Transcript 1: Two-choice questions

TEACHER: Do you think it's lettuce she's feeding to the rabbit?
CHILD 2: Yes.
CHILD 1 : Yes, it's . . .
TEACHER (*interrupts*): Do you like lettuce?
CHILD 1: Yes.
CHILD 2 (*shakes head*): No.
TEACHER (*to Child 1*): To eat? Do you?
CHILD 1 : And my rabbit likes lettuce but me mum gives her a let . . . my rabbit, lettuce.
TEACHER: But do you like lettuce?
(*Child 1 nods*)
TEACHER: . . . to eat?
CHILD 1 (*nods*): Yes.
TEACHER: Yes. Good.
CHILD 2: I don't like tomatoes.
TEACHER: You don't like tomatoes either?
CHILD 2: No.
TEACHER: Oh dear, oh dear, oh dear. Uh, do you like cucumber?
CHILD 1: Yes!
CHILD 2: Yes!
TEACHER: You do like cucumber? That's green, isn't it, like lettuce?
(*Child 2 nods*)
CHILD 1: Like that! (*points to page of book*)
TEACHER: Yes, like that bird, yes, that's right. That's a green bird (*points*).
CHILD 1: He . . . (*points*) he had a got a . . .
TEACHER (*interrupts*): Can you see another green bird?
CHILD 2: Yes.

This session is typical of what I have found not only with pre-schoolers but also with school-aged children. Pupils' responses to the teacher are mainly short and factual. Although I have not added any timing measures to the transcript, the pace of interaction was fast, pauses between speakers seldom exceeding a second or so. Where children volunteer relevant topics for discussion (as when Child 1 says, 'And my rabbit likes lettuce . . .') the teacher tends to ignore the offering as she returns to her own line of questioning ('But do you like lettuce?'), and on two occasions, even in this short extract, she interrupts a child who attempted to enter the conversation. Another feature of teaching talk which is rich in specific questions is the simple grammatical structure of both teacher and child speech. While these observations come from a 'contrived' social encounter, the same relations between teacher questions and child participation are to be found when teachers 'naturally' adopt such a style of interaction.

In the next transcript, the teacher sets out to provide more personal contributions in a discussion with the same two girls.

Transcript 2: Teacher contributions

CHILD 1: And there's some lorries picking up the sand (*points to picture in a book*).

TEACHER (*nods*): It is, yes, it's a pick-up lorry.

CHILD 1: Picking-up lorry and putting it into the lorry what drives off.

TEACHER: Oh, I see. Oh, yes, that's, that's the one that picks it up. (*points*)

CHILD 1: And that's the one that takes it away and tips it out.

TEACHER: I see.

Later

TEACHER (*pointing to picture*): I think this boy must have used a special bucket to make that shape. (*i.e. on a sandcastle*)

CHILD 1: Perhaps he has . . . perhaps he cut some wood out and put it just there.

TEACHER: Perhaps he did what?

CHILD 1: Cut some wood and put it just there. (*points to page*) It looks like wood.

TEACHER: That piece looks like wood . . . it does, doesn't it?

CHILD 2: 'Tis wood, isn't it?

TEACHER: You think it's wood as well. Yes, I think you're right. He'd get it (*i.e. the sandcastle*) nice and smooth with a piece of wood.

CHILD 1: But that's some wood . . . look that's . . . (*points to picture*)

TEACHER: I guess it's wood that he's drawing with as well.

CHILD 1: It isn't. (*giggles*)

CHILD 2: No, that isn't.

TEACHER: That isn't? Oh.

CHILD 1: No, cos that's a pencil . . . the bottom of a pencil and it's, it's makes that shape, the bottom of a pencil.

TEACHER: Oh, he's using the bottom of a pencil to make that shape. Mmmm . . . perhaps you're right.

CHILD 2: What's that one? (*points to page*)

Later

TEACHER: I think she will take them (*i.e. flowers*) home with her when she's finished playing in the sandpit.

CHILD 1: That might be her home. (*pointing*)

TEACHER: It might be . . . I thought it was in the park.

CHILD 1: It isn't a park.

TEACHER: It isn't a park? Oh. There's lots of pictures in this book, and they all seem to be about a park, so I thought that was in the park.

CHILD 1: I wouldn't. I think it was a house.

TEACHER: In a house! It could be . . . well, it wouldn't be in the house, would it?

CHILD 1: No.

CHILD 2: No. I think it's outside the house.

TEACHER (*laughing*): Outside the house, it might be, mightn't it? Yes.

CHILD 2: In the garden.

CHILD 1: I got some sand in my garden, but sometimes, when I want to . . . me mum lets me bring . . . sometimes, sand in . . . some sand in . . .

The children experienced no difficulty in sustaining the interaction: they did not need constant questioning to keep them on task. When the teacher offers speculations ('I think this boy must have used a special bucket . . .'), pupils tend to respond in kind, opining that 'perhaps he cut some wood out . . .'. Later we find disagreements and negotiation emerging as both children challenge the teacher's guess that 'it's wood that he's drawing with'. Similarly, when the teacher and the first child offer different opinions about the location of an activity (does it take place in a park or a house?), the second child suggests that it may be taking place in a garden. We also see the emergence of child questions, as when the first child asks, 'What's that one?'

Again, such effects of teaching talk have emerged in both contrived and spontaneous classroom interactions involving a wide age range of children. Note too how, in comparison with the questioning session, the utterances of both teacher and children are more extended and structurally complex. There are no signs of teacher interruption, and the pace of the interaction is also much 'gentler' with both teacher and children leaving time for their partner to respond.

Socrates versus the evidence

The use of questions in education is now so commonplace that it seems a 'natural' feature of teaching talk. The evidence I have reviewed here suggests, however, that the continuation of the long-standing emphasis on the 'Socratic method' has itself to be called into question. As Dillon (1980) observes, for Socrates questioning was a dialectical process in which both teacher and student shared a joint inquiry in the search for a truth which was unknown to both participants. This contrasts sharply with the character of most classroom questions which typically involve the pupil in an attempt to provide answers which are already known to the teacher: a quiz rather than a collaborative search for knowledge and understanding.

Alternatives to teacher questions, which include telling, speculating, suggesting, negotiating and listening, can and do promote active and relevant involvement of pupils in classroom discussion. Such alternatives free pupils to give their own views, to reveal their knowledge and uncertainties and to seek information and explanation through questions of their own. Once the pupil has helped to shape the verbal agenda, any teacher question which arises is more likely to relate to the pupil's thinking on the subject and to involve a genuine attempt on the teacher's part to solicit knowledge or ideas from the pupil. Perhaps, then, we do have the means to move closer towards the Socratic ideal. In doing so, however, we must question our own questions and tip the balance of power and control towards the pupil.

Acknowledgement

Thanks to Mrs Bennett, teacher at Dunkirk Primary School, Nottingham, now retired.

References

BRONFENBRENNER, U. (1977) 'Toward an experimental ecology of human development', *American Psychologist*, 32, 513–31.
DILLON, J. T. (1982) 'The multidisciplinary study of questioning', *Journal of Educational Psychology*, 74, 147–65.

DILLON, J. T. (1980) 'Paper Chase and the Socratic method of teaching law', *Journal of Legal Education*, 30, 529–35.

GOLDMAN-EISER, F. (1968) *Psycholinguistics: Experiments in spontaneous speech.* New York: Academic Press.

GOODY, E. N. (ed.) (1978) *Questions and Politeness.* Cambridge: Cambridge University Press.

KERRY, T. (1987) Classroom questions in England, *Questioning Exchange*, Vol 1, No. 1, 32–3.

LEES, J. (1981) 'Conversational strategies with deaf children'. Unpublished M. Phil. thesis, University of Nottingham.

LEVIN, H., SILVERMAN, I. AND FORD, B. (1967) 'Hesitations in children's speech during explanation and description', *Journal of Verbal Learning and Verbal Behaviour*, 6, 560–4.

SUSSKIND, E. (1969) 'The role of question-asking in the elementary school classroom', in Kaplan, F. and Sarason, S. (eds.) (1969) *The Psycho-educational Clinic.* New Haven: Yale University Press.

SWIFT, J. N. and GOODING, C. T. (1983) 'Interaction of wait time feedback and questioning instruction on middle school science teaching', *Journal of Research in Science Teaching*, 20, 721–30.

SWIFT, J. N., GOODING, C. T. AND SWIFT, P. R. (1988) 'Questions and wait time', in Dillon, J. T. (ed.) *Questioning and Discussion: A Multi-Disciplinary Study.* Norwood, N. J.: Ablex (pp. 192–211).

TAYLOR, I. (1969) 'Content and structure in sentence production', *Journal of Verbal Learning and Verbal Behaviour*, 8, 170–5.

WOOD, D. AND WOOD, H. (1988) 'Questioning versus student initiative', in Dillon, J. T. (ed.) (1988) *Questioning and Discussion: A Multi-Disciplinary Study.* Norwood, N. J.: Ablex (pp. 280–305).

WOOD, H. AND WOOD, D. (1983) 'Questioning the pre-school child', *Educational Review*, 35, 149–62.

WOOD, H. AND WOOD, D. (1984) 'An experimental evaluation of five styles of teacher conversation on the language of hearing-impaired children', *Journal of Child Psychology and Psychiatry*, 25, (1), 131–47.

4.5

Talk for Teaching-and-Learning

NEIL MERCER

Introduction

The National Oracy Project has generated a new and informed interest in children's collaborative learning through talk, and particularly in the educational potential of talk between children when a teacher is not present. I think members of the Project would agree that, with some notable exceptions (see Roy Corden's article in this section), they initially gave less emphasis to the functions of talk between children and teachers. This relative emphasis reflected a concern to assert the value there is in giving children control over their own learning, and a wish to encourage teachers to respect children's competence as language users. I do not wish to question those concerns or the achievements they generated. But any consideration of the value of talk for learning must also pay attention to the ways that teachers can – and should – shape children's learning. There are, therefore, two aspects of classroom talk that I want to focus on here: the ways that teachers' talk to pupils functions as a guide and support for their learning, and the role of the teacher as the planner, organiser and evaluator of children's talk activities.

Teaching and learning, or 'teaching-and-learning'?

In his article, 'The Role of Talk in Learning', Douglas Barnes says, 'Whatever teaching methods a teacher chooses . . . it will always be the pupil who has to do the learning'. This is patently true, but it is also true that:

a) the methods the teacher employs may have a profound effect on what is learned, and how it is learned;
b) good teaching means choosing methods which take account of the needs of the learner;
c) teaching requires some learning on the part of the teacher, because teachers must continually monitor their pupils' understanding in order to support the further development of their understanding.

What is more, learning in school has a special relationship to the culture of the society in which the school is located. If, like Vygotsky, you believe that 'the very essence of cultural development is in the collision between mature cultural forms of behaviour with the primitive forms which characterise the child's behaviour' (Vygotsky, 1981, p. 151), then interactions between teachers and children cannot be treated as anything other than crucial in any examination of learning in school. It is through communicating with their teachers that children become aware of the special nature of educational knowledge, as something distinct from everyday kinds of ideas and social practices. I am not intending here to demean such 'everyday' kinds of understanding, merely to distinguish them from the kinds of knowledge involved in studying science, maths, geography and so on. If we are interested in how children become educated rather than simply in how they acquire some understanding of the world in general, then the process we must be concerned with is never simply one of *learning* but of *teaching-and-learning*.

Some functions of teacher-talk

If you ask anyone who is not a teacher what the main reason why talk has to be used in a classroom is, he or she will probably say that teachers need to talk in order to tell children what they are to do, how they are to do it, when to start and when to stop. Teachers certainly do these things, and, of course, one very important function of talk for teachers is to control the behaviour of children. Indeed, in the absence of corporal punishment, talk is the main tool of control in the classroom. Educational researchers from some disciplines, notably sociologists and linguists, have shown great interest in classroom talk as a medium through which teachers attempt to control children's behaviour, and through which roles and identities are defined and maintained. However, teachers also use talk for many other purposes. They assess children's learning through talking to children and listening to what they say, and they provide children with educational experiences which would be hard to provide by any means other than talk (for example, telling stories, reading poetry, describing events, supplying factual information in an accessible form). The educational researchers mentioned above have shown much less interest in this aspect of talk, where it is a medium for sharing knowledge, and one through which adults influence the representations of reality, the interpretations of experience, which children eventually adopt.

An extremely important function of talk in the classroom is as a means for *developing shared understanding*. Through joint action and talk, participants in the process of teaching and learning build a body of common knowledge which provides a contextual basis for further educational activity. This applies to activities in which a teacher is talking with pupils, and to those in which pupils are working together. The extent to which educational knowledge becomes 'common' to teachers and pupils is one measure of the effectiveness of the educational process.

Why do teachers ask questions?

Teachers are sometimes not only accused of asking too many questions, they are also accused of behaving oddly because they ask questions to which they already know the answers. This does seem, on first consideration, to be a rather peculiar kind of language behaviour. (There are even jokes about it – Teacher: 'How many millimetres in a centimetre?' Pupil: 'If you don't know, you should be in a different job!'). Some sociologists – and some teachers – have used this discovery to criticise the extent to which teachers set up communicative patterns in the classroom which are at odds with 'normal' conversational practices, and which limit children's opportunities for self-expression and exploration through talk: but do such judgments really take into account what teachers are trying to achieve through talking to children in class?

Asking questions to which they know the answer only seems odd if teachers' behaviour is judged against some general and abstract standards of language use, whereby the only acceptable function of a question is to provide the answer to someone who doesn't already know it. Such standards cannot be appropriately applied to the classroom, because – as with all situational varieties of language – the nature and function of teacher-talk need to be considered in context. To understand teachers' unusual use of questions, we need to know why they ask them.

In order to plan and evaluate their teaching and assess the learning of their pupils, teachers need constantly to monitor children's knowledge and understanding. Most of the questions they ask are meant to serve this purpose. Research (for example, Willes, 1983) has shown that, on entering school, children very quickly become familiar with the conventions of teacher-pupil interchanges (the joke above is only funny if you know what is normal in the classroom), so we might expect there to be few misunderstandings about the kinds of questions which are being asked. However, misunderstandings about *what* is being asked may well arise because teachers often avoid asking direct, explicit questions. Consider the following sequence from a science lesson in a British secondary school classroom, in which the pupils have been doing a series of practical activities about air pressure:

TEACHER: Well we blew into it, and what happened?
PUPIL 1: All the water came out of the straw.
PUPIL 2: The water came out of the S-top.
TEACHER: All came out! Now, why? Come on! This one's easy.
PUPIL 1: Cos when you were blowing bubbles in, all the . . . air came up the straw . . . and the water with it.
PUPILS (*together*): Into the bottle.
TEACHER: Into the bottle! So was there more air in here or less air?
PUPILS (*together*): More.
TEACHER: More air, wasn't there? There was a lot more air in here. Now this air . . . wanted to do what?
PUPILS (*clash of voices*): Get out. Push water . . . push water outside to get room for itself.
TEACHER: Yes, ah. That's a very good answer.
(Barnes, 1976, pp. 73–4)

In this extract, the teacher uses questions in a kind of 'guessing game' to draw out from the children some key ideas of the lesson. The questions thus are not merely for assessment; they are *part of the teaching*. Teachers use questions not only to monitor children's understanding, but also to guide their learning. Through talk, teachers mark some knowledge and experience as significant. They also attempt to create continuities between past, present and future events in children's classroom experience. Knowledge and experience which is not considered educationally significant or valuable by a teacher will normally be marked as such in their talk, either by simply ignoring it or by dismissing it more explicitly.

Marking knowledge as significant and joint

One of the most obvious ways in which teachers mark knowledge as significant or otherwise is in their evaluative feedback to children's responses to their questions. For example, 'wrong' answers to a teacher's questions are commonly followed by one of the following events:

a) the teacher says the answer is wrong;
b) the teacher ignores the wrong answer.

The teacher is then likely to ask the question again, either in the same words or in a paraphrased form.

Teachers also mark the significance of elements of knowledge and experience in other, more subtle ways. Derek Edwards and I (for example, Edwards and Mercer, 1987) described three features of teachers' discourse which illustrate this. They are 'cued elicitations', 'joint knowledge markers', and 'reconstructive recaps'.

Cued elicitations are exchanges in which the teacher asks children questions while simultaneously providing heavy clues to the information required. This 'cueing' may be achieved by wording the question in a particular way, but it is in fact often accomplished by some other means such as intonation, pausing, gestures or physical demonstrations. The extract below, from a primary school lesson, provides a good example of this. The teacher is talking to a group of children about Galileo's studies of pendulums. (Note: non-verbal features of the discourse are shown in italics, and emphatic speech is in bold type. Pauses of less than two seconds are shown by /, and longer pauses by //.)

TEACHER: Now he didn't have a watch / but he **had** on **him** something that was a very good timekeeper that he could use to hand straight away /

Teacher snaps fingers on 'straight away' and looks invitingly at pupils as if inviting a response.

You've got it. I've got it. What is it? // What could we use to count beats? What have **you** got? //	*Teacher points on 'You've' and 'I've', then beats her hand slowly on the table, looking around at the pupils who smile and shrug.*
You can feel it **here**.	*She put her fingers on her wrist pulse.*
PUPILS: Pulse.	*Speaking in near unison.*
TEACHER: A pulse. Everybody see if you can find it.	*All copy the teacher, feeling for wrist pulses.*

(adapted from Edwards and Mercer, 1987, p. 142)

When we used the term *joint knowledge markers,* we meant teachers' use of certain ways of talking to indicate that some shared experience – something said or done – is particularly significant and relevant to a current problem or activity in the classroom. One common way in which teachers do this is by using 'we' when recalling an event, as in: 'When we did the Normans last term, we said that they came from France.' Another way is by emphasising that what a pupil has said is a particularly 'good' comment or answer (as in the extract from Barnes, 1976, above), and by perhaps referring back to this gem of wisdom later in the lesson.

Reconstructive recaps are occasions on which teachers feel it necessary to 'rewrite history'. They are accounts of past activities or events shared with the children which highlight those features which the teacher sees as being of most educational significance, and which play down aspects seen as irrelevant or confusing. Thus a teacher summarising a class discussion might decide to leave out all the 'red herrings' raised in the process. I can offer an extreme example from a secondary science class: although a series of mishaps had thwarted all but one of many attempts by pupils to create a vacuum in a bell-jar, the teacher involved subsequently referred to this occasion as simply 'the lesson in which you made a vacuum'.

Some implications for classroom practice

I have tried to describe some of the communicative functions of teachers' talk in the classroom. It seems obvious to me that education cannot be achieved without such input from teachers. However, what is crucial is the *quality* of teachers' communications with children. 'Joint knowledge markers', 'reconstructive recaps' and any other such features of teacher-talk are only useful if they help pupils make better sense of what they are trying to do in class. (Telling children to remember the lesson in which they 'made a vacuum' when they had done nothing of the sort might not score very highly against this criterion!) I mentioned earlier the important function of classroom talk for developing a shared understanding between teachers and pupils. The features which are described above point to some of the ways in which teachers attempt to create a continuous, shared and contextual basis for children's learning. The success of such attempts will, however, inevitably vary.

The analysis above also suggests that the special nature of teachers' questions is understandable if we see that they may be intended to serve more than one function. They may not only inform a teacher about the current state of pupils' knowledge, but also assist the further development of that knowledge. This gives us two possible explanations why teachers sometimes avoid direct, explicit questions: they may want to avoid 'putting words into children's mouths' because that would not test children's real understanding, or they may feel that children should be required to put some 'mental effort' into making connections between work they have done in the past and the task in hand. On some occasions, a question could even be intended to serve both these functions. Whether teachers' questions function effectively in these and other ways is a suitable subject for research. We still need to develop a theoretically sound and practically applicable method for evaluating teachers' talk as a form of intervention in children's learning. (My colleagues and I explore one approach in the second article of this section.)

My own belief is that good teachers are those who are able to help pupils see the point and purpose of what they are doing in class, and so enable them, in the tangled jungle of educational experience, to see the wood for the trees. This does not simply apply to situations in which activity is self-evidently teacher-led. The educational value of any classroom talk between children, with or without a teacher present, may hinge on how well a teacher has set up activities and environments for generating and supporting suitable kinds of talk. This point is well illustrated by a case study written by Dorothy Steel (1991), a primary teacher whose involvement with the National Oracy Project focused on the quality of talk around computers in the classroom. In discussing a group activity set up by herself and colleagues in her school, she comments:

> We had rather naively assumed that just because the children were grouped round the computer together that they would be actively collaborating. Closer observation of what was actually taking place

revealed some disturbing findings . . . Dominant personalities and fast readers dictated the rate of progress through the programs . . . this was not an atmosphere of active collaboration but one of competitiveness within groups and a very limited range of talk.

(1991, p. A223)

After some reflection, Steel and her colleagues decided that what was required was a major intervention, whereby the children were taken off the computer-based activity and instead followed a series of carefully-planned activities designed to:

a) extend the range of their experience of collaborative work;
b) develop their awareness and analytic understanding of group work (through what Steel calls 'talking about the talking').

When these children subsequently returned to the computer, both they and their teacher brought with them much new, relevant knowledge and understanding. Thus Steel comments:

Second time around I approached the program in a different light. The term spent 'talking about talking' with the children had changed my perceptions of their capabilities. I was now able to visualise 'oracy opportunities' much more readily . . . (Group activities) proved very successful and generated a lot of excitement. Each group had to come to a consensus and be able to justify their decision to other groups. Many ingenious reasons were cited and a high degree of collaboration was evident.

(p. A224)

Real progress had been made, it would seem, because of two kinds of teacher involvement in the children's collaborative activity. First, the teachers involved used an evaluation of children's observed talk to set up much more carefully structured kinds of collaborative tasks (away from, as well as at, the computer). Secondly, a teacher spent some time listening to the children's views about what they were doing, and encouraging them to become more aware of how they communicated when working together. Among other benefits, such interventions on the part of the teacher would almost certainly help the children involved to see quite what they were meant to achieve, and why the teacher wanted them to achieve it. That is, through their teacher's efforts they could become more aware of what are sometimes called the 'educational ground rules' (Edwards and Mercer, 1987, Sheeran and Barnes, 1991), the tacit expectations that underlie all educational tasks.

For pupils, the educational value of any kind of activities – including 'talk activities' like collaborative problem solving and discussions – will almost certainly depend on the extent to which they are able to understand the ground rules. I am not suggesting that children should be trained uncritically to accept these requirements of the educational system, but they do need to be helped to understand those requirements, as operated by their teachers, and to relate them to their own experience and their own ways of learning. This is itself part of the process of becoming educated, as much as is the acquisition of more specific kinds of curriculum knowledge. Some educational ground rules – those relating to the principles of scientific method, for example – represent the effort of generations in devising a system of thought which will transform experience into knowledge and understanding.

I hope, therefore, that I have justified my belief that oracy concerns should include a critical examination of the role of the teacher in talk activities. The development of children's understanding is crucially dependent on the ways teachers organise activities for talk, the extent to which they explain the point and purpose of those activities to children, and how they use talk to help children to gain an education from what could otherwise be mere experience.

References

BARNES, D. (1976) *From Communication to Curriculum*. Harmondsworth: Penguin.

EDWARDS, D. AND MERCER, N. (1987) *Common Knowledge*. London: Methuen.

SHEERAN, Y. AND BARNES, D. (1991) *School Writing: discovering the ground rules*. Milton Keynes: Open University Press.

STEEL, D. (1991) 'Granny's Garden' in *Talk and Learning 5–16, an in-service pack on oracy for teachers*. Milton Keynes: The Open University.

VYGOTSKY, L. (1981) 'The genesis of higher mental functions' in Wertsch, J. (ed.) (1981) *The Concept of Activity in Soviety Psychology*. Amonk, N.Y.: Sharpe.

WILLES, M. (1983) *Children Into Pupils: a study of language in early schooling*. London: Routledge and Kegan Paul.

'No, We Ask You Questions'

LAURA BRIERLEY, IRENA CASSAR,

PAULINE LOADER, KATE NORMAN,

IRENE SHANTRY, SIMON WOLFE

AND

DAVE WOOD

> Attention should be given to ways of improving the quality of classroom talk and using it to stimulate and challenge children's thinking. In particular, more discriminating use should be made of questioning as a classroom strategy.

This quotation, from the summary of *Primary Education in Leeds* (Alexander, 1991), confirms a trend towards more serious consideration of the effectiveness of questioning as a support to learning. Some researchers, notably J. T. Dillon and David Wood (see the article in this section), have for some years been raising a fundamental pedagogical issue: 'Does the prevalent mode of teacher talk – the question – impede children's learning, and are there preferable alternatives?' This is not just an academic debate, but one that can make a crucial difference to the ability of children to get full benefit from the curriculum.

There are, as Roy Corden demonstrates in this section (see article 4.1), many appropriate teacher discourse modes in supporting children's learning, ranging from that of listener to transmitter of information. The focus in this article is on those areas of classroom practice which require both pupils and teacher, whether in small group or whole class, to talk. Put very simply, the issue is this: children can and should use talk in interactive situations to clarify, explore, ask questions, in every way 'work on understanding'. They can do this with their peers. But they also need to be able to do it with their teachers, because in that way they can learn from their teachers' greater knowledge, expertise and experience. Teachers need pupils to talk in these ways because they can then fit their own input much more closely to their pupils' level of understanding. Children need to 'think aloud' to help them understand – teachers need children to 'think aloud' to guide their learning effectively.

But the predominant mode of teacher talk in these situations is the question, usually followed by evaluation and/or another question. And all the evidence shows that teacher questions do not generally encourage thinking aloud so much as 'getting the right answer' and short, unelaborated responses. Teachers' intentions are therefore frustrated, and learning is held back. If there are more effective alternatives, as Dillon and Wood have suggested, then these should be given much more serious attention and, at the very least, be in every teacher's repertoire.

In summer 1991, a group of teachers from the National Oracy Project met Kate Norman, one of the Project officers, to consider and respond to some of the articles in this section, with particular reference to the issue of 'questions'. The teachers involved taught children of different ages, in different areas of the country; they had different subject specialisms or interests; some had been teaching a long time; others were in the early stages of their career. What they had in common was a commitment to the use of oracy in their classroom and a particular interest in the role of the teacher in promoting it. Issues were discussed from the point of view of a practitioner – the person who actually has to implement the idea.

We began, as Neil Mercer had done, by asking why teachers used questions so intensively. We agreed with him that one reason is to 'monitor children's knowledge and understanding', but we did not agree that this was the main function of questions, feeling that they were more often used to guide learning, a function he also identifies. Within that rather broad intention, there were, we felt, several distinct, though related functions. Teachers ask questions to get children to talk, to improve their confidence and their ability to express themselves; they ask questions to stimulate thought and encourage children to make cognitive links; and, surprisingly, they ask questions in order to impart new information through processes such as 'cued elicitation'. The group believed that for all these functions there were more effective alternatives, which should be explored more fully. Discussions ranged over the complexities of the issues, and each teacher wrote a short personal account, reflecting on his or her own practice.

We were all agreed that one certain improvement in classroom practice would be for teachers to listen more, and more attentively, to children – that this on its own would meet many of the aims of questioning. Pupils would talk more thoughtfully, and the listening teacher would find out more about what children know and think. Pauline Loader, a reception teacher, reflects on the difficulties and benefits:

From twenty minutes of talk at the collage table in the nursery:

MRS RAYNER: Right. Are you going to colour those? D'you know what colour the moon is?

TERRY: White.

MRS RAYNER: Sometimes, yes . . . and sometimes a bit yellow.

TERRY: Yeah . . . a bit yellow. What, a little bit?

MRS RAYNER: Sometimes it is; sometimes it's white; sometimes a little bit yellow. What about a star?

TERRY: What's that . . . why? Sometimes is it growing into yellow?

MRS RAYNER: I think it must be something to do with how dark it is whether it looks white or whether it looks yellow.

TERRY: I'll do a bit yellow and white.

The depth and quality of this conversation between Terry, aged four, and the nursery nurse are dependent on her ability to listen. She respects and values what he has to say and they are equal partners in the talk: they speculate, question, reason, comment and sustain the conversation.

How can the same quality be achieved in a busy classroom with 30+ children and the teacher in a managerial role? It's certainly a challenging thought. A climate needs to be fostered where the children's ideas, questions and comments are nurtured. Not an easy task.

I've found it useful to grab every opportunity to give the children the floor to talk about an interest, their news or a piece of their work, and to listen intently myself. This provides a listening model for the other children so that they learn to listen respectfully to each other. I try whenever possible not to ask questions to which they know I know the answer! Often we discuss a question or a topic and we hypothesise and speculate together. I try to allow time for them to think; to formulate their ideas into words.

It's difficult sometimes not to hear the answer you want to hear. For example, we were brainstorming the topic of talk: How does talk help us learn?

PAUL: I talk . . . I've got a good brain and I can do the lessons when I'm talking.

I immediately took this up as being about the importance of thinking aloud in order to clarify your ideas. Paul did not comment, and the discussion continued . . .

DAVID: This is what happens in your mind . . . You can do thinking if you don't know what to say and then you think and talk in your brain and you know what to do.

Paul nodded. This is what he had meant.

Eventually I'm working towards a situation where they can support and sustain each other's talk by listening. Sometimes it does happen. Here's Robert and John discussing photos of themselves as babies:

JOHN: That's when I was up to mischief and I didn't get dressed . . . I went for a ride there.
ROBERT: On holiday?
JOHN: Um.
ROBERT: You're growing up, ain't ye?
JOHN: There's my sister and me.
ROBERT: Yeah.
JOHN: That's me again . . . That's my nanny and grandad . . . This is when I had my birthday.

Pauline told the group:

We were reading *My School* by Sumiko and comparing our school with the one described in the book. One page was about the teacher being kind and asking the children lots of questions. I asked, half-jokingly, if I was like that. They replied, 'No, we ask *you* questions!'

We discussed the oddity, raised by Dillon (1988), that in schools it is the people who know who ask questions and those who don't know who are expected to answer them. Irena Cassar's account explores the notion that identifying their own questions motivates pupils to learn, and also indicates to teachers what pupils do and do not understand:

My personal experience as a secondary history teacher suggests that students are capable of making valid choices about their own learning and setting their own questions. In planning for work on the topic of 'Equality/Discrimination', I decided that instead of starting with my questions which inevitably define the type of learning that follows, I would invite the students to work out and decide what questions they wanted to have answered in the ensuing lessons.

At the beginning of the unit I simply told them the topic. I asked them, first in pairs, then in fours and subsequently in sixes (known as the 'snowball' activity) to discuss and make a list of what they wanted to find out during that unit of work. One pair's questions are over the page.

1. Have you ever discriminated against anybody?
2. Has anybody ever discriminated against you?
3. How long has racism been around and who started it?
4. What do you think about discrimination?
5. Has your husband ever discriminated against you?
6. What do you think about discrimination in the Gulf War?
7. What do you think about the IRA?
8. What age do you think people should fight at?
9. Why are people prejudiced?
10. Are you or your husband racist?

These questions are mainly personal, intended to find out where I stand in relation to the topic. This shows the need pupils feel to have an honest, two-way relationship with their teacher. Teachers often ask pupils to reveal their experiences and thoughts on a topic. Pupils need to feel they have the same right.

Of ten questions they were asked to come up with, only two cover general topics: 'How long has racism been around and who started it?' and 'Why are people prejudiced?' Other groups also presented a similar balance between general questions and personal questions related to what I thought or have experienced about each issue.

The general questions were also the ones I had decided I wanted to cover in the lessons. This may appear devious. Was I, the teacher and 'expert', still controlling their learning? What I felt was important was that they were involved in the decision-making process and that this involvement would enhance their motivation to learn. It had become *their* lesson, *their* choice of what to learn.

Some of the questions written by pupils at first glance may appear irrelevant to the topic, such as those on the IRA. However, this question shows that pupils are capable of making valid connections. The fine (and controversial) distinction between the concept of freedom fighters and terrorists was not one I had had in mind when preparing for the topic. Teachers who use this type of approach may find that they have to tackle a topic for which they have made no preparation. Does that feel threatening or an exciting possibility? That will depend on the individual.

Another idea I have experimented with was the 'inverted lesson'. It had occurred to me that educational courses often leave teachers with a feeling of disappointment because queries remain unanswered. Pupils may have similar feelings at the end of a lesson or unit of work. With that in mind, I often provide them with space/time at the end of a lesson to prepare a set of questions, preferably with a partner, which I have not covered in the lesson but which interest them.

One interesting aspect of Irena's account is the set of questions that were addressed to her as an individual. One underlying theme of our discussions was the importance of the pupils perceiving teachers as 'real' people with personalities, histories, areas of expertise and areas of uncertainty. The power of some of the alternatives to questions lies in the fact that, unlike questions, they involve teachers in stating their own view, giving information, sharing their thinking. Simon Wolfe shows how giving pupils a genuine account of an experience that happened to him stimulated them to think more deeply about a literary episode:

I read David Wood's article, 'Teaching Talk', with a great deal of sympathy. He suggests that questions asked by the teacher to the class or to a large group often tend to block or close off pupil talk, and what concerns me is the sort of class atmosphere that is created by teachers asking questions to which they already know the answers. What sort of message does this give, and how confident does it make pupils to offer their ideas, to think aloud, or to feel in any way able to voice opinions?

It is possible to remove the control of direct questioning and to offer, instead, an anecdote as a means of eliciting response. We were reading *Tom's Midnight Garden*, and I built in an opportunity, when Tom enters the garden for the second time, for the class to consider why Tom is so captivated by the garden. I stopped reading and, instead, sat there and told the class a story: it was about a time when I was young and was up very early in the morning and heard the birds start singing. It was summer, about 4 am, maybe a bit earlier, and I described rushing around the house looking for a tape-recorder to record this amazing birdsong, which I thought I must be the first person in the whole world to hear.

Telling the class about this experience established a relaxed atmosphere which allowed them to share similar experiences of late night adventures. They gave these incredible accounts of looking for foxes and badgers on Hadleigh Downs; of being up very late because of illness and about the strange things that they had noticed for the very first time. There was not a child in the room who did not, very desperately, have something to share and, after telling these stories, there was not a child who did not appreciate why Tom loved being in the garden so late at night.

It is also possible for the teacher to slip into the role of non-expert (not always a very difficult role to play). Again with *Tom's Midnight Garden*, I speculated aloud about what was actually going on in the garden at night. Tom had just entered the garden and was wondering why the grass and trees and flowers appear at night to have no colour or only a very dull shade. I stopped my reading and went into role. I did know the answer, but I just said, 'I wonder why that is . . .?' I was not sure how the pupils would react, but I need not have worried. They started to speculate aloud and to help me. Had I simply asked, 'Why has the garden no colour?' I expect, at best, I would have received a direct answer, maybe from a child with a scientific background and, at worst, only blank stares. Instead, most of the thirty children took turns to think aloud and to build on the points or ideas made by others. They felt confident to offer opinions, and they were also clearly enjoying themselves.

Simon's second example raises a question we debated at length – in what circumstances is it acceptable to 'pretend' not to know in order to get pupils to think? Is saying 'I wonder . . .', when one has a fair idea of the right answer, only another form of pseudo-question? Our feeling was that there was a significant difference – that it signalled acceptance of speculation, the possibility of alternative answers in a way that a question did not. Irene Shantry's account develops this theme:

> My awareness of the value of adopting the role of the 'non-expert' grew out of a small classroom incident. While writing out an address, I said, half to myself, 'Is that how you spell Jamaica?' Then I turned to the group of five and six year old children with me and said, laughingly, 'I can't spell Jamaica. Can you?' The response was immediate: 'I can'; 'So can I'; 'I can, my aunty lives in Jamaica'; 'It's in the story'. There was a rush to the book area and several hands presented me with the book *Jamaica's Find* by Juanita Havill.
>
> I decided to build on this enthusiasm and discussed with the children the problem I had with many other words. I presented myself as a learner, thereby creating the situation where they felt that they had to do something to help me. The children shared with me some of the methods they had learned to enable them to deal with spelling. For example, to spell 'friend', simply take the first bit of 'Friday' from the class calendar and then add 'end'. Another child showed me how a dictionary could be a valuable asset. From that point, I decided to change the emphasis of my questioning strategy. 'How would . . .?' became 'I wonder how . . .?', on the premise that the way a question is asked is as important as the actual question.
>
> On another occasion I deliberately adopted the role of 'non-expert' as a way of assessing the geographical skills of a group of five and six year olds. Geography AT 1, level 2, calls for the use of geographical vocabulary, possibly in discussion of pictorial and tourist maps. I wanted to find out what the children understood without using direct questioning. As David Wood says in his article: 'If you wish to know where the learner is at or where they would like to go next, then avoid frequent questioning.' I suggested that I had a problem. I needed to go to Notting Hill Gate in London, but I did not know how to find the way. The following suggestions were offered: 'Go in a car', 'Get a bus' and, from a quiet voice, 'Get a map'. This was from a child who presents himself as shy and uncommunicative, but whose only need is thinking time. When the map was obtained the children pored over it

excitedly, their ability to navigate becoming obvious. Leo asked, 'How are you going to London?' When I told him I was going by train, he then asked, 'Which station in London?' He was looking for my starting point. He clearly understood that, in order to solve my problem, he had to know where I was starting from. The children set about the task of finding Paddington station and talked confidently about the underground symbols on the map. Once the station was located, the activity progressed to discovering the map index, looking up co-ordinates, discussing street names and arranging that I should catch a number 27 bus!

I believe this 'non-expert' approach is a very positive way of developing children's learning. It creates relationships of trust and co-operation. The children's response is very different from that to more direct evaluative questioning. They take the initiative more frequently; are no longer hesitant about speaking and are less anxious about putting themselves in the limelight. They work out the answer together and enjoy the responsibility of helping the teacher. Recently, I wondered if I was taking the 'non-expert' approach too far. Sian had written a story book and was puzzling over its title. I asked a factual question, 'What is your title to be?' She replied slowly and deliberately, 'Well, I'd like to call it "pandemonium", but I don't think mummy and daddy will know what I mean.' Then she added 'Perhaps mummy might.'

Irene comments on how children take the initiative when there is a shift in perception away from the idea of the teacher as all-knowing. Laura Brierley set out to get evidence of a teacher managing to support a group's thinking without dominating, using a variety of strategies. She also points out the enhanced assessment opportunities that being able to listen to pupils offers:

After our discussion of issues raised by David Wood, I set out to collect evidence in my Year 6 classroom of children working on a task where the teacher was present but not dominant. I tried to give 'wait time' and to use what David Wood calls 'low control moves' – speculating, suggesting or acknowledging rather than questioning – while being prepared to offer specific help when needed.

I decided to give a group of four children a picture puzzle to solve. Before beginning the discussion the children were asked to think about the puzzle on their own and do a bit of 'think-writing'. (I find this a very useful device for ensuring that children bring their individual ideas to a group discussion). A lengthy discussion then followed, which I taped. There were several silences and long sections where I said nothing at all. In the commentary that follows, I have picked out some contrasting examples of my interventions.

At the very beginning of the discussion session I was happy to allow a two minute period of silence before the first child spoke. He put forward an idea which was supported by a second child. These two children continued this pattern for a time, after which I intervened with a statement to reassure them that they were on the right track. 'OK, . . . so the idea about the man and the dog in a hit and run accident is what's made you look for dog and man's prints in the snow.'

Reassured, the children began speaking in increasingly lengthy bursts of dialogue. The children shared their initial ideas and were excited when consensus of opinion led to the solution of parts of the puzzle. I needed to say very little but decided to ask one question in order to get the children to clarify their ideas. This question was phrased so that it would not appear persuasive: 'Why would the two feet be next to each other, I wonder?' It is important to note that the children also asked questions of each other.

On one occasion, in response to a direct question, I offered an explanation, but it was rejected:

PETER: But, I mean, how come there's two exactly the same footprints going along the side like that?

TEACHER: Well, the idea of running there is quite . . . quite reasonable, because he might run on his toes.

PETER: That just doesn't look right. Cos he might have stopped there, but how come there's just keeps going two footprints and they're both the same?

At two points, the children seemed not to be moving forward in solving the puzzle. In the first case, I asked a question to introduce another aspect for consideration:

TEACHER: What's that there?

PETER: That's two footprints.

TEACHER: Where did they come from then?

PETER: Exactly. Because there's nothing leading up to it. No footprints.

MARTIN: Bicycle! When he's riding along he could put his feet down. (*a sudden insight*)

In the second case, the children had made wrong deductions. I avoided saying they were wrong, but offered an alternative way of looking at things: 'His feet needn't have been next to each other at the same time, need they?'

After twenty minutes, the children had all been actively involved in solving the puzzle. They had done this in an enjoyable way and were uninhibited by the presence of a teacher. The session was concluded with a second 'think-write', in which the children were asked to write an assessment of the sorts of thinking and talking they had done. The children's assessments of their performances in this activity closely matched my assessments of them:

'We had to think out all the possibilities then think which would have been the most likely one to have happened. We had to use the clues given and then use our initiative and brainpower and try to fit everyone's ideas together to solve the puzzle we were set.'

Children are perceptive and capable when given appropriate support. By taking a significant but low-key part in discussions, I can not only develop the children's thinking but give myself valuable assessment opportunities.

Laura pointed out that this approach is far more than just a strategy — it requires a history of respect for children's ideas. Dave Wood makes the case very powerfully that this is the fundamental requirement:

One clear difficulty for me in any consideration of teacher talk is that a good deal of cogent and relevant linguistic research has been focused exclusively on the utterance of the teacher and subsequent pupil response. I believe, though, that analysis of utterances in isolation can only give, at best, a partial view and, at worst, present a distorted picture. I have a social view of language that has been shaped and constantly reinforced by my classroom experience. Teacher-pupil dialogue does not take place in a vacuum. Classrooms are governed by powerful social conventions: by peer group pressure exerted by whole classes on individuals and by traditional expectations of what forms appropriate teacher-pupil dialogue and accepted classroom practice. Teachers have been aware of powerful peer group forces in managing classroom 'discipline' issues. How often have we all postponed discussions with individuals until the end of the lesson because the whole class or group situation did not offer what we have judged to be an appropriate context? But teachers have not always applied this knowledge in shaping learning experiences which allow children to interact with teachers in a variety of ways in a range of contexts. And we have been even less aware of the forces which act on ourselves, pulling us towards a conformity in classroom practice which can stifle talk for learning before it has had a chance to breathe.

As David Wood shows, there is much evidence that challenges the value of teacher questions. But growing knowledge about classroom discourse is now being applied by many practitioners. Teachers know that the same question can evoke an entirely different response if it is addressed to a group rather than a whole class, or to an individual privately rather than in the classroom forum. The purpose for talk, the environment in which it takes place and the nature of the audience, which includes the way in which the pupil perceives the teacher, strongly govern the response to any question posed by the teacher. The identification of prevalent and unhelpful patterns in pupil-teacher discourse is of clear importance, but it is not enough to look only at the phrasing of teacher talk. As a classroom practitioner, I would want to emphasise the crucial influence of social context.

However utterances are structured, they need to be underpinned by a strong relationship of trust and confidence between teacher and child. Pupils know that teachers carry authority vested by society and by parents and that evaluation and assessment are never far removed. Pupils know that a teacher's response can, even unintentionally, be deflating. Pupils risk exposing their thinking to a powerful and possibly judgemental adult, as well as a demanding and potentially critical peer group. Skilful management of the context for talk can limit the inhibiting effect of these social factors by building a climate which is safe, where it is acceptable to make mistakes, where individuals can move forward at their own pace, where the ideas, opinions and knowledge brought to the classroom by the pupils are valued. It is when pupils have learned that the teacher is truly willing to develop talk as part of the learning process, to appreciate spontaneity and to accept interaction which is appropriate to the situation that they can begin to take such risks. They can be free to open their thinking and to engage in what they recognise as fruitful dialogue with the teacher. The challenge for us all is in building that climate of trust in our own classrooms. The phrasing of the utterance is, in my view, relatively unimportant in comparison.

Acknowledgements

We would like to thank the pupils whose own uses of talk have helped us to extend our understanding. They come from the following schools: Glebe Infants School, Rayleigh, Essex; Tilbury Manor Infants School, Tilbury, Essex; The King John School, Thundersley, Essex; May Park Primary School, Bristol, Avon; Lyneham Junior School, Lyneham, Wiltshire; Madeley High School, Staffordshire.

References

ALEXANDER, R. (1991) *Primary Education in Leeds – Summary, Conclusions and Recommendations.* Leeds: University of Leeds.
DILLON, J. T. (1988) *Questioning and Teaching: a manual of practice.* London: Croom Helm.

Teacher Talk and Pupil Competence – A Response to Section 4

TONY EDWARDS

To provoke reflection on the 'accustomed routine', which Harold Gardiner suggests teachers might profitably unlearn, I occasionally present a profile of what those routines demand of communicatively competent pupils. Students in initial training tend to reject the account as a travesty of their intentions, as no doubt it is. Experienced teachers tend to receive it with wry amusement, recognising the portrait within the caricature. It certainly has uncomfortable resemblances to my recollections of teaching history in secondary school. According to this portrayal, as a competent pupil you have to be able and willing to:

- listen to the teacher, often for long periods of time;

- when the teacher stops talking, bid properly for the right to speak yourself, sometimes when competition for the next turn means balancing the risks of not being noticed against the risks of being ignored as too enthusiastic;

- answer questions to which the answer will be judged more or less relevant, useful and correct by a teacher who is seeking not to know something but to know if you know something;

- put up with having anyone's answer treated as evidence of a common understanding or misunderstanding, so that the teacher will often explain something again when you understood it first time or rush on when you are still struggling with what was said before;

- look for clues as to what a right answer might be from the way a teacher leads into a question, asks the question, and evaluates the responses – that last source of clues being often so prolific that even a wild guess may lead the teacher to answer the question for you;

- ask questions about the administration of the lesson but not usually about its content (and certainly never suggest that the teacher may be wrong);

- accept that what you know already about the topic of the lesson is unlikely to be asked for, or to be accepted as relevant, unless and until it fits into the teacher's frame of reference.

These 'profile components' derive from the proposition that the teacher's task is to know what pupils do not know, and to pass some of that knowledge on. This section illustrates some of the possibilities which are opened up when that task is redefined. Very different situational competences are demanded when the teacher temporarily relinquishes, or appears willing to share, the authority of the 'expert'. I want to comment briefly on aspects of that redefinition.

The distinctiveness of classroom questioning

The 'essential teaching exchange' is not the teacher telling pupils directly. It is the sequence of posing a question, eliciting an answer, eliciting a comment or elaboration or revision or some more direct form of evaluation. If questioning is extraordinarily frequent in classrooms, it is still more extraordinary in the frequency with which the teacher takes the first and third moves in that sequence (Edwards and Westgate, 1987, pp. 123–133). But the main reservations about too many 'known-answer' questions are not, as Neil Mercer suggests, that they depart from 'normal conversational practice' – which they evidently do. It is because they so often serve to focus pupils' attention away from any argument or enquiry or conclusion which might be emerging from the 'discussion', and towards whatever cues and clues the teacher might be providing as to what he or she is after. Similarly, it is hard for the teacher to listen to what the pupils are saying while he or she is listening intently for anything which might contribute or approximate to the 'right' answer being sought. The evaluation move in the teaching exchange offers rich opportunities to remake a pupil response into something which the teacher can more easily use. 'So what you're saying is . . .', the teacher may say, and before long the pupil no longer recognises the contribution as his or her own. To use the concept emphasised by Roy Corden, the teacher's response is 'contingent' on the pupil's thinking only so far as that thinking is convenient for the teacher's instructional agenda. Neil Mercer vigorously defends this use of questions to mark what is educationally 'significant', and it can be done with great skill and subtlety. Yet the two examples he cites seem heavy-handed. Knowledge certainly becomes 'joint' when 'I get you to know something which I know', and a great deal of teaching is necessarily like that. But his excellent account of how teachers and pupils construct 'common knowledge' together (Edwards and Mercer, 1987) is more appreciative than his article here of the possibilities of two-way movement to what is in part newly-constructed knowledge for all participants.

If questioning is 'the predominant technique for initiating, extending and controlling classroom discourse' (Dillon, 1982, p. 128), then it may be only professional common sense that inquiry-oriented teachers ask more and better questions, that better questions produce better answers, and that to question well is to teach well. Good questions may be defined cognitively as at a 'higher' level or, interactionally, as 'open' to an unpredictable and diverse range of acceptable responses. Either way, they are seen as determining the quality of the consequent responses.

I was interested in David Wood's scepticism about whether questions are so evidently a good thing, and whether 'better' questions are indisputably a better thing, because it compares closely with what David Westgate and I wrote about questioning for the Open University's Initial Teacher Training Course, 'Frameworks for Teaching'. David Wood notes the preponderance of right/wrong and two-choice questions, and the relative rarity with which they serve to promote reflection and encourage enquiry. He might also have noted in that context a tendency for teachers to close down potentially open questions, turning matters of opinion into matters of 'fact' (Hargreaves, 1984). But he is clearly persuaded by Dillon's lively explorations of myths about the efficacy of questioning, including the assumption that more 'demanding' questions will elicit cognitively superior answers. Not necessarily, Dillon concludes. If the question is largely an invitation to step into the teacher's frame of reference without disturbing it, and if pupils' experience tells them that their answers are there to be evaluated, then 'to ask a high-level question is to get any level of answer' (Dillon, 1982, 1988).

Borrowing similarly from Dillon, David Westgate and I suggested some alternatives to the traditional question, 'open' or otherwise, used when the teacher wished to initiate or extend discussion (Edwards and Westgate, 1988, p. 30). These include:

- making a declarative (open-ended or provocative) statement which invites a rejoinder or disagreement;

- inviting elaboration ('Could you say a bit more than that?');

- admitting perplexity when it occurs, whether about the topic itself or about a pupil's contribution to it;

- encouraging questions from pupils (rare in many classrooms);

- maintaining silence at strategic points (Dillon suggests that three to five seconds may be enough to draw in another pupil's contribution or encourage the previous speaker to elaborate on what was said).

An important interactional constraint on 'open' questions, as David Wood notes, is the fast pace of most classroom exchanges. Reflective answers to demanding questions take time to get going. They are also likely to need time to be thought through, the 'thinking aloud' characteristic of truly exploratory talk requiring patience on the part of the listeners and some protection from interruption. Not getting a usable answer quickly enough, teachers tend to redirect the question or even answer it themselves in the interests of 'getting on'. And in whole-class teaching, of course, the task of achieving and maintaining orderly discourse is likely to make 'long' pauses – anything more than two seconds, according to David Wood's evidence – seem risky, liable to be filled with unofficial and potentially disruptive talk. It is curious that none of the articles refers explicitly to the managerial inhibitions on 'open' questioning, and on 'discussion' defined as an unpredictable exploration of a topic, when large groups are being taught together. Of course, such teaching is often appropriate for purposes of exposition and explanation. But the organisational problems of managing turns and shaping meanings are liable to crowd out exploratory exchanges between teacher and pupils. The 'empowering' of pupils which Harold Gardiner and Roy Corden describe seems to require a much greater diversity of groupings, and so of 'participating structures', than many classrooms provide.

The mantle of the expert

The most powerful limitations on pupil activity come from maintaining intact the traditional boundary between knowledgeable teachers and pupils judged to be ignorant of the matters in hand until they have been taught about them. In contrast, the emphasis on listening to pupils which runs through much of this section recognises the scope for using what pupils already know and have experienced in many of the classroom tasks in which they are to be engaged. Roy Corden refers to 'responding to pupils' expertise', whether this takes the form of everyday knowledge outside the teacher's range or a reflection of some special interest. (That many Primary classes contain at least one current world expert on dinosaurs is a familiar fact of classroom life.)

The expertise may, of course, be temporarily contrived as well as cultivated. My former colleague, Dorothy Heathcote, used dramatic improvisation and role playing to 'hand over the mantle of the expert', thereby turning the teacher temporarily into a supporting player as opposed to the more usual combination of director and star performer (Heathcote, 1984). In the Schools Council's Humanities Curriculum Project and some more recent projects, pupils are given direct access to information unmediated by the teacher and some freedom to decide what parts of it are relevant to their investigations; the intention is not only to relieve the teacher of part of the burden of providing information, but also to free pupils from some of the constraints inherent in the traditional role of 'inexpert receiver'. Such direct access is seen by many enthusiasts for Information Technology as the source of a unique capacity for effecting a shift 'from teaching to learning', although there are accompanying risks that the prestige of high technology may make conveniently packaged knowledge too attractive and the response to it too deferential and inert.

However achieved, some temporary transfer of expertise is evident in many of the exchanges reported in this section. Pupils know something which the teacher does not, or they know it more vividly, and the teacher becomes an actively engaged and learning listener. Handling over the 'mantle' in this way is not abdication. The primary purpose is to create conditions in which pupils, individually or in groups, can explore and extend their own understanding at their own pace.

Flexibility in roles and relationships

The 'empowering' of pupils is obviously not all-or-nothing but temporary and provisional, and Roy Corden outlines most usefully the range of roles and relationships which become possible when 'expertise' is dispersed. His discussion directs attention to the different kinds of facilitating intervention which teachers can make, and it is an interesting exercise (in the light of the prominence given to teacher questions throughout this section) to identify what other ways of facilitating and shaping their pupils' learning the teachers use when they join in a discussion, a 'conference', or some other working group.

There is also the reminder that, on some occasions, the teacher's best contribution may be not to be there at all. Trusting pupils to achieve worthwhile learning without any intervention or supervision is difficult. Hardly less so is the self-restraint required not to outstay a welcome. The 'you have been dismissed' in Roy Corden's illustration of a teacher acting as 'information source', by invitation and with the evident intention of becoming quickly dispensable, suggests again a well-practised and shared definition of the teacher's role in tasks of that kind. I was also persuaded by his example of teacher and pupil working through a 'parallel thinking process' on what was for each of them a 'real' problem. It would have been interesting to have followed the process a little longer to see if the parallels began to converge. But the suggestion that the transcript has to be read aloud by two speakers almost simultaneously to catch anything of the exchange is in sharp contrast to the measured, classical playscript character of classroom interaction when the teacher's frame of reference is all-containing.

The approaches advocated and illustrated in this section are, of course, vulnerable to attack as manifestations of 'progressivism'. As travestied by its critics, progressivism is marked (in the sense of tarnished) by a distaste for facts, an indulgence in easy-going discussion and vague opinions, and a general retreat from the proper certainties of authoritative knowledge authoritatively taught. In practice, the wide ranging and rapidly changing forms of teacher intervention which the section portrays depend on deep, reflective understanding of how children learn. To intervene 'minimally' but appropriately, to time the interventions to best effect, to know when to transfer and when to regain the initiative, to give credit to what pupils already know by listening carefully and taking that knowledge seriously – all this displays a much higher level of professional skill than the traditionalist notion of teacher expertise, which reduces 'good teaching' to knowledge, love of subject and practice in passing on some of that knowledge.

References

DILLON, J. T. (1982) 'The effects of questions in education and other enterprises', *Journal of Curriculum Studies*, 14(2), pp. 127–152.

DILLON, J. T. (1988) *Questioning and Teaching: a Manual of Practice*. London: Croom Helm.

EDWARDS, A. AND WESTGATE, D. (1987) *Investigating Classroom Talk*. Lewes: Falmer Press.

EDWARDS, A. AND WESTGATE, D. (1988) *Language and Classroom*, Unit C2, Open University Course EP 228.

EDWARDS, D. AND MERCER, N. (1987) *Common Knowledge*. London: Methuen.

HARGREAVES, D. (1984) 'Teachers' questions: open, closed and half-open', *Educational Research*, 26(1), pp. 46–52.

HEATHCOTE, D. (1984) *Collected Writings on Education and Drama* Johnson, L. and O'Neill, C. (eds). London: Hutchinson.

Learning Through Talk
– Adults Together

5

Introduction

This section focuses on the National Oracy Project itself: its origins, current context and ways of working.

Judy Keiner traces the complex interweaving of political, institutional, financial and pedagogical influences – some going back many years – which led to the establishment of the National Oracy Project. She claims that 'if any politician can claim responsibility for the origin of the National Oracy Project, it is Sir Keith Joseph'.

Judy Keiner ends her account with the impact on the Project of the concurrent introduction of the National Curriculum, particularly the inclusion of Speaking and Listening as an attainment target in English. In the second article, Peter Latham, who is a local authority inspector, reflects on the relationship between the principles and practice of the National Oracy Project and the implementation of the various subjects of the National Curriculum. He concludes that, while there is limited explicit inclusion of oracy (particularly for older pupils), there is nevertheless implicit support for it, and he recommends readers to 'watch the verbs', 'to see such terms as "describe", "evaluate", "interpret" . . . as incitement to commit oracy'.

Hilary Kemeny and Kate Norman refer back to Douglas Barnes's model of learning in their account of the structure and ways of working of the National Oracy Project – a structure of 'interlinking groups of adults working together'. They demonstrate how the Project members found that their own learning needs echoed those of their pupils, and they attempt to answer concern about intellectual growth in curriculum development projects of this type.

Colin Biott picks up this issue in a response article, 'Towards Change in Classrooms'. He uses his own experience and the work of various theorists to analyse how teacher groups can be helped to progress, 'to find a way of fostering exploratory talk which is open and provisional . . . but which also engenders a search for new information and an interest in testing out new ideas'.

A Brief History of the Origins of the National Oracy Project

JUDY KEINER

The National Oracy Project, launched in 1987, was the most ambitious initiative of the School Curriculum Development Committee's six year life. Oracy was already high on the national educational agenda. In 1986, the Department of Education and Science had offered over £3,000,000 of Education Support Grant (ESG) to establish school-based projects on speaking and listening in seven local education authorities. Yet oracy was an unknown term outside a small constituency of educationists with interests in language and learning. To understand why it became a national priority in the late 1980s, we need both to look further back and to be aware of wider contemporary influences and imperatives.

In the history of state education in England this century, one recurrent focus of controversy is the English language itself. Public debates recur around a series of allegations of deterioration. Standards are said to be falling. Employers complain that schools are turning out pupils who can't speak properly, or who can't read, write or spell. Teachers or their trainers are said to be incompetent, or, more recently, so obsessed with other agendas that they deliberately seek not to teach key language skills. Riots or poor national economic performance may be ascribed to these failures, or (from another ideological direction) to the failure of the education system to motivate disaffected inner-city pupils, low achievers and disadvantaged ethnic minority groups. Questions are asked in the House. Enquiries are established. In the way of such things, they take some time to report, and when they do, they may recommend approaches too expensive to implement; the political agenda may have moved on. It is perhaps only when they can be seen to serve some new imperative that their time comes.

The 1921 Newbolt Report on English considered many of the issues of alleged deterioration. It recommended that the use of classroom talk as a learning strategy should form part of the repertoire of every teacher, offering ways of motivating learners. Yet HMI reports on classroom language work over the last 50 years show that this message was not widely taken up, though it was repeated in successive editions of official advice to teachers and in educational reports. Although Newbolt argued that every teacher had a responsibility for English, promotion of speaking and listening was seen as the province of the English teacher or the English lesson. The prospect of a class full of children talking to each other has traditionally been a threatening one for many teachers, signalling loss of control and even failure.

Newbolt also articulated recurrent fears about the potentially corrupting influence of the vernacular of the poorest social classes. It defended the use of stoutly respectable regional accents, while urging that teachers should work to eliminate their pupils' use of dialect forms and accents that it deemed ugly and slipshod – such as those of inner city working class areas. The study of linguistics (which had then only relatively recently been established) was already arguing that such distinctions were invalid; that all dialects were equally rule-bound and capable of conveying meaning. While linguistics was to become widely established as a respected discipline in higher education and research, its message of linguistic relativism has been widely ignored or misunderstood by the public and, until very recently, by most teachers. Forty years after Newbolt, Schools Council Examination Bulletin No. 11 was asserting that 'the language of the coffee bar is not appropriate to school' (quoted in Barnes et al., 1969) and it was only the Bullock Report (*A Language for Life*, 1975) which first advocated that teacher training programmes should incorporate elements of linguistics.

Education had by then felt the influence of linguistics through more informal methods. Some of the most far-reaching innovations in classroom practice owe their origin in part to the development of the battery-operated tape recorder. When, in the 1960s, the tape recorder became widely available, teachers and researchers in linguistics used it as an investigative tool. It became relatively easy to record and transcribe language in use in any social setting, rather than in the laboratory or recording studio. With the rapid growth of comprehensive schools, groups of teachers, fired with a new idealism about what could be achieved, built up subject associations (such as the National Association for the Teaching of English) and enrolled themselves on lengthy part-time Master's and Diploma courses. Such groups filtered the university findings about spoken language back into schools, and created an impetus which gave rise to what we can now call the oracy movement. From its beginnings, this movement set out to investigate the use of classroom language across subject boundaries.

In Birmingham, members of the University School of Education and their students, working in the linguistics tradition, recorded classroom talk and set out to provide models of educational discourse. Out of this work came an influential set of papers (1965), in which Andrew Wilkinson first formulated the term 'oracy', a term analogous to literacy as a prerequisite for successful learning. Synthesising the findings of linguistics and cognitive psychology, the argument was that learners need to learn through talk, particularly through working co-operatively in small groups.

In 1965 came a new public examination, the Certificate of Secondary Education, aimed at a wider range of pupils and involving new modes of learning and assessment. In order to devise means of oral assessment for this examination, the Schools Council funded the Oracy Research Unit, run by Andrew Wilkinson and colleagues from 1967–72. This, however, had only a limited impact on classroom practice.

In Leeds, a group of teachers on a course led by Douglas Barnes began to tape and transcribe their friends' lessons, investigating how teachers' questions and strategies for promoting enquiry helped their pupils learn. In London, members of the London Association for the Teaching of English were doing similar work, trying to describe the conditions which most contributed to successful learning. Working with Harold Rosen, they drew up the first 'Language Policy Across the Curriculum'. Part manifesto, part practical recommendations, it called for classroom learning to be organised in small groups, with pupils being encouraged to use their own language, tentatively and inexplicitly. The publication of *Language, the Learner and the School* (1969) and Barnes's *From Communication to Curriculum* (1976) in the new Penguin Education series gave this work a much wider impact, particularly among student teachers of that period. Very slowly, as new teachers became Heads of Department, there was an increasing presence of small group learning approaches in the comprehensive school, but it was overwhelmingly focused on English and Humanities.

There was remarkable agreement in this work that it was the language style of the school which needed to change rather than that of the pupils. However, throughout the 1960s and 1970s, ideas about pupils' language deficiencies, not so very different from those articulated in the Newbolt Report, continued to inform research and development and to be widespread in schools. The Schools Council had been set up partly to promote and fund curriculum development as well as assessment developments such as the 1967 Oracy project. The most substantial development of primary oral language work funded by the Council during that period was directed by Joan Tough at Leeds University. The project, Communication Skills in Early Childhood, concentrated on developing communication skills in those children who were supposed to lack them (see, for example, *Listening to Children Talking*, 1976). Through its sponsorship of projects in the humanities, science and personal and social education, the Council promoted the spread of group teaching strategies in subjects other than English. Its only project explicitly devoted to the promotion of oral language as a cross-curricular strategy in secondary schools was the Weston Language Development Project (1979). Disappointingly, research commissioned by the Council showed that the long-term impact of most of its projects was minimal.

The Economic and Social Research Council funded a substantial research project, led by Douglas Barnes and Frankie Todd, on communication and learning in small groups (1977). Yet the research's classroom impact beyond English teaching was as disappointing as that of the Schools Council. While all these initiatives were enthusiastically promoted by HMI, teacher training institutions and subject associations, they were actually adopted in very few schools.

It was another public controversy about language, this time about a supposed decline in standards of reading achievement, which led the then Secretary of State for Education, Mrs Margaret Thatcher, to establish the Bullock Committee to enquire into the teaching of English in 1973. Its report (*A Language for Life*) endorsed the use of oral language and small group teaching strategies. It insisted that language was a cross-curricular responsibility and recommended that all schools should adopt language policies. It concluded:

We welcome the growth in interest in oral language in recent years, for we cannot emphasise too strongly our conviction of its importance in the education of the child . . . But there is still a great deal to be done. A priority objective for all schools is a commitment to the speech needs of their pupils and a serious study of the role of oral language in learning.

(DES, 1975, § 10.30)

Unfortunately, this report was published at a time when Britain was facing its gravest financial crisis since World War II. No funds were forthcoming to support the recommendations of the report. Most teacher training institutions implemented Bullock's recommendation that all students should have more extended training in all aspects of language. LEAs and schools did adopt language policies, but in many cases they existed only in filing cabinets. Different agendas were appearing during the 1970s, with more fundamental questioning of the education system itself. Unemployment rose sharply. To what extent was the school system failing to prepare pupils for work? Strikes and inner city unrest in multi-ethnic communities increased. Was the school system serving its least advantaged members properly? Britain was now a member of the EC and, unlike the majority of its fellow members, was unable to produce any hard comparative evidence of what pupils were achieving, or even of what they were learning. Could control of education any longer be left in the hands of LEAs, and the curriculum in the hands of teachers?

James Callaghan's famous Ruskin College speech of 1976 called for a national 'great' debate on the curriculum. From the debates that followed there emerged a new vocationalism. The preparation of young people for the workplace became an educational imperative. This was to lead to the establishment of the GCSE examination with its emphasis on new, criterion-referenced curricula and examinations and, ultimately, to a system of national accreditation for all vocational qualifications.

The Bullock Report had also recommended the establishment of a programme to devise national tests of reading achievement. Amid opposition from teaching unions and many educationists, an Assessment of Performance Unit (APU) had been set up at DES in 1975 and had been given the brief of devising and carrying out appropriate tests to measure a nationally valid sample of pupil achievement in English, Mathematics and Science at seven, eleven, thirteen and fifteen. Continuing professional hostility in the early stages had caused the tests at age seven to be dropped, yet it was those at age eleven which attracted the greatest interest. These offered an approach to rigorous assessment of primary pupils which avoided the artificialities of the old eleven-plus system. APU developed tests of speaking and listening based, as with the other tests, on presenting pupils with problem-solving situations and cases to argue. A key aim was the production of situations with 'natural, genuine communicative purpose or outcome'. They attracted admiration in some quarters – particularly amongst those responsible for developing examinations – and criticisms from others, such as Maybin (1988), who saw the tasks chosen as too artificially imposed.

Throughout the late 1970s and early 1980s, a series of HMI reports provided evidence that there was a disappointingly narrow range of attention to the development of speaking and listening skills in primary and secondary schools. The research of Galton, Simon and associates (1980) into the relationship between educational achievement and classroom teaching styles confirmed that small-group learning in primary schools, deemed by its opponents to have been one of the unproven experiments imposed by the Plowden Report, was only to be found in a small minority of schools. Over the same period of time, however, HMI – and in particular those responsible for English – also acted as an important bridge between the enthusiastic groups of teachers intent on developing oral work in the classroom and the officers of the DES and LEAs.

From 1979, radically-minded Conservative administrations accelerated initiatives which were to help promote oracy. Pressure was put on LEAs to develop clear curriculum policies and to ensure that they were implemented in schools. Moves began to review and extend the range of school qualifications and the types of information made available to future employers. If any politician can claim responsibility for the origin of the National Oracy Project, it is Sir Keith Joseph, Secretary of State for Education from 1983–6. His preoccupation with the results of social disadvantage gave the impetus for a range of initiatives, long advocated by DES and HMI, aimed at the lowest-achieving 40% of the secondary school population. The Lower Attaining Pupils (LAP) programme was intended to promote more effective teaching and learning methods, applicable to real-life situations.

Among these was the Wiltshire Oracy Project. This was originally aimed at potential early school leavers and had a strong emphasis on developing forms of oral assessment. A few months before launching the LAP initiatives, Sir Keith's comments gave explicit priority to curriculum development in oracy:

> We ought to attach much more importance to improving our children's proficiency in speaking and listening, as well as in reading and writing.
> (Speech to Council of Local Education Authorities, July 1982.)

The Wiltshire Oracy Project ran from 1984–90 and, in its later years, covered the primary and secondary age range. Starting with small groups of schools, pupils and teachers, it set out to organise teaching and learning across different curriculum areas so as to give value and status to what pupils had to say. Key strategies included the creation of opportunities through which pupils could become, and then speak as, experts to adults and other learners. Its assessment activities sought to demonstrate that natural and genuine communicative outcomes could only be assessed in situations in which the learners could have time to consider, rehearse and speak interactively.

The Project was generally seen as successful by HMI and officials in DES and SCDC. Yet this was a particularly difficult time for innovation in education. Teacher industrial action grew, culminating in a long and damaging strike over proposed new conditions of service which, for the first time, obliged teachers to carry out record-keeping and attend meetings outside school hours. Just as the dispute was finally resolved, the launch of GCSE brought with it the requirement for every secondary teacher to be trained in new assessment and reporting methods, including oral assessment.

Radically new forms of funding were introduced for in-service training. The tradition of seconding individual teachers for one term or one year courses was replaced with a system through which LEAs provided or delegated to schools funding for in-house training days for the staff as a whole. Very substantial new Educational Support Grants were offered for competitive tender to LEAs for DES-specified curriculum development priorities. Amongst those announced for 1986 was the £3,000,000 funding for oracy development referred to above, with specifications which had obviously been influenced by the experience of the Wiltshire Oracy Project.

The time of oracy had clearly arrived, and plans for the National Oracy Project were finalised by the School Curriculum Development Committee (SCDC), the successor body to the Schools Council. SCDC had been running a very successful project since 1985, the National Writing Project; many of the member LEAs on this project had been unsuccessful in bidding for ESG oracy funding. When agreement was finally secured in 1987 for the National Oracy Project, it was agreed to include over thirty authorities, some working in consortia, and for the Project to run until 1993. The starting point would be a warm-up phase, drawing on a selection of the National Writing Project authorities which had an interest in continuing their work into oracy.

In 1987, the Conservatives won a General Election with a manifesto which included proposals to establish a National Curriculum and a new assessment system, and to change the system for funding schools. The programme of educational reform which was set in motion was arguably the most radical since the 1902 Education Act set up LEAs. Its most fundamental change was the move from a concept of educational opportunity provided according to age, ability and aptitude to one of statutory individual entitlement to a ten-subject curriculum. The curriculum development and examinations framework of the SCDC and Secondary Examination Council (SEC) was replaced by new statutory bodies, the National Curriculum Council (NCC) and the Schools Examination and Assessment Council (SEAC). Expert groups were set up to devise an overall assessment framework and to develop proposals for curriculum content. The curriculum for English brought speaking and listening onto the statutory agenda of every classroom, and accorded it equal weight with reading and writing. Teachers were required to record and assess each pupil's progress in speaking and listening against ten levels of attainment. Other subject groups also proposed giving official status to activities requiring oracy.

As with many other aspects of the National Curriculum, the models of best practice which HMI had found only in a minority of schools were now being demanded of every school and every teacher. Those who had worked for so long to establish a National Oracy Project could scarcely have imagined that, within months of its launch, the profession would look to it to provide rapid answers to fundamental questions about the implementation and assessment of what had suddenly become a statutory classroom requirement. The challenge the Project faced was indeed formidable.

Acknowledgements

I am particularly grateful to Elizabeth and David Grugeon for helpful comments on earlier drafts of this article. I would also like to thank members of the National Oracy Project Evaluation team for continuing discussions on oracy projects past and present, and the many former members of the National Oracy Project whose insights have been so helpful.

References

BARNES, D. (1976) *From Communication to Curriculum*. Harmondsworth: Penguin.

BARNES, D. AND TODD, R. (1977) *Communicating and Learning in Small Groups*. London: Routledge.

BARNES, D., BRITTON, J. AND ROSEN, H. (1969) *Language the Learner and the School*. Harmondsworth: Penguin.

DES (1975) *A Language for Life*. London: HMSO.

GALTON, M., SIMON, B. AND CROLL, P. (1980) *Inside the Primary Classroom*. London: Routledge.

MAYBIN, J. (1988) 'A critical review of the DES Assessment of Performance Unit's Oracy Surveys', *English in Education*, Vol 22, No. 1.

SCHOOLS COUNCIL (1979) *Learning Through Talking 11–16 (Schools Council Working Paper 64)*. London: Evans.

TOUGH, J. (1976) *Listening to Children Talking*. London: Ward Lock Education/ Drake Educational Associates.

WILKINSON, A., DAVIES, A. AND ATKINSON, D. (1965) *Spoken English*. Educational Review Occasional Papers No. 2, University of Birmingham School of Education.

5.2

Oracy and the National Curriculum

PETER LATHAM

If someone had said as recently as five years ago that oral work would soon enjoy equivalent status to reading and writing in the English curriculum, my confident response would have been 'not in my lifetime'. If they had then gone on to predict that oral communication would find a firm (even statutory) foothold in all areas of the curriculum, I would probably have adopted the condescending, sceptical expression of a believer doubting the potential faith of others.

But you only have to go as far as the second level of the first attainment target for mathematics to find: 'Pupils should talk about work or ask questions using appropriate mathematical language.' Or the second level of the first attainment target for science: 'Pupils should ask questions ... suggest ideas and make predictions ... .' Oracy has become an educational theme restated with the arrival of each National Curriculum folder.

My work as an LEA inspector has involved regular, planned visits to primary, secondary and special school classrooms over the period in which, subject by subject, the National Curriculum has come into view. My LEA, Croydon, has over the same period been a member of the National Oracy Project, so I have had the opportunity to explore how a focus on oracy can assist the delivery of the National

Curriculum. The relationship between the National Curriculum and the work of the Project has been more than one of peaceful co-existence. In key areas, the 'dialogue' between them has been positive and challenging for teachers, children and others involved in education. Statutory requirements have provided status and a specific curriculum framework for oracy. In turn, the National Oracy Project has presented a necessary counter-balance to the 'top-down' model of curriculum planning. It has done so by exemplifying and reaffirming the expertise of the increasing number of teachers who have come to value oracy as a key element in effective learning.

At a personal level, the growing status of oracy in educational practice has made my job and that of my colleagues significantly easier. In a classroom where active, purposeful talk is the norm, children are more willing and able to explain, even to a total stranger, what they are doing and why. The contrast with the classroom where tasks are uniformly presented by the teacher and dutifully completed by the pupils is plain to see. In the latter, questions from a visitor about 'what' and 'why' are, I have found, likely to be met with half-formed, hesitant responses from pupils about 'having to finish things', about 'doing the work for the teacher' and then, perhaps, about putting away the (written) outcomes in a folder or in another collection of work.

In the former classroom, by contrast, the children's level of achievement has been easier to 'inspect' through their developed oral responses. What is more, such achievement, realised and exemplified through active discussion and negotiation in a range of groupings, has usually been of a higher standard than that of the classroom where oracy has yet to become a focus for curriculum provision.

If the occasional visitor is able to learn more about pupil performance in the classroom where oracy flourishes, how much more illuminating must the opportunity be for the regular adult presence, the teacher, who is attentive to what children are telling him or her and each other? At a practical as well as theoretical level, it has become increasingly apparent that, faced with growing demands for assessment of attainment, the teacher who values and encourages children's oral skills will always be more aware of what they really know, understand and are able to do.

This point was underlined for me by some teachers' responses to the Key Stage 1 standard assessment tasks for summer 1991. There were, as widely reported at the time, many practical difficulties with the first SATs. Even so, positive comments were made by a number of teachers about how the process of closely observing children exploring their ideas through talk had prompted them to review their own classroom practices and planning. For example, '. . . it made me think about the sort of directions, questions and explanations I give' and, in another case, '. . . it made me look at grouping children and grouping them more flexibly'. A focus on oracy has had a positive impact on classroom management and approaches to planning and assessment. Teachers have gradually acknowledged that, in planning and practising the explicit requirements for oracy in the National Curriculum, they have uncovered its potential to inform their work more widely.

However, in offering such affirmation I am reflecting mainly on changes in primary and especially Key Stage 1 classrooms. Despite many positive developments and some notable exceptions, it remains the case that the overall influence of oracy diminishes in all subjects as the child grows older. There are fewer explicit statutory demands for oral work in later key stages, although I think it is important to 'watch the verbs' and to see such terms as 'describe', 'evaluate', 'formulate', 'interpret', 'plan', 'respond' and many others in pro-grammes of study and statements of attainment as incitement to commit oracy. In a curriculum too long weighed down by written recording without a sense of audience or purpose, the immediacy and interaction implied by these active verbs holds out the possibility of a more challenging curriculum at all levels.

But this diminution also misses a vital point about the National Curriculum – that oracy has to be addressed at two levels: explicitly, in terms of attending to programmes of study and statements of attainment; but also implicitly, in supporting certain key assumptions which underpin the National Curriculum about the processes of teaching and learning throughout the Key Stages.

One such implicit assumption is that learning is likely to be most effective when children are active in formulating their own questions and developing their own strategies for solving problems or making use of information. In this context, knowledge is seen as something to be interpreted, negotiated and applied, rather than simply to be gained. The main medium for such negotiation has to be talk. I have observed, for example, a group of infants setting up a role-play area in their classroom, to represent a café. They had to decide how much space would be needed for furniture; whether the table available would be big enough for the plates, cups, etc. they were to use. The measuring and reorganisation of materials in such an activity led to sustained, purposeful discussion among the children as they 'used and applied' mathematics according to National Curriculum requirements.

At the other end of compulsory schooling, such expectations of independent learning have equal relevance. To give an example, a group of Year 10 (fifteen year old) pupils volunteered to conduct research on varieties of 'talk' that occur in the workplace. They were going to spend a morning at two different companies.

With their classmates, they prepared a number of questions to structure their enquiries. Examples were:

- How do people of the same status talk to each others?

- How do they talk to someone of senior rank?

- Is it different if they work together a lot?

- Do men talk politely to women?

- Does speech alter if men are talking to a woman in a higher position to them?

- Is canteen talk more relaxed?

- What qualities do employers look for in their staff (in terms of competence in oral communication)?

The sophistication of the questions themselves, and of the discussion which generated them, impressed the class teacher. The explicit audience and purpose for the work appear to have given it particular impetus.

This opportunity of exploring talk through talk will provide useful, contextualised insights into the pupils' competence in relation to English attainment target 1 (Speaking and Listening). It will, in particular, offer a focus for considering the 'knowledge about language' strand of the English programmes of study. This promotes consideration of how language use changes according to social context, for example, at level 7: '. . . show in discussion an awareness of the appropriate use of spoken language, according to purpose, topic and audience'. The work can now be further developed using pupils' own research findings and their role as 'experts' in presenting to others what they have learned.

A second assumption which, I suggest, underpins the National Curriculum is the need to acknowledge and use what children already know as a basis for extending their learning. For example, the report of the English working party, *English for Ages 5 to 16*, makes clear statements on the need to value, from the earliest stages, the knowledge and experience of language which children bring to school. Similarly, in mathematics, children are encouraged to build conceptual understanding through their own forms of expression. The teacher will intervene to refine these forms into more 'mathematical language' when the pupils are ready.

In Croydon, the value of using what children know has been

particularly highlighted as an oracy issue in the teaching of the visual arts. In the following extract, three Year 2 children are discussing with their teacher a well known classical painting, 'Holyday', by Tissot.

ALISON: They can't be trees, they must be . . . perhaps there is a bridge up there.

TEACHER: You think it's a bridge that goes up there?

MICHAEL: I think it is because I can see some black there.

ALISON: It must be a station where trains go, cos you see steps and you see rivers sometimes when we go to collect mummy.

TEACHER: Yes, Anthony?

ANTHONY: Cos there might be some steps down the side.

TEACHER: Do you think it might be a railway bridge though, would you choose to have a picnic underneath a railway bridge?

ALISON AND MICHAEL: No.

TEACHER: Where does it look as though it might be?

MICHAEL: The bridge might break.

ALISON: When I went on train one day, mummy stayed for a little while, and then Philip drove the car to collect mummy, but we couldn't find her for quite a long time and mummy buying me little ornament, a little thing.

TEACHER: A bell?

ALISON: And it can make a noise and it's fragile.

TEACHER: Can you see something in the picture that would be very fragile?

MICHAEL: There's a teapot.

TEACHER: What does it look as though it's made of?

MICHAEL: China?

TEACHER: Do you think it's made of china, Anthony?

ANTHONY: No, it's made of metal . . .

The conversation moves freely between anecdotal comments and close observational study of what is in the painting. The teacher encourages both, recognising how mutually supportive they are. The children are 'seeing' more by relating the images to what they know and have experienced. Furthermore, in building up their art vocabulary, the teacher takes words from the children's descriptions of their experience, and enlists them, opportunistically, into the shared reading of the painting.

In a sustained exploratory discussion, the teacher is preempting superficial judgements of the 'I like this, I don't like that' kind and enabling more durable, more developed views to be shaped. The medium for that shaping is talk. It is, I suggest, a particularly fine example of understanding and evaluating art as required by the National Curriculum.

A third assumption within the National Curriculum, which this example also illustrates, is that *reflection* has to be an essential aspect of learning. Thus, for example, the Physical Education attainment target includes 'evaluation' as a major aspect, and the Art attainment target 1 for Key Stage 3 requires pupils to be able to 'modify their work as it progresses, reviewing its development and meaning, and explain the reasons for change'. Reflection is increasingly recognised as a way of supporting sustained, critical thinking, of helping pupils to make explicit to themselves, as well as to others, what they know, understand and can do.

'Planning', reflecting on what needs to be done as well as on what has been done, is accorded similar status. For example, planning a scientific investigation becomes an increasingly high level activity, as we move through the National Curriculum statements of attainment in Science. The immediacy of these processes of 'reflection' and 'planning' – as well as, especially in the latter case, the interactive contexts which they assume – clearly carry the implicit expectation that oracy will be the main means by which they are to be realised.

The fourth and final assumption built into the National Curriculum which I want to draw out is one which, I think, underlies all the others. It is also one where the National Oracy Project has made its most significant contribution to classroom-based teaching and learning. It is that, in most respects, learning is a social and collaborative enterprise. The programmes of study for Speaking and Listening state the need for 'planning situations and activities which should cover: working with other children and adults – involving discussion with others; listening and giving weight to, the opinions of others . . .'

The activities outlined in this article, each of which has been recently observed in classrooms (the infants planning their role-play area; the Year 10 pupils preparing their questions for use in the workplace; the middle infants discussing a famous painting), all work because the participants' interest (including that of the teacher) in the materials and ideas is enhanced by curiosity about what others are thinking. There is a social as well as a cognitive return in terms of what is learned. These are mutually dependent, not separable aspects of the process. In each case, the young children and the older pupils have interacted more easily and more purposefully because of the quality of the task. In turn, the level of achievement is raised collectively and individually by implicit recognition of the advantages of working together. It is collaboration in the strictest sense of the word.

In Croydon, the National Oracy Project has also provided a focus for adult collaboration. Three years ago, as a participating LEA, we set up a cross-curricular, cross-phase Steering Group to share ideas on how best to promote oracy in our schools. The group consisted of primary and secondary headteachers, advisers, inspectors, a representative of local industry, and a parent. The areas of special educational needs and English as a second language were also represented. In addition, we took an early opportunity to co-opt our adviser for the Language in the National Curriculum Project (LINC) to support, at local level, the creative dialogue between the two projects in terms of use of, and knowledge about, language. Termly meetings provided an opportunity to review in-service provision for oracy, to share anecdotal evidence of a kind which I have offered above, and to clarify our own understanding about oracy from a range of subject-specific and community perspectives.

As the formalised part of our work was coming to an end in the summer of 1991, the group was increasingly recognising the value of highlighting the importance of oracy in the whole school curriculum to wider audiences, both within and beyond the schools, and, in particular, with governors and local employers. There remains much to do in this respect as well as in terms of ensuring that opportunities for oral work are sustained throughout all Key Stages.

Through our various contacts with schools, we continue to be convinced that classrooms where oracy has had real impact are more interesting and intellectually challenging places to be. The National Curriculum now enables oracy to be explicitly and implicitly valued as an essential aspect of effective education. We are all learning more as a result.

Acknowledgements

I should like to thank: Judy Elliott of Keston Infants School, Old Coulsdon, for the transcript of 'Holyday'; Brian Symons of Edenham School, Croydon, and Caroline Conniff, Advisory Teacher, for the 'workplace questions'.

Adults Working on Understanding

HILARY KEMENY

AND

KATE NORMAN

> ... we are beginning to see change not simply as a technical problem but as a cultural problem that requires attention to context and the creation of shared meaning within working groups.
>
> (Ruddock, 1991, p. 30)

In her review of Schools Council Projects, Jean Ruddock characterises two distinct types:

- large-scale, centrally funded, national curriculum projects;

- school-based curriculum development activities.

The National Oracy Project possesses features of both types. It was large-scale and, at least partially, centrally funded. It was deliberately designed to stimulate and support local classroom-based development while at the same time taking responsibility for national dissemination. This article describes what the Project has achieved in its development phase and reflects on the factors that have contributed to that achievement. We shall also be exploring how adults – teachers, co-ordinators, advisers, project officers – have learned to 'share meanings' through the structures and approaches of the Project.

Structure

In planning the National Oracy Project, the School Curriculum Development Committee drew heavily on the way that its sister project, the National Writing Project, had been designed and carried out. This led to the following basic structure:

- LEAs 'bidding in', making a commitment to fund a full-time co-ordinator and to support a number of teachers from different schools meeting together regularly.

- Member LEAs, deliberately selected to represent a wide range of institutions, pupil ages, curriculum areas and interests in oracy.

- Teachers, schools and LEA groups, encouraged to pursue their own investigations and produce their own outcomes.

- A small central team of a director, three project officers and administrators, supporting local initiatives and publishing and widely disseminating the work of teachers.

- Oversight from a steering committee and a parent body (the National Curriculum Council).

- A long time-scale, including four years for development and two years of dissemination.

Five interrelated aspects of this structure and its implementation can be identified as significant. These are: teacher ownership; collaborative ways of working; the use of talk as a vehicle for adult learning; sufficient time; and mechanisms through which the classroom changes made by individual teachers could become part of a wider reflective process. The quality of these aspects was greatly influenced by the nature of oracy itself. Principles that applied to pupils' use of talk were also assumed to be appropriate to adults – the Project learned to 'practise what you preach'.

Ownership

Commenting on the first type of curriculum development model, Jean Ruddock says:

> ... the focus was on the mass-produced curriculum package and its

transmission, its installation and its integrity. The ownership of meaning remained with its originators. (. . .) The central curriculum development teams (. . .) did not work hard enough at finding ways of bringing teachers into the world of curriculum deliberation that they created and inhabited. In particular, they did not do enough to help teachers see that curricula can be designed to embody hypotheses about learning that teachers can test in the particular conditions of their own classrooms.

(op cit.)

The National Oracy Project structure was designed to start from teachers' concerns and to establish teacher ownership from the outset. The Project had no initial INSET programme or package of materials. This was a situation which many teachers found uncomfortable. It was common in early meetings for co-ordinators to be pressed, 'Just tell us what you want us to do.' But it was felt to be particularly crucial with a topic like oracy, which is hard to 'grasp', that people established their own areas for investigation, tried to find answers to their own questions. As Dionne Connor, a teacher from the Clwyd Project, said in conversation with Gordon Baddeley, project officer:

GORDON: So what's your role in all this? Have you had to rethink what your . . . job is as a teacher?

DIONNE: Yes, because when you first come out of college, you've got so many people who can tell you things as though they are fact, and they're right . . . about teaching. I found originally I was trying to please everybody else and not knowing how exactly I wanted to teach, myself. And that's why I think the Oracy Project has helped me so much because it didn't offer, it didn't say, 'Look, this is what you do and this is how you do it.' It's helped me enormously because I've found that . . . it's given me ideas and, as I've tried them out, I've learned and then been able to expand it, rather than taking someone else's ideas and copying them – which doesn't work. It's given me a whole approach . . . it's kind of evolved.

The Project continued to emphasise a strong commitment to the fundamental importance of teachers' own classroom-based work, for example through its journal, *Talk*, which consists almost entirely of teachers' own accounts, and through the use at conferences of teachers as workshop presenters.

Collaboration

A highly significant aspect of the process has been the emphasis on collaboration – indeed the whole Project can be seen as composed of interlinking groups of adults working together. In many LEAs, at least two teachers were nominated from each member school. This provided mutual support and a base from which to influence others.

The Hampshire Oracy Project, for example, had built into its design a specific commitment that the two teachers from each secondary school involved should be from different departments. The LEA co-ordinator, Valmai Wainhouse, reflecting on how the teachers had worked together, had these points to make:

> What I was clear about from the start was that I didn't want the Oracy Project to be identified with the English department. I was particularly pleased to involve colleagues from, for example, Technology, Religious Studies, Business Studies, Modern Foreign Languages and Physical Education.
>
> The pairs of teachers began fairly modestly with starting points such as:
>
> - observing each other in the classroom;
>
> - tracking a pupil over a period of time;
>
> - asking pupils how they perceived talk as a learning tool;
>
> - comparing and developing strategies for collaborative learning in their classrooms.
>
> It was the responsibility of these pairs of teachers to begin to involve others, at least within their own departments; more by instinct than design, perhaps, certain 'ways in' to doing this began to evolve. For instance, we used existing initiatives within the school:
>
> - The English and Science Departments were collaborating on joint GCSE written coursework, so it was logical to try to extend this to oral work.
>
> - There were existing field trips and visits where we could build in talk activities.
>
> - Regular visitors to the school gave us a chance to consider active listening.
>
> - Assessment of and through talk was a major focus of our work, and concerns with GCSE and the onset of a National Curriculum highlighted this.
>
> Each pair of teachers, along with me as local co-ordinator, was also expected to take on the responsibility for encouraging greater awareness within the school of the value of oracy. Where they have been able to do this most successfully, I think it has been because of the support of the senior management team and the developing and sharing of home-grown materials.
>
> The project has taught me a lot about the value of working with a

team of teachers in this way. Much of the teachers' early work was by no means innovative, but the point was that it was new to them and enabled many of them to go on to really push forward their own thinking, particularly about the way children learn most effectively. They were able to do this through sharing and reflecting upon their observations with their school project partner and with the network of teachers in the Hampshire Oracy Project. What I have tried to do is to set up a network which in terms of its professional support has modelled for the teachers the kinds of approaches that will work in schools. The network has gained strength through regular meetings where social as well as professional bonds are strengthened.

Learning through talk

The Project's ways of working can be related directly to the model of learning through talk, outlined in Douglas Barnes's article, 'The Role of Talk in Learning', and exemplified in relation to children by other writers. It was a working assumption of the Project that what worked for children probably worked for adults as well. Often, meetings were deliberately organised to model approaches to peer-group learning that would work with pupils. But it went deeper than a question of 'modelling' to a firm conviction that this was the most effective way for anyone to learn.

Douglas Barnes points out, 'The readiest way of working on understanding is often through talk, because the flexibility of speech makes it easy for us to try out new ways of arranging what we know'. The structure of the Project gave teachers opportunities over time to *explore*, *present* and, most importantly, *reflect* through talk in a variety of supportive groupings. Teachers were able to make sense of new concepts by trying them out in their own classrooms, assimilating or accommodating them into their existing understanding. They also had the opportunity to discuss their thinking, to move from the personal to the general with others on the same journey. As confidence grew, people were ready to share their new understandings with wider audiences.

As well as having individual and consortia LEA members, the Project has encouraged the establishment of other 'linked groups' of teachers, working on some aspect of oracy. Their main contact with the Project nationally has been to receive journals and newsletters, and to report back to the Project from time to time on what they have been doing. In Sheffield, a linked group of teachers convened by Sue Horner, advisory teacher for English, focused on children's perceptions of talk in Years 1–7. The group set up investigative activities in classrooms and met to share and discuss findings.

Reflecting on their involvement in the group, teachers made the following comments:

> I have found the group most supportive, even when I haven't done the 'homework' or done it all wrong! Discussing various aspects of oracy with a like-minded and sympathetic group has helped to fix its importance in my mind. The group has always been open and honest about the realities of teaching in inner-city schools yet somehow maintained an optimistic air. I know that the opportunity to talk about an area of the curriculum and focus on that specifically over a fairly long period of time is, for me, a helpful way of absorbing new ideas and putting them into practice, even in a limited way. When I did make time for the 'homework', I always learned something from it in the classroom and when we looked at everyone's work in the group.
>
> The other major area of learning for me has got to be listening. I feel I am better, though still not good, at listening to the children in my class. I know in my mind that it must be valuable in assessing children, but somehow the nagging feeling that I ought to be doing something instead of listening is difficult to ignore. There are so many demands on our time, but I am convinced now that listening to my children is one of the most valuable activities I could be doing. Insights are developing into how individual children are developing, thinking or feeling.

Time

An essential factor making for success with this sort of approach is time. The time-span of three or four years for most LEAs allowed all involved to work on their understanding: to learn, not to have to be told. Alan Howe, looking back over his time as Director of the Wiltshire Oracy Project, summed up in an interview how he thought this process worked:

> Typically the pattern in the Wiltshire schools involved, in both the primary and secondary sectors, is an initial stage where teachers are questioning, unsure, uncertain, prepared to have a go, prepared to try things out. Then, interestingly, you get to a stage (and this isn't fast) where a lot of teachers suddenly get very enthusiastic and they say things like, 'Yes, do come in next week, I am doing oracy in that class' or, 'It's no good you coming in tomorrow, I won't be doing oracy tomorrow'. They do talk in terms of 'doing oracy' which seems to be a necessary stage people go through, that they start to put a box around

it. Then there comes a point where teachers begin to say, 'Well, actually it's all about learning, isn't it?' and 'I hadn't realised how this fits in with all I'm doing', and then the project is moving. That takes time, possibly a year of teachers getting working, trying things out, getting a lot of support, looking at the evidence, talking to their colleagues, working with critical friends and so on.

As for the whole school, it seems to me from the experience that I've had that there is another phase, where teachers then reach a point where they are ready to talk with others, to share that experience with others, to write about it, to present workshops, to run INSET and to talk at staff meetings, and all those things where they move from working with their own practice towards working with others and helping others take that on. So it may be in the second year of involvement that work really begins to take off. It begins to move across the curriculum, because the teachers who were initially involved have confidence in their own work. They are then able to talk with others about what they're doing, and they can share their expertise around.

(Howe, 1990)

Mechanisms for development

Jean Ruddock suggests that working groups of teachers who are able to create new meanings for themselves may be the key to effective curriculum development and sustained change. However, as Pam Czerniewska, director of the National Writing Project, points out:

> . . . curriculum development which starts from practice and tries to build itself within existing structures is a very messy process . . . You can never be quite sure where you have got to and can easily become complacent amid the testimonials from teachers delighted simply to have talked to each other.

(1989, p. 155)

And Michael Fullan (1990) warns against a too-ready acceptance of the value of teachers' collaborative working, quoting Little (1989):

> Bluntly put, do we have in teachers' collaborative work the creative development of well-informed choices or the mutual reinforcement of poorly informed habit? Does teachers' time together advance the imagination and understanding of their work, or do teachers merely confirm one another in present practice? What subject philosophy and subject pedagogy do teachers reflect as they work together? How explicit and accessible is their knowledge to one another?

(p. 22)

Responsibility for ensuring that teachers' groups in the National Oracy Project did not simply 'recycle ignorance' fell mainly to local co-ordinators. Douglas Barnes discusses the challenge for teachers in helping pupils to try out new ways of thinking that may be disturbingly different from those they are used to while at the same time needing to give more responsibility to those learners to explore their own dilemmas. This fine balance is very much what the Project co-ordinators had to achieve with their teachers. Co-ordinators have suggested that this was often a case of 'contingent responsiveness' to the teachers – taking time to reflect back on a classroom experience, providing a photocopy of a relevant article at just the right moment, knowing when a particular teacher could be persuaded to present something at a staff meeting. The relationship is clearly not that of teacher and pupils, but there are elements of the skilful teacher role, as exemplified in Section 4: the importance of responsive listening; not intervening too quickly but being prepared to lead when necessary; asking the challenging question.

Cristina Bennett, who changed from being a Project teacher in Wiltshire to being one of the Project's co-ordinators in that county, said:

> Working as a co-ordinator put me in a completely different role, I was now a key person in the support system for teachers planning for talk. The move from working with secondary to primary didn't affect the way I worked, nor the way I thought. In short, regular contact for planning and for classroom work together – reviewing approaches with a small number of teachers is a positive formula for working well. Obviously the nature of my work depended on the needs of the teachers. Therefore, the initial meeting to talk together through what they were interested in doing was vital; some teachers needed me as a sounding board for ideas; some wanted me to evaluate what they were doing and talk through approaches to change. One other vital aspect to all this was TIME. Change does not happen quickly. Thus, my role as co-ordinator was more about working with teachers, getting them to think about what they were doing in their classrooms and what other possibilities they might consider to encourage purposeful learning.

As well as supporting individual teachers, co-ordinators planned and managed group meetings. Here also there were sensitive judgements to be made. How much pre-planning could a co-ordinator do without taking too much responsibility away from members? What was the appropriate balance between the sharing of members' own investigations and the input of new ideas, say from a visiting speaker? Many co-ordinators found it valuable at times for the group to be working towards a definite outcome – a local publication or conference, for example – but did this external pressure to make a presentation cut short deeper explorations? There might be a tension between the feelings of group solidarity based on shared experience and the need to widen the Project's influence. Co-ordinators, many of them doing this sort of job for the first time, developed great skill in balancing these conflicting pressures to create a dynamic process of investigation, development and consolidation leading to the generation of new questions.

Co-ordinators themselves also need their supportive peer group meetings. Central team members, as well as giving individual support to local co-ordinators, organised various opportunities for co-ordinators to work together. As Judy Keiner has pointed out (in the first article in this section), the emerging National Curriculum put unforeseen pressures on the Project to provide instant guidance. 'What is the Project saying about assessment?' was the most obvious question. The response was to work on such questions together in issue-focused groups, writing groups and national co-ordinators' conferences. As answers emerged from discussion of evidence provided by the Project (see, for example, the account by Andy Milton in article 1.1), these were fed back in the form of publications and input at INSET sessions.

Steering groups, both local and national, brought to Project deliberations the views of people with an informed interest in oracy as well as the more objective stance of those not concerned with everyday implementation. (Peter Latham's article in this section discusses an example.) One invaluable role of these groups was to review and authenticate publications.

A continuing process of national publications not only fulfils the brief for wider dissemination but also plays a significant part as a stimulus for intellectual growth. The materials published – newsletters, journals, occasional papers, books and videos – expose teachers' work to an audience beyond the Project and, through an inevitable process of selection and editing, begin to highlight the main principles and areas of development. These feed back into further reflection on practice, and a developmental upward spiral of understanding continues.

When one looks back to the questions being raised at the start of the Project and compares them with current concerns, the progress becomes clear. To give one example: many worries were expressed in early meetings about 'off-task talk'. 'If I allow time to discuss, they'll just talk about last night's TV.' But reflection on practice began to refine thinking on this issue. In the first place, teachers found from observation that off-task talk didn't happen as much as they had feared if the task was right and if children appreciated the value of talk and had helped to establish the ground rules. Through examination of transcripts, we all came to understand better the significance of personal anecdote in making sense of a general concept. We also learned from experience the importance of social talk in the processes of group cohesion for child or adult. Finally, Janet Maybin, in an influential presentation at a co-ordinators' conference, argued that 'off-task' talk, usually ignored in research into children's school language, was in fact a fundamental aspect of learning to become part of a culture.

In this way, certain talks, articles, journal centrespreads or tape recordings (like the one of Wayne and Christopher in article 1.1) take on an emblematic significance as marking mileposts – aspects now established – which become starting points for further development. Shared meanings based on common experience become well founded within the circle of members of a project. The challenge for those charged with wider dissemination is to find ways for teachers and others not previously involved to obtain access to the 'meanings' without having to go through the entire process.

Acknowledgement

We should like to thank all the National Oracy Project co-ordinators who have discussed these issues with the authors.

References

CZERNIEWSKA, P. (1989) 'National Writing Project: a story of curriculum change' in Murphy, P. and Moon, B. (eds) (1989) *Developments in Learning and Assessment.* Sevenoaks: Hodder and Stoughton.

FULLAN, M. (1990) 'Staff Development, Innovation and Institutional Development' in Joyce, B. (ed.) (1990) *Changing School Culture Through Staff Development.* Alexandria, Virginia: ASCD.

HOWE, A. (1990) 'Short steps and big leaps', *Oracy Issues 5*, Autumn 1990, National Curriculum Council/National Oracy Project.

LITTLE, J. W. (1989) *The Persistence of Privacy: Autonomy and Initiative in Teachers' Professional Relations.* Paper presented at American Educational Research Association Annual Meeting.

RUDDOCK, J. (1991) *Innovation and Change.* Milton Keynes: Open University Press.

Towards Change in Classrooms: Working on Understanding in Teacher Groups

COLIN BIOTT

The purpose of this article is to comment on the contribution of the National Oracy Project to ideas about curriculum development, with particular reference to the types of reflection which may be encouraged through exploratory talk. I shall discuss issues about the co-ordination of teacher groups by addressing two questions. First, how can a group explore value issues rather than merely rehearse individual members' old ways of talking about fixed ideas? Second, what counts as progress and quality in teachers' discussions?

I began to 'work on understanding' in teacher groups when I was involved in the Schools Council Humanities Curriculum Project during the late 1960s and early 1970s. My more recent experience is of the co-ordination of teachers' action research groups and other groups which are undertaking enquiries into their own practice as the core of a Masters degree programme. Like Hilary Kemeny and Kate Norman (in the previous article), I have learned from this work that teacher development is an integral and essential part of the 'messy processes' of curriculum development. These processes of development are messy because curricula, and even single lessons, are not simply the linear and logically sequenced products of pre-planning. This does not deny the usefulness of good planning, but it does acknowledge that classroom action is complex, uncertain and unique. The 'developed curriculum' is never as tidy as it looks in a glossy ring binder. However closely we might think that we have followed our plans, childrens' learning opportunities are enhanced or limited by our judgements and responsive actions during lessons. Because so much is happening at the same time, and because so much of it is inter-related, we cannot be certain that we have disentangled and responded to the most important 'bits' of the action.

It follows that curriculum development is most usefully seen as a form of enquiry in which the best ideas we have at the time are tested out in specific classrooms. A key principle underlying the use of teacher groups in the National Oracy Project was that by talking together, teachers might improve their individual and collective capacities to create new meanings of what they see, especially that which has become ordinary and familiar to them. This view of professional development underplays or rejects the idea that progress comes best when teachers learn to apply new techniques, or when they introduce new materials, or serve as the testers of a particular theory. The fostering of oracy in classrooms is not seen as merely a theoretical or technical problem. It has been assumed to be closer to what Schon (1987) has called an 'indeterminate zone of practice', full of 'uncertainty, uniqueness and value conflict' (p. 6). Even with the statutory orders and helpful non-statutory guidance of the National Curriculum, it is important to hold on to the idea that improvement of teaching is still dependent on improvement of day to day interpretations of classroom action as it unfolds – what Schon has called 'reflection in action'.

Teachers' insights into teaching deepen through the continual, progressive interplay between doing things and thinking about them, rather than separating the two processes. A basic assumption of the Project was that the teachers could sharpen their capacities for this kind of professional understanding through what Douglas Barnes in his article has called 'reflection that is enabled by talk outside the event', and what Schon terms 'reflection on action'.

If 'reflection that is enabled by talk' is at the heart of changing the ways that we see what is already familiar and ordinary, then we must consider the form and quality of the reflection processes themselves. We cannot assume that every teacher group that meets to reflect on its teaching will achieve the same ends. It depends what we mean by reflection. Mezirow (1981) has provided a useful framework for thinking about types of reflection based on his work on adult learning. He has been particularly interested in the place of reflection in what he calls 'perspective transformation' and because of this his ideas are of direct relevance to those of us who try to support teacher groups. He divides his framework into two parts: forms of reflection which are part of our ordinary consciousness, and those which are more demanding and critical. His interest in the latter is because it can free us from old ideas and help us to reconstruct new ones.

Turning his framework into a set of questions for the co-ordinators of teacher groups, we might ask ourselves about the kinds of reflection we are trying to foster. At the first level, Mezirow lists three forms: 'affective reflectivity' or becoming aware of how we feel about what we have been doing; 'discriminant reflectivity' or assessing the effects of what we have been doing; and 'judgemental reflectivity' which is becoming aware of our own judgements of what we like or dislike. It is likely that most teacher groups which have worked together for some time will have used these types of reflection in reviewing oracy activities in classrooms.

The second, and more demanding, level of group reflection is harder to achieve and so is less common. As co-ordinators of groups, we might ask ourselves whether we are encouraging Mezirow's three types of critical reflection. First, does the group use 'conceptual reflectivity' to become conscious of the constructs and concepts it uses to evaluate what its members have been doing or thinking? Secondly, does the group use 'psychic reflectivity' to learn how its interests, values and biases influence the ways that it perceives things? Thirdly, and lastly, does it use 'theoretical reflectivity' to become aware of how its conceptual and psychic reflections are based upon taken-for-granted and embedded cultural assumptions which impede the emancipation of thought and prevent 'perspective transformation'? In the rest of this article, I shall discuss some of the processes of critical reflection by which teacher groups might become emancipatory and transforming rather than self-confirming and cosy.

Tackling value issues

In the previous article, Hilary Kemeny and Kate Norman are rightly cautious about oversimplifying what teacher groups might achieve because of the possibilities of merely 'reinforcing poorly informed habit' or 'recycling current ignorance'. From my own experience, it seems that there are a number of possible strategies which co-ordinators might adopt to reduce the likelihood of this happening. One of the things which makes exploratory talk difficult for teachers in Project groups is that the topic often brings out justification or advocacy for one particular kind of practice. Where this meets with approval, the assertions grow ever stronger. In Mezirow's terms, there may be plenty of affective, discriminant and judgemental reflectivity, but it is difficult for anyone to challenge or even to question the apparent orthodoxies.

What makes the role of the co-ordinator demanding in these circumstances is the task of finding a balance of support and challenge. For example, we know that much can be learned from teachers' stories of their own experiences. However, it can be problematic to encourage teachers to talk about their own practice when the group has no evidence other than those personal accounts and before it has worked together long enough to be able to engage in a critical analysis of someone else's personal anecdotes. Sometimes the speaker conveys an expectation of applause or seems merely to want the sympathy of fellow strugglers. In these comforting circumstances it can feel insensitive to respond in any other manner. Because of a lack of Mezirow's conceptual and theoretical reflectivity, the underlying biases and values are rarely identified in a form which renders them open to critical discussion. This is a serious weakness since the use of oracy across the curriculum is riddled with the doubts and contradictions of different subject cultures, as well as its own uncertainties. It seems essential to uncover the value-laden nature of any interpretations and judgements which we make.

With this in mind, an alternative approach is for the co-ordinator to provide tangible evidence to which all participants have equal access. At the beginning, it may be important to have some anonymous evidence, such as a recording and/or a transcript of unknown children engaged in exploratory talk. This should not be offered as a model of good practice and the co-ordinator who provides it should not be expected to express a point of view about the material. His or her commitment should be to the quality of the processes by which the group analyses the evidence, being concerned about such things as helping the group to find, maintain and review its focus, to stay close to the evidence and to identify the underlying values which underpin various points of view about it. If a group has not got beyond affective and judgemental reflection on its own practice, this approach may help to reveal the hidden value orientations of group members in a form which enables them to be talked about. Moreover, it provides a shared foundation for raising awareness of the nature and potential of conceptual and theoretical reflectivity. It can also help the group to talk about its emerging character and to make its own ground rules explicit. It encourages the group to ask itself questions about what counts as rigour in exploratory talk which aims to contribute to curriculum development.

What counts as progress and quality in teachers' exploratory discussions?

Hilary Kemeny and Kate Norman quote Pam Czerniewska's observation that 'you can easily become complacent amid the testimonials from teachers delighted simply to have talked to each other' (p. 269). This raises questions about what counts as progress and quality in teachers' discussions which aim to promote curriculum change rather than offer therapy. I have written elsewhere (Biott, 1988) about the kinds of questions which co-ordinators might ask when reviewing progress. In this brief article, I concentrate on one aspect which seems relevant because of Douglas Barnes's comment that 'exploratory talk does not provide new information', and Hilary Kemeny and Kate Norman's example of 'contingent responsiveness' in 'providing a photocopy of a relevant article at just the right moment'. The question for the co-ordinator is: How can exploratory talk, and the practice of curriculum development through enquiry, become better informed?

Lawrence Stenhouse (1983) addressed this question when developing an approach to the informed discussion of controversial issues in classrooms in the Schools Council Humanities Curriculum Project. There were at least three key principles which helped to maintain the exploratory nature of the discussion whilst developing intellectual rigour. First, new information was treated as evidence to elucidate whatever issue was being discussed and not to prove a point or to close the exploration. Secondly, evidence was to be evaluated in terms of whether it helped towards understanding of different viewpoints or ideas, and not simply whether it was considered to be true or false. Thirdly, the person providing the information was not expected necessarily to agree with its message or to be pushed into a corner when defending it. There is a degree of artistry in judging when to introduce new material, but there is also a case for being guided by a set of principles such as these which are explicit to the whole group.

It is important to find a way of fostering exploratory talk which is open and provisional and explores embedded assumptions and value differences, but which also engenders a search for new information and an interest in testing out new ideas. As well as trying to add new dimensions to exploratory talk, co-ordinators need to be alert to the kinds of responses which impede progress. The following examples illustrate the sort of difficulties I have in mind.

When being asked to discuss a video recording of a lesson, group members may make appeals to special status or confine the scope of a topic so that they can claim superior knowledge, such as in the remark, 'Well, when you've worked round here as long as I have you know that just wouldn't work with our children.' This can be even more of a problem when such claims to special status are used to limit the contributions of other people in the same group 'who haven't worked round here at all'. Similar ploys may also be used to marginalise outsiders who are invited into schools or groups. I have mischievously imagined one teacher saying of Paul McCartney, if he happened to come to teach a music lesson, 'I'd like to see him on yard duty!'

Another kind of claim to superior knowledge can come from those who try to close a line of enquiry by suggesting that the issue under discussion is already resolved because it's in somebody's book. Their references seem to place the ideas beyond criticism. One strategy is to treat their ideas as starting points for enquiry and not as conclusions. This tends to maintain their commitment to group learning while allowing others to explore the ideas critically from the basis of experience and evidence. Group members become more equal if all have access to the same evidence.

Sometimes a group needs to be helped to get beyond descriptive judgements if it is to progress towards understanding. In one such group, the teachers had watched a video recording of an anonymous lesson based on group talk. One of them asked when it had been filmed. 'Oh,' he said, 'if it was that far into the term there's not enough display on the walls, then.' When asked why display was important to him, he said it was mainly to motivate and encourage the children and to give them pride in their work. These concepts became a focus for further discussion, and we needed to have another look at the video to explore more deeply what was happening in the lesson. The group's talk was gaining depth, direction and continuity as the concepts of motivation and pride were reconsidered and used in the analysis. We felt we needed further evidence because we wanted to check how the children were making meaning of what we thought might be the teachers' intended and unintended messages. Our discussion of abstract concepts and our questions about what would count as satisfactory evidence formed both an impetus and a framework for planning further enquiry. A number of the group wanted to try things in their own classrooms and to bring evidence to analyse in the next group session.

Conclusion

In this article, I have tried to make a case for an approach which is based mainly on the use of evidence, and which explores value issues and concepts. This kind of demanding discussion is not arid or exclusively cerebral. It can also engender creative and imaginative talk. For instance, when struggling at the edges of their understanding, teachers often tell stories to explain what they mean. This is rather like the butler in Ishiguro's novel, *The Remains of the Day*, who tells stories involving other butlers to work out what they mean by the concept of 'dignity'. New ways of seeing can come in surprising ways, especially when we are open to trying different ways of making and conveying meaning. Aiming for quality does not stop us enjoying ourselves and having a laugh, but it does require us to know when we are being facile, indulgent or simply opinionated.

Those of us who spend a lot of time trying to engage in exploratory talk can usually remember times when it has suddenly become deeper, or more sharply focused, or more exciting. I have noticed how it often tends to happen when a real dilemma has been identified and when it is seen as important by most group members. Mezirow has called this a 'disorientating dilemma'; an essential feature in 'perspective transformation' in adult learning. He has also argued that it helps if learners sense a problem but recognise that it is not exclusive to themselves. Taken together, the 'disorientating dilemma' and the shared problem are two of the factors which seem to form a key point in the kind of teacher development and curriculum development being encouraged in the National Oracy Project. Successful groups seem to have both the patience to reach that point and the resilience to go further.

References

BIOTT, C. (1988) 'Collaborative Enquiry in Staffrooms and Classrooms', *Forum*, Vol. 30, No. 2 pp. 56–8.

ISHIGURO, K. (1989) *The Remains of the Day*. London: Faber & Faber.

MEZIROW, J. A. (1981) 'A Critical Theory of Adult Learning and Education', *Adult Education*, Vol. 32, No. 1, pp. 3–24.

SCHON, D. (1987) *Educating the Reflective Practitioner*. San Francisco: Jossey Bass.

STENHOUSE, L. (1983) *Authority, Education and Emancipation*. London: Heinemann.

ENDPIECE

The Centrality of Talk in Education

GORDON WELLS

In many ways this is a celebratory volume. And for good reason. The centrality of talk in education is finally being recognised. Not simply in theory – in the exhortations of progressive-minded academics – but mandated at all levels and across all subjects in a national curriculum. From my Canadian position on the sidelines, I have watched, with mixed emotions, the sequence of political events which has eventuated in this happy state of affairs, and which is carefully documented in Judy Keiner's article in Section 5. The account is fascinating. It is also instructive about the unpredictable – and essentially unprincipled – nature of educational change, when this is directed from 'above'.

But just as important as a cause for celebration is the fact that, as a result of the approach adopted by the National Oracy Project, the meaning in practice of that claim about the centrality of talk is being addressed by thousands of teachers in a variety of exploratory and innovative ways. Through the examples of their work that are included in this volume, we are presented with a very different picture of educational change to that which is directed from above. This educational change can be brought about through the efforts of practising teachers, networking with each other and supported by advisers and administrators who believe in the potential for improving pupils' learning experiences that is inherent in teachers' self-directed professional development. As one who shares this belief, I am delighted to have been asked to review the work of the National Oracy Project, as it is represented in the articles which make up this volume.

Talk has, in fact, been receiving more attention in recent years in quite a number of countries. In North America, an important influence has been the work of the 'whole language' movement, with its emphasis on the functional interrelatedness of reading, writing and talking in relation to all areas of the curriculum (Goodman 1987). Similar developments have taken place in Australia (Cambourne, 1988) and in New Zealand (Corson, 1988). An increased valuing of talk has also occurred as a by-product of attempts to introduce a more collaborative style of learning in the classroom, with students working in small groups rather than in the traditional 'recitation' mode, directed by the teacher from the front of the classroom. Various forms of 'cooperative learning' have been pioneered in the United States (Johnson, Johnson and Holubec, 1988; Slavin, 1990), in Canada (Brubacher *et al.*, 1990), in Australia (see Forrestal, this volume), and in Israel (Sharan and Shachar, 1988), and all have emphasised the essential role of talk in small group learning.

However, old traditions die hard, particularly when they are reinforced by countervailing pressure groups urging a return to mastery learning of basic skills and prescribed content. In practice, therefore, many primary and most secondary classrooms are still places in which learners' talk is seen as something to be strictly controlled and directed, rather than as a resource to be encouraged and exploited as a powerful means of learning. Reviewing the current place of speaking and listening in the classroom for the *Handbook of Research on Teaching the English Language Arts*, Pinnell and Jaggar write: 'surveys show oral language curricula in the United States have changed little since the 1960s' (1991, p. 700). This is certainly not the case in Australia, Canada and New Zealand, which have been more strongly influenced by the work of those in Britain associated with the emphasis on 'language across the curriculum' (e.g. Barnes *et al.*, 1969; Barnes, 1976; Britton, 1970; Rosen and Rosen, 1973; Torbe and Medway, 1981). However, it still remains true that, in all these countries, at a national level, a recognition of the centrality of talk in education – in practice as well as in policy – still has to be achieved. The current situation in Britain, therefore, where both the National Curriculum and the National Oracy Project are attempting to bring about such a change nationwide, is likely to attract a great deal of international attention.

In article 5.2, Peter Latham characterises the relationship between these two agencies of change by means of a metaphor drawn from mechanics. The work of the National Oracy Project, he writes, has been a valuable counterbalance to the 'top-down' model of curriculum planning represented by the National Curriculum. And I certainly agree that a top-down approach, if it is to be successful, needs to be complemented by one that is practice-based and bottom-up. However, I believe that the wide range of teacher enquiries through which the National Oracy Project has been carried out is related to the National Curriculum in an organic, as well as a mechanical, way. To substantiate this claim, I want to explore the assumptions about learning in the National Curriculum that have led to the valuing of oracy, and then to relate these to the approach to curriculum development that has been adopted in the National Oracy Project. In the process, I shall offer some comments on some of the issues raised in earlier articles of this volume.

Discourse as means and goal of learning and teaching

In the article already referred to, Latham identifies four assumptions about learning which, in his view, underpin the requirements for attention to spoken language that are found at all Key Stages and in all subject areas of the National Curriculum. They are the following:

1   '. . . learning is likely to be most effective when (learners) are active in formulating their own questions and developing their own strategies for solving problems or making use of information.' (p. 258)

2   '(There is) a need to acknowledge and use what (learners) already know as a basis for extending their learning.' (p. 259)

3   '. . . reflection has to be an essential aspect of learning . . . helping (learners) to make explicit to themselves, as well as to others, what they know, understand and can do.' (p. 261)

4   '. . . learning is a social and collaborative enterprise.' (p. 261)

These four assumptions stem from a coherent theory of learning and teaching which, originating in the work of Piaget and Vygotsky and extended and developed by scholars in a wide range of disciplines*, is

---

*For example, Piaget (1954), Vygotsky (1978), Barnes (1976), Britton (1970), Bruner (1971), Moll (1991) and Wood (1988).

gradually gaining ascendancy in educational thinking. This theory, if followed through to its logical conclusions, is likely to bring about a revolution in classroom practice. Stated briefly, the theory can be articulated in terms of three basic principles, each of which is empirically well-supported.

First, knowledge is not a commodity existing in some pure and abstract realm independently of particular knowers, but a state of understanding achieved through the constructive mental activity of individual learners. Even when 'transmitted' by an authority, in the form of a teacher or textbook, therefore, knowledge does not enter the mind of the learner in the form transmitted; rather, learners progressively construct their own knowledge by bringing what they already know to bear on new information in order to assimilate or accommodate to the new and to extend or modify their initial understanding.

Secondly, although it results in an individual resource for interpretation and action, this process of knowledge construction is essentially social and cultural in nature. For it is through participation with more mature members of the community in socially significant, purposeful activities that learners encounter the knowledge and skills that are valued in their culture, as these are enacted in the problem-solving strategies deployed and in the discourse that accompanies, and in some cases constitutes, the activity. And by thus engaging with others in collaborative action and in the co-construction of meaning, learners are assisted to take over these cultural resources and make them their own. Moreover, because this process of 'appropriation' involves the active transformation of the information provided by the other participant(s) in the activity, the learner's resulting knowledge is never a straightforward copy, but a new, personal reconstruction. As a result, it may go beyond the 'model' in its potential for finding novel and creative solutions to the original problem and even for formulating and tackling problems not previously envisaged.

Thirdly, in all these activity settings, collaborative problem-solving – and the learning it engenders – is mediated and facilitated by cultural practices and artefacts. These include artefacts such as wheels, levers, clocks and microscopes, and modes of representation such as pictures, diagrams and musical notation, as well as such social practices as co-ordinating action and dividing responsibility for the task according to expertise and availability. All of these are 'tools' which, as members of the culture, we inherit, but which were invented by problem-solvers in previous generations.

Of these culturally inherited mediating tools, it is generally agreed that the most important is discourse – that is to say, the interactive and constructive meaning-making that occurs in purposeful linguistic interaction with others. First, the words and structures of the linguistic code that is used provide a conventional resource for referring to the objects and events that are at issue in the activity in which the participants are engaged; they also enable the participants to refer, reflexively and reflectively, to the discourse itself. Secondly, discourse is itself a form of action. For, in producing and responding to the linked and reciprocally related moves that make up a sequence of discourse, participants are able to act on each other, guiding and influencing each other's understanding of, and involvement in, their joint endeavour.

However, neither commonality of reference nor co-ordination of action is assured simply by the use of the same linguistic code. As a result of their different backgrounds and different life experiences, as well as their different concerns in engaging in the interaction, participants in discourse always 'speak with different voices' (Bakhtin, 1986). In order to communicate successfully, therefore, they must constantly strive to achieve and maintain a shared, *intersubjective* understanding of the matter at hand (Rommetveit, 1979). And it is because of the adjustment of perspective that is required as one attempts to 'see' as the other person sees – as evidenced by what he or she says – that discourse provides such a powerful occasion and means of learning. Furthermore, when internalised, the discourses one has engaged in *intermentally* with others become a personal resource for *intramental* problem-solving and reflection, through what Vygotsky referred to as 'inner speech'.

Talk as a tool for learning and teaching

The importance of discourse – or conversation, as it is more commonly called – has long been recognised with respect to the pre-school years. It is through what can be thought of as a form of 'apprenticeship in conversation' that children learn both the language system and the cultural ways of making sense of experience that constitute the 'meaning potential' of that system (Halliday, 1975; Lock, 1980; Rogoff, 1990; Wells, 1980, 1986; MacLure, this volume). However, it is only in recent years that explicit acknowledgement has been given to the important role that spoken discourse continues to play, throughout the years of schooling and beyond, in mediating the culturally valued knowledge and skills that learners encounter and are expected to master. To be sure, the significance of written discourse in this respect has long been recognised, at least implicitly; hence the perennial concern with standards of literacy. However, acquisition of the written mode of language use in no way reduces the importance of the spoken mode, for the two modes stand in a complementary, rather than a mutually exclusive, relationship to each other. Moreover, it is quite largely through talk about texts that children first discover how to use the tool of written discourse and, throughout our lives, our engagement with written texts continues to be accompanied by talk about them (Chambers, 1985; Wells, 1990).

This belated recognition of the importance of spoken discourse in education may seem surprising when one considers how large a proportion of time is spent, in every classroom, in talking and listening. However, the explanation is probably to be found, on the one hand, in the individualistic and competitive ethos that has typically prevailed in schools and, on the other, in the misguided model of communication that has been almost universally taken for granted in Western societies since the rise of empiricist philosophy. In a nutshell, what is assumed according to this model, is that communication is essentially a matter of information transfer. This belief is based, in turn, on four further assumptions:

1) language functions like a conduit, transferring thoughts bodily from one person to another;
2) in writing and speaking, people insert their thoughts or feelings in the words;
3) words accomplish the transfer by containing the thoughts or feelings and transferring them to others;
4) in listening or reading, people extract the thoughts and feelings once again from the words.

            (Reddy, 1979, p. 290; quoted in Wertsch, 1991, p. 72)

Such a simple transmissional theory, however, is completely incompatible with the sociocultural theory of knowledge construction outlined above. Furthermore, it has been demonstrated empirically – particularly with respect to reading – that the interpretation of a text that is constructed in the act of reading or listening is not a copy of what was in the mind of the originator but the outcome of a transaction between the cues and constraints provided by the linguistically organised signal and what the reader/listener brings by way of prior knowledge, cultural expectations engendered by the context and his or her current personal preoccupations (Rosenblatt, 1988). Or, as Wertsch (1991) puts it with reference to spoken discourse:

... for communication to occur, one must always listen to what the speaker says, but what the speaker says does not mechanistically generate an exclusive interpretation.

(p.79)

Thus, while it is true that one function of a text is to enable the listener to reconstruct the speaker's meaning as accurately as possible, there is a second and equally important function, which is to provide the occasion for the generation of new meaning, as the listener makes sense of what the speaker says by responding to it in terms of his or her existing knowledge and current purposes. It is in this second 'dialogic' function that a text acts as what Lotman (1988) calls a 'thinking device' as, in successive turns, each participant strives to contribute to the jointly constructed conversational meaning in a manner which both does justice to what the previous speaker has said and extends the discourse in terms of his or her own understanding.

Educational discourse therefore needs to give due emphasis to both these functions. And since, traditionally, it has been the transmissional function which has dominated discourse in the classroom, the balance now needs to be rectified with much more attention being given to the dialogic function (Tharp and Gallimore, 1988).

Consider, for example, the situation that arises when new information is encountered through observation or reading, or in the utterances of the teacher or some other speaker. Because each learner makes sense of this 'text' in terms of what he or she already knows, there will inevitably be a variety of alternative interpretations. If the teacher operates only in terms of a transmission model of communication, he or she will assume that everybody has understood the information in the same way – or, alternatively, has simply *failed* to understand – and the divergences will go undetected. If, at this point, on the other hand, a dialogic perspective is adopted, the teacher will encourage these different interpretations to be brought out into the open so that their bases in pupils' prior beliefs can be explored. Further evidence can then be presented in order to prompt pupils to question those beliefs and either to modify them in the direction of those that are culturally accepted or to make explicit for themselves and for others the grounds of their disagreement. (This can be seen happening in several of the extracts discussed in this volume.)

Furthermore, when pupils are encouraged to express their own thoughts and opinions under these dialogic conditions, they provide the teacher with evidence about their current levels of skill and understanding and this, in turn, enables the teacher to be contingently responsive in the help he or she provides. Thus, by adopting a dialogic perspective, teachers are better able to 'scaffold' their pupils' learning (see Maybin, Mercer and Stierer, article 4.2) or, in Vygotsky's terms, to address their teaching to the pupils' 'zone of proximal development'.

Learning to participate in the discourse of the disciplines

So far, I have focused on discourse as the *means* of enacting the teaching-learning relationship. But, viewed from a slightly different perspective, it can be seen to be also the *goal* of education.

One way of looking at the school curriculum is as the systematic provision of opportunities for successive generations to be apprenticed into some of the different 'disciplines' that our culture treats as being of particular value. Each subject discipline constitutes a way of making sense of human experience that has evolved over generations and each is dependent on its own particular practices: its instrumental procedures, its criteria for judging relevance and validity, and its conventions of acceptable forms of argument. In a word, each has developed its own modes of discourse. To work in a discipline, therefore, it is necessary to be able to engage in these practices and, in particular, to participate in the discourse of that community.

Unfortunately, the discursive nature of knowledge construction is all too often lost in the accounts of the different subject disciplines that are presented to pupils in school. Either the focus is on the inventions or discoveries of great individuals or, still worse, the subject is presented as a set of timeless truths which have an impersonal and unchallengeable authority. In either case, what is lost is an understanding of the influence of the cultural and historical context in determining what problems are addressed in any period, what presuppositions are brought to bear on them and what semiotic tools are available for use in their solution. And, more importantly, pupils get no sense of the dialogue between the members of the specialist community through which the process of 'composing and revising' the 'story' of the discipline is carried on (Rosen, 1984).

In a very important sense, then, to be, for example, a physicist or historian is to engage in the discourse of physics or history, and to be able to 'do' either 'subject' involves being able to use the specialist discourse genres that have been shaped within the relevant communities as the essential semiotic tools for collaborative meaning-making. Like the child's conversational learning of and through language in the pre-school years, therefore, learning in school can be seen quite largely as a continuing apprenticeship in discourse, as he or she participates in, and takes over, the different discourse genres – that is, ways of making meaning – that are encountered in the various subjects of the curriculum (Halliday and Hasan, 1989).

In the preceding discussion, I have made no distinction between spoken and written discourse, although there clearly are important differences from this point of view between the genres in any discipline, both in their forms and in their contexts of use. Because publication is the most visible mode in which academic dialogue is carried on, it is not surprising that it is the written genres which have received most attention (for example, Martin, Christie and Rothery, 1987). However, as I have already mentioned, the published text almost always emerges from a prolonged preparation in the oral mode, in the form of seminars, discussion at conferences and the much less formal conversations that occur between peers in the course of conducting an experiment, carrying out an archaeological dig, or examining a historical document or the output from a computer analysis of questionnaire data. While the spoken genres of conversation or of debate do not correspond in any simple way to the written genres of exposition, critical review, and so on, there are nevertheless important commonalities between the spoken and written genres in any discipline. Equally importantly, it is in the fully dialogic mode of spoken discourse, with its dependence on the maintenance of intersubjectivity, that what is written and read can most readily be related to individuals' personal experience, and differences in beliefs or interpretations uncovered, explored and either resolved or refined to the point where they can be made the basis of further inquiry.

Similarly, in the classroom, while it is an important goal of schooling that pupils should learn to use the written genres of the different subject disciplines, both as readers and as writers (Christie, 1984), this should not lead to an undervaluing of talk. For spoken discourse has an essential role to play in mediating the pupils' apprenticeship into the discipline, both as a medium in which to respond to and prepare for work on written texts (Barnes, 1976) and, more generally, as an opportunity for 'talking their way in' (Halliday, 1975) to ways of making sense of new information, however encountered, in forms that, with the assistance provided by the teacher, gradually incorporate the essential features of the discourse of the particular discipline (Newman *et al.*, 1989; Lampert, 1989; Lemke, 1990).

Oracy: some problematic issues

In the preceding pages, I have tried to develop, in outline, a rationale for the attention to spoken language that is required by the National Curriculum. To do so, I have appealed to a theory of learning and teaching that is rooted in a view of knowledge as personally constructed through social interaction and mediated by culturally inherited semiotic tools, the most important of which is discourse. And it is a similar view of the instrumental significance of spoken discourse for learning and teaching which, I believe, has inspired the work of the National Oracy Project.

However, as several writers in this volume make clear, there are still areas which remain problematic, both as a result of other social forces which are powering the current eruption of curriculum reform, and as a result of the inexperience of many teachers in realising the general curriculum recommendations about oracy in specific classroom practices.

One particular note of concern that can be heard throughout the volume has to do with the requirements of assessment. As Judy Keiner reminds us in her historical overview (in article 5.1), the first funded research project with 'oracy' in its title was aimed at devising 'modes of oral assessment' for the new CSE examination. Since this concern to assess oracy has been carried over into the National Curriculum, there is a justifiable fear that the term will continue to be understood, by some people at least, as denoting a set of skills in oral language that need to be assessed. However, as Douglas Barnes points out (in article 2.1), if the testing of these skills is divorced from the curricular topics that have excited the pupils' interest and from contexts in which talk about such topics, undertaken with responsive co-participants, has a genuine purpose for them, then there is a danger that their skills of oracy will remain untapped – and therefore unrecognized. Such testing would, furthermore, convey a message about the place of spoken language in the classroom which runs counter to the emphasis on oracy as a tool for learning, which it is one of the goals of the National Curriculum to promote.

A second, and related, set of issues concerns the 'heterogeneity of voices' (Wertsch, 1991) that is found in any community and, indeed, in any discourse. The first type of heterogeneity – that is to say, the existence of variation between individuals in accent and dialect, and even in preferred language, that is found in any multicultural, class-based society – is introduced by Douglas Barnes in the article already referred to and discussed at length by Tony Edwards (article 2.2) and Richard Bain (article 2.3). Edwards argues that teachers and others in positions of power should avoid making negative judgements about the abilities of pupils on the basis of their use of languages or dialects other than the authorised standard dialect of English, and Bain urges teachers to encourage pupils to develop a positive attitude to their own dialect or language. The tension between these recommendations and the more prescriptive tenor of the National Curriculum attainment targets pertaining to spoken language still remains, however, and is particularly strongly felt by teachers of bilingual children, as is made clear in article 2.6 by Mary Morrison and Perminder Sandhu.

The issue of gender, as it relates to the differential participation of girls and boys in some classroom activities, can also be seen in terms of the privileging of one set of voices over others, as is clearly brought out in Hilary Kemeny and Gemma Moss's discussion of gender issues in article 2.7. Alan Howe and Jenny Des-Fountain (article 3.2) present a particularly interesting example of this problem arising in a science unit, in which the girls' voices tend to be suppressed when they are working in a group with boys. When working later in a single-sex group, on the other hand, they show themselves well able to make their own sense of the task they have been set.

Several articles also address the second type of heterogeneity – that between different registers and genres, as they may be used by the same individuals on different occasions according to the contexts in which they find themselves and their own roles within them or, within the same context, by people who have varying degrees of expertise with respect to the topic under discussion. One particularly important type of heterogeneity, as far as schooling is concerned, occurs with respect to the genres used in the different subject disciplines. Being able to use the genre appropriate to the curricular activity in progress may be as important a part of being communicatively competent in school as is being able to use the appropriate social register in the typically asymmetrical power relationship that obtains between teacher and pupils in the classroom (cf. Edwards, article 2.2) – although, ironically, success in learning to manage the former is likely to be impeded if too much attention has to be given to the latter.

Yanina Sheeran and Douglas Barnes address this issue of discipline-based genres quite directly. They ask: 'are the language and thought patterns of specialist subjects somehow inextricably interwoven? . . .

or should our efforts be mainly directed towards the demystification and demotion of language so remote from everyday living?' (see article 2.5).

Obviously, an answer to the first question demands a lengthier consideration of the thorny issue of the relationship between using language and thinking than there is space for here. However, whatever the position one adopts on the issue of the role of language in the intellectual activity of individuals, what seems to me incontrovertible is that it is only by entering into the social discourse used by members of a particular community that one can hope to discover and appropriate their ways of making sense of experience. To the extent that the modes of discourse of different subject disciplines involve different sets of 'ground rules', specialist terms and structural patterns, which may at first seem to be in conflict with those with which pupils are familiar, it will almost certainly be advantageous for them to receive help in learning the new registers and genres. In this sense, it is very much the teacher's responsibility to 'demystify' what is strange and difficult to grasp, and to build bridges between pupils' everyday ways of talking and those used within the subject disciplines. Article 1.5, by Jenny Des-Fountain and her colleagues, offers an interesting exploration of ways of providing this apprenticeship with respect to the discourse of history.

But perhaps the most important point to make is that, as with different social dialects, there is nothing intrinsically better or worse about the different genres that may be used to talk about the same domain of experience. 'Common-sense' ways of talking and thinking are as valid as those of physicists or historians. Which is more appropriate, however, depends upon the activity in which the participants are engaged. For example, common-sense ways of talking about balance may be most helpful to someone learning to ride a bicycle, but, in the task of designing a new bicycle, those involved will probably find it more helpful to discuss their problems in genres closer to those used by physicists and mathematicians in order to make sense of essentially the same phenomena.

In their article, Sheeran and Barnes seem to arrive at very much the same conclusion. While there may be some features of the specialist genres that they would like to 'demote', such as the impersonal passive construction in the writing of scientific reports, they agree that pupils need to be given access to the genres of the specialist disciplines. And this is not simply in order to fit in with teacher expectations and get good grades, valid reasons though these are. It is because, as I suggested earlier, it is only by learning to talk in these ways that they will be able to join in the discourse of the discipline and take over the ways of thinking that are made public in that discourse.

As several authors in this volume point out, however, the extent to which pupils are given this opportunity depends on the ways in which they encounter these specialist genres and the help they receive in making sense of them. Since space is limited, I should like to look at just one aspect of classroom discourse from this point of view, and that is the occurrence of questions.

Questions in the classroom

As David Wood amply documents (article 4.4), questions have always been the teacher's stock in trade. In one North American study, teachers were found to ask an average of two questions per minute. And, of these, a high proportion were display questions, that is to say, questions to test whether the pupils know what the teacher knows rather than to help the teacher learn something from the pupils. The Bristol Study (Wells, 1986) found that, already by the first term of school, about 20% of the teacher utterances that children received, either individually or as members of a group or whole class, were questions and, of these, two thirds were requests for display.

But the imbalance does not stop there. In a display question exchange, the teacher not only asks the question in the first slot (of the exchange), but also takes the third and last slot to evaluate the answer, often also modifying or elaborating on it from his or her perspective. Again, the same study found that, overall, only 17% of teachers' utterances picked up and extended the meanings expressed in children's previous utterances whereas as many as 39% were elaborations and developments of meanings that they themselves had previously initiated. The study reached the same conclusion as Wood, that is that, if teachers really want to hear what pupils think and if they genuinely want to encourage pupils to ask questions of their own, they should use a less controlling discourse genre. As Pauline Loader puts it (article 4.6), teachers should 'give the children the floor . . . and listen intently'.

But, some may want to argue, that is not what teaching is about. In their view, the teacher's role is to ensure that pupils are presented with the culturally valued knowledge which is specified in the curriculum and are encouraged to reconstruct it as accurately as possible. To achieve this goal, the most appropriate discourse genre is one to which pupils as well as the teacher contribute, but with the teacher in control of the meanings that are made. This is very much the view of Newman, Griffin and Cole (1989), who see the three-part structure of the display question exchange as being 'quite nicely designed' for this purpose. While the exchange as a whole is 'collaboratively constructed', it has the particular merit of having 'a built-in repair structure in the teacher's last turn so that incorrect information can be replaced with the right answers' (p. 127).

The article by Neil Mercer which immediately follows the one by Wood can be read as presenting an argument along these lines. Teachers' display questions are justified as an effective means of 'monitoring children's knowledge and understanding', 'guiding their learning' and 'marking knowledge and experience which is considered educationally significant or valuable'. The overall aim is for the teacher's knowledge to become 'common knowledge' (Edwards and Mercer, 1987), constructed according to the 'ground rules' of educational discourse; and these are inculcated, indirectly, through the opportunity that this discourse genre provides for the teacher to frame and shape pupil responses in the first and last move in each exchange.

From their more extended writings, however, it is clear that Mercer and Wood both subscribe to the same social constructivist theory of learning and teaching as was outlined earlier in this article (see Edwards and Mercer, 1987, and Wood, 1988). How, then, can they present arguments in their respective articles for points of view that seem to be in conflict with respect to the teacher's role in classroom discourse? The answer is to be found, I think, in the tension which is inherent in the theory itself.

To be able to act effectively in the world – and to succeed in school – pupils need to appropriate the ways of acting and thinking that are 'common knowledge' within their culture. That is to say, they need to encounter and receive assistance in internalising the use of the mediating tools which are drawn upon in collaborative problem-solving. This, as Mercer emphasises, requires input from teachers and others who already have this knowledge so that pupils may be helped to make sense of the tasks they are set and enabled to perform them appropriately. In Newman *et al.*'s phrase, they need to be able to arrive at the 'right answers'. To provide this guidance is a very important part of the teacher's task and one which deserves the sort of detailed attention that it receives at the hands of Mercer in article 4.5 and by Maybin, Mercer and Stierer in article 4.2.

On the other hand, learning and teaching should not be concerned *only* with cultural reproduction. Nor should the problems pupils tackle always be selected from those to which the teacher already knows the right answer. It is equally important that pupils gain confidence in their ability to find their own solutions to problems, since they will not always be able to turn to someone else for the answer. As important as teacher input, therefore, is the opportunity for pupils to pose their own problems, either individually or in collaboration with their peers, and to ask questions to which they themselves wish to find answers. For, as Irena Cassar shows (article 4.6), it is when learners have a real desire to understand, and one which comes from a purpose of their own, that they most actively engage in making sense of new information, transforming it in the process of incorporating it into their own mental models. And in this act of transformation lies the potential for new ways of thinking, new ways of solving problems, that can ultimately enrich and extend the culture's existing repertoire.

Not all new ideas are valid, of course; often they are incomplete or internally inconsistent. But the best way for learners to discover when their solutions to problems are inadequate is by being taken seriously – by being encouraged to formulate their ideas in their own terms, and to put them to the test in action or in discussion. The same aim of encouraging pupils to become independent thinkers who formulate and attempt to solve their own problems underlies Terry Phillips's arguments (article 3.3) for pupils to 'interrogate the tasks' they are set, in order to clarify for themselves the nature of the task demands and to take responsibility for deciding how best to carry them out.

By contrast, as Wood emphasises, if their ideas are habitually suppressed just because they do not conform to the teacher's expectations, and if their questions are discouraged because they interfere with the teacher's pre-planned development of the topic, pupils will be denied the opportunity to take ownership of their own ideas and to develop the discourse skills necessary to provide reasoned arguments to defend them. Instead, they will learn that the ground rules for effective participation in classroom activities place a much higher value on conformity than on originality, on convention rather than on effectiveness. As a result, they will remain dependent thinkers and, in the larger scheme of things, it will be society that is the loser.

The key question therefore is: are these two requirements inevitably in conflict? Or, more narrowly in the context of this discussion, do teacher questions necessarily suppress pupil initiative, both in saying what they really think and in asking the questions to which they themselves want answers? The answer is clearly 'no' – as several contributions to this volume make clear. However, to determine which sorts of questions are successful in encouraging pupils to contribute more actively to classroom discussion and to take the initiative in formulating and solving their own problems, it is necessary to consider both the contexts in which the questions are asked and the asker's reasons for asking them.

As Dave Wood, a secondary school teacher observes (article 4.6), 'the same question can evoke an entirely different response when it is addressed to a group rather than a whole class, or to an individual rather than in the classroom forum.' If the teacher can build a climate which is safe, in which pupils' ideas and opinions are valued, and in which it is acceptable to make mistakes, 'the phrasing of the utterance is . . . relatively unimportant in comparison'. And as Irene Shantry, an infant school teacher, demonstrates (article 4.6), asking how to get to Notting Hill Gate can lead five and six year olds to apply their existing knowledge in a focused, goal-oriented manner when they believe that the problem is one to which the teacher is genuinely seeking a solution.

One way of looking at the contexts and purposes for questions is in terms of the 'locus of expertise'. As Roy Corden's examples make clear (article 4.1), the force of a question is linked to the way in which expertise is assumed to be distributed in the group. In everyday conversation, questions are usually posed by non-experts to those who are believed to possess the relevant expertise and they are answered on the same assumption. Departures from this norm do occur, of course, but they almost always convey additional messages about the speaker's judgement of the competence of the person questioned (Labov and Fanshel, 1977). In considering when a question might appropriately be asked in the classroom, therefore, without implying a doubt about the expertise of the addressee, we might usefully draw upon the distinction proposed by Labov (op. cit.). Conversational topics in dyadic conversations, he suggests, can be classified as either 'A-events' (things that A alone knows about), 'B-events' (things that B alone knows about) or 'AB-events' (things that both A and B know about). The situation in the classroom is somewhat more complex, of course, because of the greater number of participants. Nevertheless, with this proviso, it is possible to use this basic framework, as in Table 1 opposite, to distinguish a variety of possible configurations of 'locus of expertise' that are likely to occur.

In this table, Category 1 represents the situation in which only the teacher has expertise, for example at the beginning of a new unit of work (although, on further investigation, it would probably almost always emerge that this situation was in reality a version of 5 or 7). In Category 2, the teacher again has the expertise and wants to know whether one or more of the pupils has also acquired it. In 3, one of the pupils – or a group that has been working together – has expertise that is shared by no-one else in the class; while in 4, the situation is

Category	Locus of Expertise		
	Teacher	*Focal Pupil*	*Other Pupils*
1	Yes	No	No
2	Yes	?	?
3	No	Yes	No
4	Yes	Yes	No
5	Yes	Yes	Yes
6	No	No	No
7	Yes	Partial	—

Table 1. Configurations of 'Locus of Expertise' in the classroom

similar to 3, except that the teacher also shares the expertise. In 5, everyone in the class has expertise with respect to the topic at issue; while in 6, the opposite is the case – nobody in the classroom has expertise relevant to a topic that at least one participant is interested in. Finally, in 7, one or more pupils has some expertise, but this is either incomplete or it differs in some significant way from that of the teacher.

Categories 1 and 2 seem to be the ones that have received the most attention, both as contexts in which, traditionally, the bulk of teacher questions have occurred, and also as the focus of the debate about the appropriateness of teachers' questions as an aid to pupil learning. However, as Table 1 makes clear, there are other configurations of expertise in which the asking of questions could be of benefit to both the asker and the provider of information.

In 3 and 4, for example, really interesting questions are likely to be forthcoming from peers after they have listened to an account of what another pupil, or a group, had learned from carrying out an inquiry and, as most of us can attest, there is probably no better way of consolidating one's understanding than having to explain what one has learned to those who know less than oneself. Several of the reports from teachers in this volume make reference to situations of this kind, almost always in positive terms. It is also an important component of the Australian approach to small group learning reported by Peter Forrestal (article 3.4).

In these same situations, teacher questions can also have similar positive outcomes, as is illustrated by the example from Irene Shantry already referred to and the accounts that Harold Gardiner gives of his conversation with the fifteen-year-old fishing expert and of the teacher questioning a fifth year boy about his engineering technology project for which he had made a fabric-testing machine (article 4.3). Pupils get a real sense of satisfaction from being able to 'teach' their teachers something that they do not already know, and teachers can also enjoy learning from their pupils. The fact that the teacher may already share the pupils' expertise, as in Category 4, need not significantly change the situation, for there will no doubt be some areas in which the pupils' knowledge outstrips the teacher's, if only on how they came to know what they know.

Category 5 is, in many ways, the situation of 4 writ large. Everybody has knowledge about the topic, but it is almost certain that no two people have identical knowledge. There is thus an excellent opportunity to compare what different people know and to work towards the formulation of overarching statements that can contain the range of detailed information contributed by the different members of the group while reaching towards the organising principles of the relevant discipline(s). A version of this sharing of relevant experience is, in essence, the strategy that Simon Wolfe reports having adopted with great success (article 4.6).

As well as being an occasion to review the substantive content that has been addressed over the course of a curricular unit, such reflective discussions, to which all participants have relevant expertise to contribute, also provide an excellent opportunity to consider the procedures used, including different discourse genres, and their relative effectiveness for different purposes. Mercer (article 4.4) quotes from the case-study by Dorothy Steel to make a similar point: as she says, 'the term spent "talking about talking" with the children had changed my perceptions of their capabilities'. From the rest of her account it is clear that the children, too, had benefited from the experience. Such 'meta-talk' has tended to occur rather rarely in classrooms yet, as John Johnson and his co-authors suggest, it is, in fact, 'the richest resource ... for developing and improving the quality of teaching and learning' (article 1.1).

Although mutual ignorance (Category 6) may seem to be at the other end of the spectrum of expertise from the situation described in the previous paragraph, it offers very similar opportunities for reflective and exploratory talk. How often a major piece of research starts with the question 'I wonder why ...?' or 'I wonder what would happen if ... ?', to which nobody knows the answer. In the past, teachers have often been unwilling to allow time for the consideration of such questions, or still less to ask them themselves, for fear of revealing their own ignorance – of being unable immediately to provide the 'right answer'. But once they recognise the value of creating, in the classroom, a collaborative community of inquirers, such occasions are seen for what they are – an opportunity for asking 'real' questions. As Antonio Bettencourt (1991) writes about the learning and teaching of science:

> Understanding starts with a question, not any question but a real question . . . Said in another way, a real question expresses a desire to know. This desire is what moves the questioner to pursue the question until an adequate answer has been found (i.e. made). Desiring to know opens ourselves to experiencing what is new as new and the already known as renewed under new aspects.

In fact, there are likely to be few questions to which nobody in the class can contribute a tentative opinion, and so the posing of such 'I wonder' questions, by a pupil or the teacher, can be the basis for valuable discussion in which speculation is encouraged, and suggestions, both substantive and procedural, are evaluated for their possible relevance for the 'making' of an adequate answer. In a classroom of ten year olds in which I observed some very effective work on the theme of living creatures, the unit began with just such a question about the sorts of learning that the pupils might engage in when carrying out their projects. A lively discussion ensued, and the suggestions offered were recorded on the blackboard as a set of hypotheses to be tested in practice. At the end of the unit of work, this list was revised to see whether, in the light of experience, it needed any revisions. The following is an excerpt from the conversation between Kathryn and two friends as they reviewed the activities in which they had engaged. I have rarely heard such sophisticated metacognitive discussion in school – not even in the staffroom.

MARI: But 'created'.
JANICE: 'Created', I don't really get that.
MARI: Do you know what 'created' means?
KATHRYN: Yeah, you made it. Like, er . . .
JANICE: Then that's just like you made models? (*referring to the previous category*)
KATHRYN: I created an idea. (*trying out the collocation*) You can say it with ideas, but you can't model an idea like you can model things. But creating . . .
JANICE: Yeah, but if you have an idea about . . .
KATHRYN: Creating a thought . . .

JANICE: But if you have an idea of . . .

KATHRYN: Like creating a story . . .

JANICE: But if you have an idea of a lion – you can model a lion. So that's part of the thing.

KATHRYN: Yeah, so 'created' also meant 'model'. Almost the same thing.

(Wells, Chang and Maher, 1990, p.117)

The final configuration in Table 1 (Category 7) is in many ways the most challenging for the teacher who wishes to intervene in a pupil's process of coming to know, in a way that provides help and support without usurping the pupil's responsibility for the task in which he or she is engaged. The problem, as Branko Deronja put it in his report of the inquiry he carried out on his role in supporting problem-solving in dramatic play with his class of five and six year olds in Toronto, is to know when teacher intervention is 'assistance' rather than 'interference' (quoted in Wells, in press).

I have recently been involved in a lengthy discussion of this issue on a computer e-mail (electronic mail) network run by Michael Cole from the University of California at San Diego. The following comment, which was made by Ken Goodman in response to several preceding messages about whether learning physics involves students in (re)inventing Newtonian concepts, makes this distinction between assistance and interference in terms of 'mediation' as opposed to 'intervention'. Since it is so much to the point, I should like to quote it at length.

In intervention it is never Newton but the teacher's interpretation of Newton which the teacher is intent on the student coming to agree with. In mediation the teacher tries to support the development of schemes which will move toward scientific understanding by involving students in experiences in which they will experience the forces at work and bring their own inventions into their attempt to make sense of the phenomena. If Newton is right – and my questions or comments lead the student to examine Newtonian conventions – then the student may move toward them, or may move in another, perhaps tangential, direction. As a mediator, I'll push the student to examine that new view. But what if Newton is wrong – or more commonly what if I as a teacher am not quite right about Newton? It may be that my student will come up with an insight that goes beyond my view of Newton. It may even be that my student may go beyond Newton. The key in all this is that as teacher I recognise I can never control learning but I can powerfully support it.

(Goodman, 1991)

The article in this volume by Janet Maybin, Neil Mercer and Barry Stierer addresses this issue in terms of the metaphor of 'scaffolding', which, in their most stringent definition, they characterise as assistance with a task that results in the learner 'having achieved some greater level of independent competence as a result of the scaffolding experience' (article 4.2). As they show in their examples, when teachers ask questions with this purpose in mind, they can, as Goodman puts it, 'powerfully support' pupils' learning. The same point is made by examples quoted in several other articles in this volume.

In concluding this review of the value of questions in learning and teaching, therefore, I should like to suggest that, rather than trying to limit the quantity of teacher questions, it may be more profitable to attempt to identify the contexts in which, and the purposes for which, the asking of questions by pupils or teachers can genuinely help learners to clarify and solve problems which they are working on and stimulate their continuing desire to inquire and understand. And, in this context, it must be emphasised that teachers as well as pupils can learn from the discourse that takes place in the classroom (Duckworth, 1987). Nor should attention be focused exclusively on utterances that have the surface form of questions. As Wood argues, there is a wide range of alternative ways of engaging in thought-provoking dialogue, and in some contexts there may be more effective alternatives to those that are conventionally written with a terminal mark of interrogation.

Clearly, this is an area that – as part of the more general aim to improve the opportunities for learning through talk – is in need of further investigation. And it is to the model for carrying out such investigations that has been developed in the National Oracy Project that I wish to turn in the final section of this article.

Teachers as learners and agents of change

One of the most impressive features of this volume, when it is compared with most other reports of large-scale curriculum projects, is that, throughout its pages, one hears the voices of teachers – of the practitioners who give substance to the abstractions contained in the curriculum documents. Several of the articles have been written by teachers, or by partnerships of classroom and advisory teachers and, in almost all the other articles, reference is made to particular investigations carried out by teachers, often with quotations from transcripts of episodes of talk recorded in their classrooms. I mention this, not simply because it adds to the quality of the book as a whole – which it certainly does – but because it is indicative of the philosophy that has inspired this project. We can be sure that the teachers' role in the partnership is valued when their voices are heard clearly in the final published report.

However, what is unique about this particular volume is its largely fortuitous, but entirely appropriate, relationship to the co-occurring policy-based reform of education represented by the National Curriculum. That policy calls for a much greater attention to the role of spoken language in education and, by a happy coincidence of timing, this report from the National Oracy Project explores and exemplifies what such an attention can mean in practice.

Any major educational reform requires a concomitant commitment to the professional development of those who are required to implement the intended change. This is particularly so when the planned change involves, not only the content of the curriculum, but also the manner in which the teaching-learning relationship is enacted. All too often, however, such professional development is conceived as retraining, which is 'delivered' in the transmission mode that, throughout this volume, has been argued to be an inadequate basis for learning. Yet learning is what educational change is essentially about: teachers learning to think and act differently on the basis of the enhanced understanding they have constructed of the issues raised by the policy change.

What this theory of learning implies for teachers – as much as for the pupils they teach – has been spelled out in considerable detail in several of the articles in this volume. In particular, it means encouraging teachers to 'problematise' the relationship between learning, teaching and the curriculum – that is to say, encouraging them to treat the relationship as a matter that they can actively address in their own classrooms and schools, through systematic inquiry and through discussion with colleagues who are similarly engaged. Or, to repeat Bettencourt's way of putting it, through the asking of real questions and the pursuit of them through action and reflection until an adequate answer has been made.

This is what the teachers who have been involved in the National Oracy Project have done, ably supported by advisory teachers, academics and members of the central team. And the results, as manifested in the articles they have contributed to this volume, and in the many contributions to the Project's newsletter and journal, demonstrate the effectiveness of this mode of professional development. In case after case, they report on the insights they have gained, on their revised estimates of their pupils' capabilities, and on the changes they have made in their practice, with beneficial consequences for those they teach. What is more, as they have grappled with the requirements of the National Curriculum in the contexts of their own classrooms, they have begun to put flesh on the bare bones of the policy statements, in the form of case studies of individual children's use of oral language, of examples of effective contexts for learning through talk, and of ways of enabling assessment of and through talk to be simultaneously an occasion for further learning. They have also begun to identify and propose solutions to some of the problems that inevitably arise in the implementation of change.

In article 1.1, John Johnson and his colleagues point out, somewhat apologetically, that the work of the hundreds, even thousands, of teachers who have been associated with the Project has not produced the sort of findings nor followed the methodological practices associated with large-scale 'traditional' research. Since this and similar criticisms have been levelled against this form of activity by a number of academic researchers (for example, Applebee, 1987) who argue that it is not proper research, it is important to emphasise, as Johnson and his colleagues go on to do, that this is not its purpose. Whether it is described as action research, teacher research, classroom-based inquiry or reflective practice is not important. What is important, however, is that it has its basis in practice. Teacher research, conducted in the context of professional development, arises out of the professional concerns of individual teachers and has as its purpose to improve their practice. It is also concerned with the development of theory, but primarily with the personal theory of the teacher, as this is enriched and extended through the interplay of observation, action and reflection that occurs in the prosecution of his or her problem-based inquiry. And, once again, the goal of such theory development is to enrich the basis for the many decisions that are called for in day-to-day practice (Elliott, 1991; Wells, in press).

However, emphasis on personally-selected, problem-based inquiry does not mean that this sort of research has no contribution to make to the wider educational debate. Every one of the articles in this volume that reports on a teacher's inquiry throws new light on an issue of more general concern. Mary Morrison and Perminder Sandhu's study of a group of Panjabi-speaking children (article 2.6) and Anne Knight's case-study of Shopna (article 1.3), for example, both extend our awareness of the way in which bilingual children draw on their dual sets of communicative resources in different classroom contexts; they also suggest that there would be considerable benefit for such children if they were enabled to use their greater competence in their first language to support their learning activities in English. Their inquiry thus contributes to the more general debate about the role of the first language in the education of bilingual children and lends support to the view that first language competence should be maintained and, if possible, exploited as a resource for learning in school (Cummins and Swain, 1986). Or, to take another example, the contributions by Pauline Loader and Laura Brierley (article 4.6) and the study by Dorothy Steel reported by Mercer (article 4.5) all illustrate the value of engaging with children in 'talking about talking' as a way of helping them to gain greater awareness and control of their strategies for thinking and communicating. In so doing, they provide a different slant on the more general issue of the importance of metacognition, which has been addressed by academic researchers, for example under the rubric of 'reciprocal teaching' (Palincsar and Brown, 1984) and 'co-investigation' (Scardamalia and Bereiter, 1983).

This latter example once again underlines the parallels between the types of oracy-based learning that teachers have been investigating in their classrooms and the learning strategies that they themselves have adopted. Just as pupils learn from talking about talk so, too, do teachers. An important feature of the design of the National Oracy Project as discussed by Colin Biott (article 5.4) has thus been its provision for teachers to meet together to discuss their inquiries and to engage in reflective talk about their own styles of talking in the classroom.

In a somewhat similar, although smaller, project with which I have been associated in Canada*, this was probably the most frequently mentioned benefit of participation. In one school, the four or five teachers who were involved in the first year of the project started to meet regularly to discuss their reading around the individual inquiries they were carrying out. Out of this grew a proposal influenced by similar work by Aidan Chambers with teachers in Britain (Chambers, 1985) to combine their inquiries under the school-wide theme of 'talk about books'. By the time the first project conference was held in the middle of the second year, almost every teacher in the school had been drawn in, many of them working in pairs on the same topic. At the conference, ten of a staff of twenty, including the school Principal, took part in a two-hour symposium, at which they reported on their work to date. Over the course of their very varied presentations, two notes were repeated time and again: the value of paying attention to their children's talk as a way of learning about their children's learning, and the value of talking with each other to discover the significance of what they had learned. The same has obviously been

---

*'Talk: a medium for learning and change' involving eight elementary schools in the Peel Board of Education and funded by the Ontario Ministry of Education.

true for many of the teachers involved in the National Oracy Project, as is made clear in the passages Hilary Kemeny and Kate Norman quote from the reports of local project co-ordinators and directors (article 5.3). What is also made clear in their article is the crucial function of those who have worked in a supporting role. The following quotation from Cristina Bennett in that article would no doubt be echoed by many others:

> Regular contact for planning and classroom work together; reviewing approaches with a small number of teachers is a positive formula for working well. Obviously the nature of my work depended on the needs of the teachers. Therefore, the initial meeting to talk together through what they were interested in doing was vital; some teachers needed me as a sounding board for ideas; some wanted me to evaluate what they were doing and talk through approaches to change.

With minor changes, this could have been written by one of the teachers in the project about his or her way of working with pupils in the classroom. At all levels, the same principles of teaching apply, when teaching is interpreted as helping learners to achieve their goals of action and understanding with the aid of the tools that the culture makes available. And at all levels, too, the co-construction of meaning through dialogue is found to be indispensable.

In quoting the assumptions about learning, at the beginning of this article, that Latham had gleaned from the documents of the National Curriculum, I deliberately substituted the term 'learner' for the more specific terms, such as 'children', that were used in the original. By now my reason for doing so will be fully apparent. In the words of the title of the book produced to honour James Britton, one of those most responsible for the recognition now given to oracy, 'the word for teaching is learning' (Lightfoot and Martin 1988). And the theory that is implied by those assumptions applies as much to teachers as it does to pupils in school classrooms.

Those working in the National Oracy Project have placed oracy in an educational context and exemplified it as a vital mode of learning; as such, they have indeed provided a 'necessary counterbalance to (the) "top-down" model of curriculum planning' so clearly illustrated by the National Curriculum. But, more importantly, they have provided a proof of the validity of the theory of learning on which the curriculum recommendations are based by applying it in the professional development of teachers, on which the successful implementation of the curriculum model depends.

This may come as something of a surprise to those of the politicians and planners, responsible for the framing of the policy, who subscribe to a more hierarchical model of curriculum development. But in its demonstration of the problem-oriented, collaborative, and dialogic nature of knowledge construction, this active involvement of teachers in the interpretation, in practice, of the emphasis on oracy in the National Curriculum augurs well for the quality of the learning and teaching transactions through which that curriculum will be enacted.

References

APPLEBEE, A. (1987) 'Musings … Teachers and the process of research', *Research in the Teaching of English*, 21: 5–7.

BAKHTIN, M.M. (1986) *Speech Genres and Other Late Essays*. Austin: University of Texas Press.

BARNES, D. (1976) *From Communication to Curriculum*. Harmondsworth: Penguin.

BARNES, D., BRITTON, J. AND ROSEN, H. (1969) *Language, the Learner and the School*. Harmondsworth: Penguin.

BETTENCOURT, A. (1991) *What it Means to Understand Science*. Michigan State University, School of Education. Unpublished Paper.

BRITTON, J. (1970) *Language and Learning*. London: Allen Lane.

BRUBACHER, M., PAYNE, R. AND RICKETT, K. (eds) (1990) *Perspectives on Small Group Learning: Theory and Practice*. Oakville, Ontario: Rubicon Publishing Inc.

BRUNER, J. S. (1971) *The Relevance of Education*. London: Allen and Unwin.

CAMBOURNE, B. (1988) *The Whole Story: Natural Learning and the Acquisition of Literacy in the Classroom*. Auckland: Ashton Scholastic.

CHAMBERS, A. (1985) *Booktalk*. London: The Bodley Head.

CHRISTIE, F. (ed.) (1984) *Children Writing*. Geelong, Vic.: Deakin University Press.

CORSON, D. (1988) *Oral Language Across the Curriculum*. Clevedon, Avon: Multilingual Matters.

CUMMINS, J. AND SWAIN, M. (1986) *Bilingualism in Education*. London: Longman.

DUCKWORTH, E. (1987) *'The Having of Wonderful Ideas' and other Essays on Teaching and Learning*. New York: Teachers College Press.

EDWARDS, D. AND MERCER, N. (1987) *Common Knowledge: the Development of Understanding in the Classroom*. London: Routledge.

ELLIOTT, J. (1991) *Action Research for Educational Change*. Milton Keynes: Open University Press.

GOODMAN, K. (1987) *What's Whole in Whole Language*. Portsmouth, NH: Heinemann Educational Books.

GOODMAN, K. (1991) *E-mail message, XLCHC*, 29 April 1991.

HALLIDAY, M. A. K. (1975) *Learning How to Mean*. London: Edward Arnold.

HALLIDAY, M. A. K. AND HASAN, R. (1989) *Language, Context and Text: A Social-Semiotic Perspective*. Oxford: Oxford University Press.

JOHNSON, D. W., JOHNSON, R. T. AND HOLUBEC, E. J. (1988) *Cooperation in the Classroom*. Edina, Minnesota: Interaction Book Co.

LABOV, W. AND FANSHEL, D. (1977) *Therapeutic Discourse*. New York: Academic Press.

LAMPERT, M. (1989) 'Choosing and using mathematical tools in classroom discourse', in Brophy, J. (ed.) *Advances in Research on Teaching*, Vol. 1. Greenwich, CT: JAI Press Inc.

LEMKE, J. (1990) *Talking in Science*. New York: Academic Press.

LIGHTFOOT, M. AND MARTIN, N. (eds) (1988) *The Word for Teaching is Learning: Essays for James Britton*. London: Heinemann Educational Books.

LOCK, A. (1980) *The Guided Reinvention of Language*. London: Academic Press.

LOTMAN, Y. M. (1988) 'Text within a text.' *Soviet Psychology*, 26 (3): 32–51.

MARTIN, J. R., CHRISTIE, F. AND ROTHERY, J. (1987) 'Social processes in education: a reply to Sawyer and Watson (and others)', in Reid, I. (ed.) *The Place of Genre in Learning: Current Debates*. Geelong, Vic.: Deakin University Press.

MOLL, L. C. (ed.) (1991) *Vygotsky and Education: Instructional Implications and Applications of Sociohistorical Psychology*. Cambridge: Cambridge University Press.

NEWMAN, D., GRIFFIN, P. AND COLE, M. (1989) *The Construction Zone: Working for Cognitive Change in School*. Cambridge: Cambridge University Press.

PALINSCAR, A. S. AND BROWN, A. L. (1984) 'Reciprocal teaching of comprehension-fostering and comprehension-monitoring activities.' *Cognition and Instruction*, 1: 117–75.

PIAGET, J. (1954) *The Construction of Reality in the Child*. New York: Basic Books.

PINNELL, G. S. AND JAGGAR, A. M. (1991) 'Oral language: speaking and listening in the classroom', in Flood, J., Jensen, J. M., Lapp, D. and Squire, J. (eds) *Handbook of Research on Teaching the English Language Arts*. New York: MacMillan (pp. 691–720).

REDDY, M. J. (1979) 'The conduit metaphor: a case of frame conflict in our language about language', in Ortony, A. (eds.) *Metaphor and Thought*. Cambridge: Cambridge University Press.

ROGOFF, B. (1990) *Apprenticeship in Thinking*. Oxford: Oxford University Press.

ROMMETVEIT, R. (1979) 'On the architecture of intersubjectivity', in Rommetveit, R. and Blakar, R. (eds.) *Studies of Language, Thought and Communication*. London: Academic Press.

ROSEN, C. AND ROSEN, H. (1973) *The Language of Primary School Children*. Harmondsworth: Penguin.

ROSEN, H. (1984) *Stories and Meanings*. National Association for the Teaching of English.

ROSENBLATT, L. M. (1988) *Writing and Reading: The Transactional Theory*. Berkeley, CA: Centre for the Study of Writing, Technical Report No. 13.

SCARDAMALIA, M. AND BEREITER, C. (1983) 'Child as coinvestigator: helping children gain insight into their own mental processes', in Paris, S. G., Olson, G. M. and Stevenson, H. W. (eds.) *Learning and Motivation in the Classroom*. Hillsdale, NJ: Lawrence Erlbaum.

SHARAN, S. AND SHACHAR, H. (1988) *Language and Learning in the Cooperative Classroom*. New York: Springer Verlag.

SLAVIN, R. E. (1990) *Cooperative Learning: Theory, Research and Practice*. Englewood Cliffs, NJ: Prentice Hall.

THARP, R. AND GALLIMORE, R. (1988) *Rousing Minds to Life*. Cambridge: Cambridge University Press.

TORBE, M. AND MEDWAY, P. (1981) *The Climate for Learning*. Montclair, NJ: Boynton/Cook.

VYGOTSKY, L. S. (1978) *Mind in Society*. Cambridge, MA: Harvard University Press.

WELLS, G. (1980) 'Apprenticeship in meaning', in Nelson, K. E. (ed.) *Children's Language*, Volume 2. New York: Gardner Press.

WELLS, G. (1986) *The Meaning Makers: Children Learning Language and Using Language to Learn*. Portsmouth, NH: Heinemann Educational Books. (Sevenoaks: Hodder and Stoughton, 1987)

WELLS, G. (1990) 'Talk about text: where literacy is learned and taught.' *Curriculum Inquiry 20 (4)*: 369–405. Reprinted in Wells, G. (in press).

WELLS, G. (in press) *Talk and Text: Multicultural Communities of Literate Thinkers at Work*. (provisional title) Portsmouth, NH: Heinemann Educational Books.

WELL, G., CHANG, G. L. AND MAHER, A. (1990) 'Creating classroom communities of literate thinkers', in Sharan, S. (ed.) *Cooperative Learning: Theory and Research*. New York: Praeger. Reprinted in Wells G., in press.

WERTSCH, J.V. (1991) *Voices of the Mind*. Cambridge, MA: Harvard University Press.

WOOD, D. (1988) *How Children Think and Learn*. Oxford: Blackwell.

List of Contributors

Richard Bain is a secondary English teacher and a former member of the Shropshire Talk Project. He worked as LINC co-ordinator in North East England and is currently English adviser for Gateshead.

Douglas Barnes was until 1989 Reader in Education at the University of Leeds. His publications include *From Communication to Curriculum* (Boynton-Heinemann, 1992) and *Practical Curriculum Study* (Routledge and Kegan Paul, 1982), and (as co-author): *Language, the Learner and the School* (Boynton-Heinemann, 1990); *Communication and Learning in Small Groups* (Routledge and Kegan Paul, 1977); *School Writing: Discovering the Ground Rules* (Open University Press, 1991); *Versions of English* (Heinemann, 1984). In 1984 he was awarded an OBE.

Colin Biott is Reader in Education at Newcastle Polytechnic where he leads the MEd degree. Recent publications include *Semi-detached Teachers* (Falmer Press, 1991) and, with Jennifer Nias, *Working and Learning Together for Change* (Open University Press, 1992).

Laura Brierley is deputy headteacher of Lyneham County Junior School in Wiltshire.

Greg Brooks works at NFER. He taught for ten years, and from

1981 to 1989 was a member of the APU Language Monitoring Project, with principal responsibility for oracy assessment.

Irena Cassar teaches History and Humanities at Southend High School for Girls.

Roy Corden was the co-ordinator for the Staffordshire Oracy Project. He is now Senior Lecturer, Language in Education, at Nottingham Polytechnic.

Jenny Des-Fountain is Deputy Headteacher of Elizabeth Garrett Anderson School in the London Borough of Islington. She was local co-ordinator for the National Oracy Project in Waltham Forest, Havering and Essex from 1988 to 1991.

Tony Edwards is Professor of Education at the University of Newcastle upon Tyne. After teaching History in London secondary schools, he worked in the Universities of Exeter and Manchester before moving to Newcastle in 1979. Among his books are *Investigating Classroom Talk* (with David Westgate) (Falmer Press, 1987); *The Language of Teaching* (with John Furlong) (Heinemann, 1979); and *Language in Culture and Class* (Heinemann, 1976).

Peter Forrestal is a freelance educational writer and consultant and a publisher with Chalkface Press. He is based in Perth, Western Australia.

Harold Gardiner was an English teacher, HMI and, at his retirement, staff inspector for English. He thereafter acted as 'participant evaluator' for the Wiltshire Oracy Project and was on the Steering Committee of the National Writing Project and the National Oracy Project. Harold Gardiner died in 1991 soon after finishing his article for this book. His support and advice have been very much missed.

Alan Howe is currently English Adviser for Wiltshire LEA. Before that, he worked for the National Curriculum Council as a Project Officer for the National Oracy Project and as Professional Officer for English. He has written two books on talk: *Expanding Horizons* (NATE, 1987) and *Making Talk Work* (Hodder and Stoughton, 1992).

Rebecca Hutton was co-ordinator of the Salford Oracy Project. She is now an Advisory Teacher in the Salford Language Support Unit. Publications (with John Paine) include *Terms of Talking and Listening* (Salford, 1989), *Terms and Turns of Talking and Listening* (Salford, 1991).

David Jackson teaches in the King John School, an 11–16 Essex comprehensive. He is head of history and has responsibility for co-ordinating curriculum continuity and progression with the local primary schools and post-16 institutions.

John Johnson was Director of the National Oracy Project from 1987 to 1991. Author of a number of Project publications, he has also written articles and INSET materials on GCSE. He is currently Senior Adviser for the London Borough of Waltham Forest.

Judy Keiner is Senior Lecturer in Education, Department of Educational Studies and Management, University of Reading. She is co-director of the National Oracy Project Evaluation Team.

Hilary Kemeny was a Project Officer for the National Oracy Project from 1988 to 1991 and edited several NOP publications. She has been an advisory teacher and taught in secondary schools. She is now Deputy Headteacher of South Camden Community School.

Anne Knight is a class teacher and language co-ordinator at Newport Infants School, Waltham Forest, London.

Peter Latham is a General Inspector with the London Borough of Croydon. His particular areas of interest are English and Drama.

Pauline Loader has taught Nursery, Reception and Year 1 children. She is currently working at Southend Observation Unit.

Maggie MacLure is Lecturer in Education at the University of East Anglia. She has been involved in research, assessment and curriculum development in oracy, across the age ranges.

Janet Maybin works as a Lecturer in the Open University School of Education. She has written for a number of Open University Courses on language and literacy and has also published articles on her own research into children's informal collaborative talk.

Neil Mercer is Director of the Centre for Language and Communications in the School of Education at the Open University. He wrote *Common Knowledge* with Derek Edwards (Methuen, 1987), and led the team which produced the INSET pack *Talk and Learning 5–16* (Open University, 1991).

Mary Morrison has taught in many different schools. She was Project Co-ordinator for Bradford from 1988–91 and is currently Senior Lecturer in English in Education at Huddersfield Polytechnic.

Gemma Moss is author of *Un/Popular Fictions* (Virago, 1989), a critical reappraisal of girls' use of the romance genre in their writing. She is research fellow at the Institute of Education, University of London.

Kate Norman has taught in primary schools in London and Glasgow. She was co-ordinator of the Early Literacy Project in Manchester before becoming a Project Officer for the National Oracy Project. She is the author of *Teaching Talking and Learning in Key Stage One* (NCC, 1990).

Terry Phillips is a lecturer at the University of East Anglia. He has taught in primary and middle schools. His funded research includes investigations of argumentative talk, talk around the computer, and the role of talk in the assessment of competence in professional education.

Perminder K. Sandhu was the co-ordinator of the 'Bilingualism and Education Project' in Bradford (1985–8) and became a development officer for the national STAIR (Standard Tasks and Assessment Implementation Research) pilot project, which produced bilingual SAT materials. She is now an advisory teacher in Bradford's Multicultural Support Service, conducting action research on bilingualism and learning with the University of Manchester.

Irene Shantry is in her third year of teaching at May Park County Primary School in Bristol, Avon.

Yanina Sheeran is A Level Co-ordinator at Keighley College of Further Education. She worked for many years as Head of Humanities in a comprehensive school. She has also been a Lecturer in Education at Leeds Polytechnic and conducted post-graduate research on language at Leeds University. She is co-author, with Douglas Barnes, of *School Writing* (Open University Press, 1991).

Barry Stierer is a Staff Tutor in the Open University School of Education. He has worked on a number of national research projects, mainly in the area of reading and language assessment.

Gordon Wells is Professor of Education, Ontario Institute for Studies in Education, Toronto, Canada. He is author of *The Meaning Makers* (the report of the Bristol Study of 'Language and Learning at Home and at School') (Hodder and Stoughton, 1987), *Talk and Text: Multicultural Communities of Literate Thinkers at Work* (Heinemann Educational Books, in press) and editor (with J. Nicholls) of *Language and Learning: an Interactional Perspective* (Falmer Press, 1985).

Mark Williams is Deputy Headteacher at South Benfleet County Primary School, Essex. He has taught for eleven years and has a particular interest in children's language experiences.

Simon Wolfe is a secondary English teacher, currently teaching at the William de Ferrers school in Essex.

Dave Wood is Head of English, Madeley High School, Staffordshire.

David Wood is Professor of Psychology at Nottingham University. His principal publications include *How Children Think and Learn* (Blackwell, 1988) and, with Heather Wood, Amanda Griffiths and Ian Howarth, *Teaching and Talking with Deaf Children* (Wiley, 1986).

Lynda Yard was the Croydon co-ordinator for the National Oracy Project and is now an Advisory Teacher for English. Publications include chapters in *Reading for Real* (Wade 1990), *Spotlight on Spelling* (Pinsent 1989) and *Talk and Learning* (Open University 1991).

Index